Chicago Public Library

Form 178 rev. 11-00

D1367644

Yigang Pan
Editor

Greater China
in the Global Market

Greater China in the Global Market has been co-published simultaneously as *Journal of Global Marketing*, Volume 14, Numbers 1/2 2000

Pre-Publication
REVIEWS,
COMMENTARIES,
EVALUATIONS . . .

"**A** thorough review of state-of-the-art research on China. Whether you are concerned about country-entry issues, direct investment or consumer culture, this book contains valuable insights. Dr. Pan has put together a terrific group of researchers that examines China strategies from all different angles."

Bernd Schmitt
Founder
Center of Global Brand Leadership
Columbia Business School
New York

"**A**s more companies struggle to learn the secrets of success in the increasingly important Chinese marketplace, the papers in this book promise important insights and lessons. I found the chapters about the best ways and best times to enter the Chinese market, and how to be relevant to the changing Chinese consumer, to be extremely interesting. Solid, valuable scholarship."

Professor Rajeev Batra, PhD
S.S. Kresge Professor of Marketing
University of Michigan Business School
and Area Director for Marketing
Davidson Institute

Greater China
in the Global Market

Greater China in the Global Market has been co-published simultaneously as *Journal of Global Marketing*, Volume 14, Numbers 1/2 2000.

The *Journal of Global Marketing* Monographic "Separates"

Below is a list of "separates," which in serials librarianship means a special issue simultaneously published as a special journal issue or double-issue *and* as a "separate" hardbound monograph. (This is a format which we also call a "DocuSerial.")

"Separates" are published because specialized libraries or professionals may wish to purchase a specific thematic issue by itself in a format which can be separately cataloged and shelved, as opposed to purchasing the journal on an on-going basis. Faculty members may also more easily consider a "separate" for classroom adoption.

"Separates" are carefully classified separately with the major book jobbers so that the journal tie-in can be noted on new book order slips to avoid duplicate purchasing.

You may wish to visit Haworth's website at . . .

http://www.HaworthPress.com

. . . to search our online catalog for complete tables of contents of these separates and related publications.

You may also call 1-800-HAWORTH (outside US/Canada: 607-722-5857), or Fax 1-800-895-0582 (outside US/Canada: 607-771-0012), or e-mail at:

getinfo@haworthpressinc.com

Greater China in the Global Market, edited by Yigang Pan, PhD (Vol. 14, No. 1/2, 2000). *Contains the most up-to-date information on business and marketing, particularly marketing strategies, in China. It is a must read for academics and business practitioners with an interest in China.*

Marketing in the Third World, edited by Denise M. Johnson, PhD, and Erdener Kaynak, PhD, DSc (Vol. 9, No. 4, 1996). *Readers learn about market orientation, market infrastructure, economic constraints, government regulations, internationalization processes of public-sector enterprises, and performance differences between foreign and domestic manufacturing firms.*

Greater China
in the Global Market

Yigang Pan, PhD
Editor

Greater China in the Global Market has been co-published simultaneously as *Journal of Global Marketing*, Volume 14, Numbers 1/2 2000.

International Business Press
An Imprint of The Haworth Press, Inc.
New York • London • Oxford

Greater China in the Global Market has been co-published simultaneously as *Journal of Global Marketing*, Volume 14, Numbers 1/2 2000.

The Haworth Press, Inc., 10 Alice Street, Binghamton, NY 13904-1580 USA

Cover design by Thomas J. Mayshock Jr.

Library of Congress Cataloging-in-Publication Data

Greater China in the global market/Yigang Pan, editor.
    p. cm.
    "Greater China in the global market has been co-published simultaneously as Journal of global marketing, volume 14, numbers 1/2 2000."
    Included bibliographical references and index.
    ISBN 0-7890-1188-3 (alk. paper)–ISBN 0-7890-1189-1 (alk. paper)
    1. Marketing–China. 2. Investments, Foreign–China. 3. Consumption (Economics)–China. I. Pan, Yigang. II. Journal of global marketing.
HF5415.12.C5 G74 2000
658.8′00951–dc21

00-046155

Indexing, Abstracting & Website/Internet Coverage

This section provides you with a list of major indexing & abstracting services. That is to say, each service began covering this periodical during the year noted in the right column. Most Websites which are listed below have indicated that they will either post, disseminate, compile, archive, cite or alert their own Website users with research-based content from this work. (This list is as current as the copyright date of this publication.)

Abstracting, Website/Indexing Coverage .... Year When Coverage Began

- *Contents of this publication are indexed and abstracted in the ABI/INFORM database, available on Bell & Howell Information & Learning's ProQuest@www.umi.com* 1999

- *Anbar Management Intelligence Abstracts* 1988

- *AURSI African Urban & Regional Science Index* 1999

- *BUBL Information Service, An Internet-based Information Service for the UK higher education community <URL:http://bubl.ac.uk/>* 1995

- *Business Education Index, The* 1994

- *Business Periodicals Index (BPI) <www.hwwi/son.com>* 1999

- *Cabell's Directory of Publishing Opportunities in Marketing (Comprehensive & Descriptive Bibliographic Listing with Editorial Criteria and Publication Production Data for Selected Marketing & Marketing-related Journals)* 1995

- *CNPIEC Reference Guide: Chinese National Directory of Foreign Periodicals* 1995

- *Contents Pages In Management (University of Manchester Business School), England* 1988

(continued)

Special Bibliographic Notes related to special journal issues (separates) and indexing/abstracting:

- indexing/abstracting services in this list will also cover material in any "separate" that is co-published simultaneously with Haworth's special thematic journal issue or DocuSerial. Indexing/abstracting usually covers material at the article/chapter level.
- monographic co-editions are intended for either non-subscribers or libraries which intend to purchase a second copy for their circulating collections.
- monographic co-editions are reported to all jobbers/wholesalers/approval plans. The source journal is listed as the "series" to assist the prevention of duplicate purchasing in the same manner utilized for books-in-series.
- to facilitate user/access services all indexing/abstracting services are encouraged to utilize the co-indexing entry note indicated at the bottom of the first page of each article/chapter/contribution.
- this is intended to assist a library user of any reference tool (whether print, electronic, online, or CD-ROM) to locate the monographic version if the library has purchased this version but not a subscription to the source journal.
- individual articles/chapters in any Haworth publication are also available through the Haworth Document Delivery Service (HDDS).

Greater China in the Global Market

CONTENTS

ABOUT THE EDITOR

Yigang Pan (PhD, Columbia University), is Scotiabank Professor of International Business at Schulich School of Business, York University, Toronto, Canada, and is on the faculty of School of Business, University of Hong Kong (2000-2002). His area of research is on market entry strategies. In the past several years, he has published extensively in this area, particularly in the context of China. He is one of the leading contributors to *Journal of International Business Studies* in the past six years. Currently, he is an active participant of several large-scale research projects about marketing in China, including business strategies, and consumers in China.

Introduction
to Greater China
in the Global Market

Yigang Pan

SUMMARY. In March 1998, I started the long process of publishing this volume. After a year and six month's work, this book is going to be published. Included in this publication are nine outstanding articles that address different aspects of marketing in Greater China today. I am very pleased to be part of this effort to bring the best of the work in front of the readers. *[Article copies available for a fee from The Haworth Document Delivery Service: 1-800-342- 9678. E-mail address: <getinfo@haworthpressinc. com> Website: <http://www.HaworthPress.com>]*

KEYWORDS. Marketing, Greater China

From time to time, we publish the state-of-the-art research on a particular area. This special volume focuses on marketing strategies in Greater China. The nine outstanding articles that are included in this volume represent the latest work of several researchers. To my amazement, several scholars who are senior and well-known in the academic and business communities remain very active in their path-

Yigang Pan (PhD, Columbia University) is Scotiabank Professor of International Business at Schulich School of Business, York University, Toronto, Canada, and is on the faculty of School of Business, University of Hong Kong (2000-2002).

[Haworth co-indexing entry note]: "Introduction to Greater China in the Global Market." Pan, Yigang. Co-published simultaneously in *Journal of Global Marketing* (International Business Press, an imprint of The Haworth Press, Inc.) Vol. 14, No. 1/2, 2000, pp. 1-5; and: *Greater China in the Global Market* (ed: Yigang Pan) International Business Press, an imprint of The Haworth Press, Inc., 2000, pp. 1-5. Single or multiple copies of this article are available for a fee from The Haworth Document Delivery Service [1-800-342-9678, 9:00 a.m.- 5:00 p.m. (EST). E-mail address: getinfo@haworthpressinc.com].

breaking work. I am very pleased to present to you the latest work by John Farley of Dartmouth College, John Child of Cambridge University, and Rohit Despandé of Harvard University. I am also very pleased that the next generation Chinese scholars do outstanding work as well. It is truly my pleasure to offer this volume to the reader. I am sure it is a must read for those front-line marketing executives in China as well as corporate decision makers in the headquarters at home.

In March 1998, I took upon the task of editing a special collection on marketing strategies in Greater China. The call for papers was distributed through AIB and ACR newsletters in 1998. It was also distributed at conferences. The response from the field was great.

A total of nine papers are published in this special volume, from a pool of 27 papers that were submitted. This set of papers represents the latest research from scholars that are interested in the marketing issues in China. These nine papers are written by authors from the United States, Hong Kong, Japan, Britain, and New Zealand. I am particularly honored to include the work from senior and well-known scholars such as John Farley, John Child, and Rohit Despandé. I am also very delighted to have the contributions from younger scholars such as Yadong Luo, Doren Chadee, Nancy Wong, and others. In the following, I will briefly introduce each paper.

Despandé and Farley examine the innovation, market orientation, and organization cultures and climate of firms in Shanghai. This follows in the stream of work on market orientation, which John Farley pioneered in the late 1980s and early 1990s. In their study, they surveyed a sample of 100 senior managers in Shanghai-based companies. They also compared the findings in China to what they found in Japan. It is interesting that they found that compared to the Japanese, the Chinese firms are on average relatively Bureaucratic, but are also relatively Entrepreneurial. Within China, joint ventures are more Competitive and less Bureaucratic than State-Owned Enterprises. The better performing Chinese firms follow a pattern which they have found elsewhere in the industrial and industrializing world. Specifically, the successful Chinese firms are innovative, market oriented, and have cultures and decision-making climates which are externally oriented. There are, however, distinctly identifiable patterns in both the values of the individual managers and in the nature of the Chinese organizations which distinguish them from samples of managers from other Asian nations.

Yan and Child discuss how to manage the value chain activities in joint ventures in China. In this project, they try to understand how foreign partners manage joint ventures. They examine the differences in the resource profile and experience of 67 Sino-foreign joint ventures located in the two sectors: non-consumer electronics and fast moving consumer goods [FMCG]. They found out that foreign partners are likely to find more flexibility, and a greater opportunity to influence joint venture management in the FMCG sector compared with non-consumer electronic sector. The physical and infrastructural features of the sectors appear to be particularly consequential for managing an investment in China, and they may be more significant than institutional factors.

Luo explains the choices of entry modes in China today. These entry modes include equity joint ventures, wholly foreign owned subsidiaries, contractual joint ventures, umbrella companies, acquisitions, representative offices, branches, build-operate-transfers, licensing and franchising. The merits and limitations of each entry mode are discussed. Based on his own experiences, Luo offers practical advice on entry strategies for international executives active in the Chinese market.

Lin offers empirical evidence on this issue of modes of entry. He examines the antecedents of market entry strategy as well as market environmental, transaction-specific, competitive strategic factors and organizational capability that influence the choice of market entry mode. His empirical findings were based on a survey of 251 Japanese companies. He shows that experiential knowledge of firms has an immense impact on the choice of entry mode in China. Also, he shows the important influences of risk-absorption capability and risk-dispersion mechanism on the choice of entry mode into the Chinese market.

Li addresses an important issue facing foreign firms that have not yet entered China, i.e., the timing of entry into China. The paper reviews the literature on first-mover advantages and the recent empirical research. It then attempts to theorize on why timing of market entry matters in the context of foreign direct investment. Apart from drawing upon the four recent studies in this area, Li focuses on the auto industry in China and the case of Volkswagen to illustrate the importance of early entry into an overseas market. Overall, it gives a nice treatment on this particular issue of entry timing.

Chadee and Zhang examine the export to China and importance of guanxi. They argue that even though more and more western business people are becoming increasingly aware of the importance of guanxi in doing business in China, its potential impacts on the performance of business are still not well understood. They adopt the path analysis to assess the impacts of guanxi on export performance of a sample of New Zealand firms exporting to China. The results show that guanxi variables significantly facilitate trade partnering, business negotiating, and problem solving and generally contributes positively to the overall export performance of firms.

Turning to understand the customer side of the marketing strategies, we have two intriguing papers. The one by Gould and Wong examines the changing trend of Chinese consumers. The authors adopt an unconventional research method by seeing the changes that have taken place in China that was depicted in a movie. They argue that cultural intertextuality, that is the hybridizing construction of global and local meanings, was central. This intertextuality had two emergent themes: (1) longstanding versus postmodern narratives and (2) a Sinicization or Chinese indigenization of meanings. They propose to take more indigenous-oriented view of Chinese consumers.

Wang, Chen, Chan and Zheng investigate the issue of promotion and brand equity in China. Their study investigates the influence of hedonic values on the consumer behavior of young Chinese. The results show that hedonic values are negatively associated with utilitarian orientation and positively associated with novelty seeking, responsiveness to promotion stimuli, and preference for foreign brands. Personal income moderates the relationship between hedonic values and brand consciousness. Conceptual importance and managerial implications are discussed.

Finally, Ouyang, Zhou and Zhou review the publications in top marketing and business journals that relate to Greater China in the past twenty years and give us a snapshot of who is who in the area. Specifically, they examine publications in leading English language academic journals from 1978 to 1998. They summarized the papers that have been published, identified the contributing individuals and institutions, examined the importance these journals have given to China-related marketing research, and compared the research with research published in leading journals in other business disciplines. The paper concludes by discussing the future of research on marketing in China.

I am grateful to the reviewers who offer their valuable and timely services. I am also obliged to all the authors who submitted their work to this special volume. Finally, I thank the editor, Dr. Erdener Kaynak, for this opportunity.

Market-Focused Organizational Transformation in China

Rohit Deshpandé
John U. Farley

SUMMARY. To help us develop an understanding of successful Chinese companies as they emerge into a more market-oriented economic environment, a sample of senior managers in 100 Shanghai-based companies were asked to profile their own values and to evaluate their companies in terms of innovation, market orientation and the nature of their

---

Rohit Deshpandé is Sebastian S. Kresge Professor of Marketing, Harvard Business School, Boston, MA 02162 and served as Executive Director of the Marketing Science Institute from 1997-1999. His previous faculty positions were at Dartmouth College and the University of Texas at Austin. He has an MBA from Northwestern University and a PhD from the University of Pittsburgh. His research is on cross-national and cross-cultural marketing problems in knowledge management, advertising, Market Orientation, and organizational culture. John U. Farley is Henkel Professor of Industrial Marketing, China-Europe International Business School, Shanghai, China and C. V. Starr Senior Research Fellow, Amos Tuck School, Dartmouth College, Hanover, NH 03755. He has an MBA from the Amos Tuck School and a PhD from the University of Chicago, and has served as Executive Director of MSI. His research, which focuses on measurement and modeling of markets and marketing management, has been published in journals in the behavioral and management sciences as well as marketing, and in six books.

The authors are indebted for support of this project to the China-Europe International Business School, to the Center for China and East Asia of the Amos Tuck School, and to the Division of Research of the Harvard Business School. They are also indebted to Rex Duh who provided valuable material on the contemporary Chinese economy and on not heretofore available research on Chinese Organizations.

[Haworth co-indexing entry note]: "Market-Focused Organizational Transformation in China." Deshpandé, Rohit, and John U. Farley. Co-published simultaneously in *Journal of Global Marketing* (International Business Press, an imprint of The Haworth Press, Inc.) Vol. 14, No. 1/2, 2000, pp. 7-35; and: *Greater China in the Global Market* (ed: Yigang Pan) International Business Press, an imprint of The Haworth Press, Inc., 2000, pp. 7-35. Single or multiple copies of this article are available for a fee from The Haworth Document Delivery Service [1-800-342-9678, 9:00 a.m. - 5:00 p.m. (EST). E-mail address: getinfo@haworthpressinc.com].

7

organizational cultures and climates. There are, of course, distinctly identifiable patterns in both the values of the individual managers and in the nature of the Chinese organizations. In comparison to a similar sample of Japanese firms, the Chinese firms are on average relatively Bureaucratic, but are also relatively Entrepreneurial. Within China we find that Joint Ventures are more Competitive and less Bureaucratic than State-Owned Enterprises. We find that the better performing Chinese firms follow a pattern which we have found elsewhere in the industrial and industrializing world, and which we now call the "Universal Market-Focused Model." Successful firms, compared to other Chinese firms, are innovative, market oriented, and have cultures and decision-making climates which are externally oriented. There are, however, distinctly identifiable patterns in both the values of the individual managers and in the nature of the Chinese organizations which distinguish them from samples of managers from other Asian nations. *[Article copies available for a fee from The Haworth Document Delivery Service: 1-800-342-9678. E-mail address: <getinfo@haworthpressinc.com> Website: <http:// www.HaworthPress.com>]*

KEYWORDS. International marketing, market orientation, corporate culture, innovation, performance

A great deal of contemporary interest is focused on the process of transforming planned economies to be more market oriented. In particular, much interest is focused on China, not only because it is such a large and important country, but because it appears that the transformation is proceeding much more smoothly than elsewhere–Russia, for example. Successful transformation depends both on government policy which enables the transformation and on the ability of firms–some old and some new–to respond to the new economic environment. Successful transformation will also depend both on the managers as individuals and on the nature of the organizations in which they work.

Chinese organizational transformation has been an important part of increasing international interest in the types of organizations which function effectively in various cultural environments, and particularly in whether there are generalizations about what firms can do to improve performance (Farley and Lehmann 1994; Bowman, Farley and Schmittlein 1998). Recent research, for example, has indicated that quite different kinds of organizational cultures may exist in different countries, but that increased innovation and more outwardly focused organizational cultures can apparently improve performance in many different cultural settings (Deshpandé, Farley and Webster 1993, 1997; Deshpandé and Farley 1998, 1999b).

The purpose of this paper is to investigate the extent to which results of this stream of organizational research are applicable in the highly dynamic Chinese environment. In doing this, we attempt to replicate, in the Chinese context, elements of previous studies elsewhere on performance. We approach the research in three steps:

1. Descriptions of the values and perceptions of Chinese culture which a sample of Chinese managers bring to their organizations. These are compared with results of similar research in Thailand to help establish Chinese managers' uniqueness on these matters.
2. Comparisons of aggregate Chinese results on corporate culture and climate, innovativeness and market orientation with results of similar studies in Thailand and Japan (Deshpandé et al. 1993). This step helps establish uniqueness of Chinese organizations in transition.
3. Comparisons within Chinese firms of good performers with other firms, and comparisons of State-Owned Enterprises and Joint Ventures. How Chinese State-Owned Enterprises face the new economic environment has received a great deal of attention both domestically and abroad in the past decade.

CONCEPTUAL BACKGROUND AND HYPOTHESES: THE "UNIVERSAL MARKET-FOCUSED MODEL" OF PERFORMANCE

Understanding managerial behavior is important to understanding Chinese firms both to market to them effectively as customers and to deal with them effectively in the market place as competitors. A framework for analysis of important aspects of such behavior was first applied in Japan (Deshpandé et al. 1993). It posits that firms which perform well to share the following characteristics:

1. A greater degree of **Market Orientation** in which the customer is placed first in the set of stakeholders with which the firm deals.

2. Organizational Cultures and Climates above average in terms of external orientation–for that society–towards markets and to external sources of ideas, for example.
3. Innovation, particularly with regard to new products and services.

These do not exhaust the many factors related to good performance, but they do focus on often-neglected marketing and organizational factors (Capon, Farley and Hoenig 1997).

The Marketing Science Institute, a leading US-based non-profit marketing think tank, has recognized the need for integration of Organizational Culture, Market Orientation and Innovation by designating the understanding of customer-focused organizations, including the underlying corporate cultural factors, as one of their highest research priority areas (Marketing Science Institute 1996).

As cross-national work in this framework has proceeded (Deshpandé et al. 1997), we have come to call this a sort of "Universal Market-Focused Model" of marketing organizational factors as they relate to firm performance. That work also shows that the appropriate comparisons are relative within rather than across countries, an unsurprising reflection in firm management of elements of national culture. It is thus important to note here that such a model does not ignore substantial differences that exist between firms in different countries (i.e., the 'national culture effect'). *However, our observation is that the most successful firms share similar relative dimensions of management practice which are conditioned on the national culture effect.* This is consistent with the argument by Ohmae (1985) and by Yip, Johansson and Roos (1996) that a global (corporate) culture is neutral between countries or nationalities, and is contrary to Newman and Nollen's (1996) perspective that firms should adapt their management practices away from the home country standard toward the host country culture (importantly, Newman and Nollen studied subsidiaries within a single U.S. firm while the current study examines several firms within a single country). To the extent that we are exploring China, a country in economic transition, we might expect what Ralston, Holf, Terpstra and Kai-Cheng (1997) refer to as "crossvergence" with Chinese values influencing other cultures and values of others influencing China.

China, as it emerges from central planning and into a form of market socialism, offers a unique setting for an application of the

"Universal Market-Focused Model." It is not immediately clear that firms in centrally planned economies are recognized in any tangible way for market orientation or for innovation. It is also not evident that externally-oriented organizational cultures serve a firm well in a highly bureaucratic centrally-planned economy. However, the "Universal Market-Focused Model" has proven itself robust enough in tests in very different cultural settings that it deserves a test in the Chinese managerial environment as well.

The four elements of the model each have a history in terms of both theory and measurement by the use of scales. Operationalizations are discussed in detail later in this paper, and the actual scale items are in Appendix A.

Market Orientation. The concept of Market Orientation is the central element of the management philosophy based on the marketing concept (Drucker, 1954; Levitt 1960; Webster 1988) and is presumed to contribute to long-term profitability, although there has been relatively little testing of this presumption.

We define Market Orientation as the set of cross-functional processes and activities directed at creating and satisfying customers through continuous need assessments. Deshpandé and Farley (1998) have attempted to integrate three different but related approaches that have been developed to measure Market Orientation (Kohli and Jaworski 1990, 1993; Narver and Slater 1990; Deshpandé et al. 1993). They show that the three approaches produce similar substantive results and that the three scales related to the three approaches are reliable and are highly correlated when used on the same subjects. They also show that the three approaches produce similarly reliable results when used cross-culturally (Farley and Deshpandé 1998, 1999c).

Hypothesis 1. Chinese firms with higher Market Orientations should perform better.

Organizational Innovation. In one of his most-cited passages, Peter Drucker (1954) wrote that "there is only one valid definition of business purpose: to create a customer . . . It is the customer who determines what the business is . . . Because it is its purpose to create a customer, any business enterprise has two–and only these two–basic functions: marketing and innovation." Economists have also noted the aggregate importance of organizational innovation (Mansfield 1977). Others have linked organizational structure and strategy through innovation to performance (Capon, Farley, Hulbert and Lehmann 1992), suggesting that a firm needs to be innovative so as "to gain a competitive edge in order to survive and grow." Innovation has been shown to be a key element of better firm performance in several countries (Deshpandé et al., 1993, 1997; Deshpandé and Farley 1999c; Grönhaug and Kaufmann 1988).

> Hypothesis 2. More innovative Chinese firms should perform better.

Organizational Climate. Organizational climate is an enduring quality of the internal environment of the firm experienced by its members, which influences behavior and can be described in terms of attributes of an organization (Tagiuri and Litwin 1968). It has a long and distinguished history in organization research and in popular books on firm performance.

Corporate culture and climate are closely related; Schneider and Rentsch (1988), for example, see culture as "why things happen" and climate as "what happens." Empowered climates which encourage communication, participation, decentralization, friendliness and trust have been positively related to performance in Western industrial firms (Capon, Farley, Hulbert and Lei 1991; Capon, Farley and Hoenig 1997), but it is not clear whether these patterns will be found elsewhere.

> Hypothesis 3. Chinese firms with stronger Organizational Climates should perform better.

Corporate Culture. Corporate culture, the pattern of shared values and beliefs that help individuals understand organizational functioning (Deshpandé and Webster 1989; Weick 1985), is perhaps the most difficult of the concepts under study here. We start with four classifications of culture developed from work by Quinn and others (Quinn 1988; Quinn and McGrath 1985; Quinn and Rorbaugh 1983; Campbell 1977; Cameron and Freeman 1991). Figure 1 shows that four culture types map into two dimensions. The two dimensions represent the merging of two theoretical streams from organizational behavior–systems-structure and transaction cost. The vertical axis describes a continuum from organic to mechanistic processes, and the other axis describes internal versus external organizational positioning. The external positioning is especially part of effective marketing:

- Competitive Culture characterized by an emphasis on competitive advantage and market superiority.
- Entrepreneurial Culture emphasizing innovation and risk-taking.
- Bureaucratic Culture characterized by regulations and formal structures.
- Consensual Cultures emphasizing loyalty, tradition and internal maintenance.

In practice, actual organizations turn out to be a mixture of these four types; Japanese firms, for example, turned out to be relatively high on Consensual and Competitive cultures, about average in terms of Bureaucracy but very low on Entrepreneurial Culture (Deshpandé et al. 1993). Firms from other Industrial economies have quite different profiles (Deshpandé et al. 1997).

The fact that there are two dimensions complicates hypothesizing about the relationship of Organizational Culture with performance. Entrepreneurial and Competitive cultures should perform best, with some bias towards the Competitive Culture because of its emphasis on performance. Bureaucratic and Consensual cultures should both per-

FIGURE 1. Dominant Characteristics of Organizational Culture Types

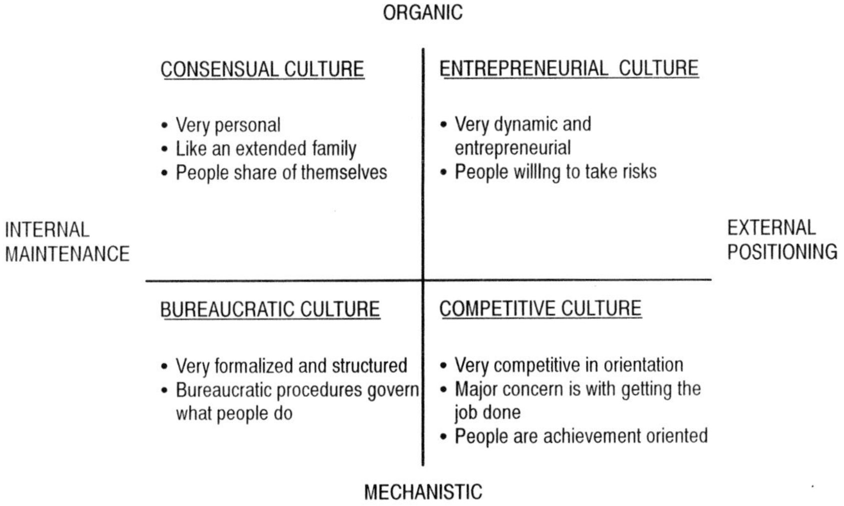

ORGANIC

CONSENSUAL CULTURE	ENTREPRENEURIAL CULTURE
• Very personal • Like an extended family • People share of themselves	• Very dynamic and entrepreneurial • People willlng to take risks

INTERNAL MAINTENANCE   EXTERNAL POSITIONING

BUREAUCRATIC CULTURE	COMPETITIVE CULTURE
• Very formalized and structured • Bureaucratic procedures govern what people do	• Very competitive in orientation • Major concern is with getting the job done • People are achievement oriented

MECHANISTIC

Source: Adapted from Cameron and Freeman 1988; Quinn 1988; and Deshpandé, Farley and Webster 1997.

form less well, the Consensual culture perhaps a bit more so because of its heavy emphasis on internal matters.

> Hypothesis 5. Among Chinese firms, differences in Organizational Culture should be related to differences in performance. Extending the results of Deshpandé et al. (1993,1997), firms with more Competitive and Entrepreneurial cultures should outperform firms with more Bureaucratic and Consensual cultures.

CHINESE MANAGEMENT IN TRANSITION

The excellent performance of the Chinese economy, with near double-digit percentage growth each year of this decade, is well-documented (Table 1). Our primary interest is with individual firms operating in this environment and with individual managers within those

TABLE 1. Number of Industrial Firms and Share of GDP by Ownership Type

	1979		1990		1994	
	Number of Firms	Share of GDP	Number of Firms	Share of GDP	Number of Firms	Share of GDP
State-Owned Enterprises	N/A	55.9%	104,400	43.5%	102,000	35.90%
Collectively-Owned Enterprises	N/A	44.1%	1,668,500	20.3%	1,863,000	26.9%
Individually-Owned Enterprises	N/A	0.0%	6,176,000	32.8%	8,007,400	28.6%
Others (Shareholding, Joint Ventures, Joint Ownership)	N/A	0.0%	8,800	3.4%	44,500	8.6%

Source: *China Statistical Yearbook* 1995, p. 375 and *Jingji Cankao Bao* 1997 Mar. 18

Gross Output Value of Industry: (Unit–1 billion Yuan)

1991	1992	1993	1994	1995
2662.5	3459.9	4840.2	7017.6	9189.4

Source: *China Statistical Yearbook*, 1996, p. 401

firms, but we must interpret our results in terms of changes in contemporary Chinese economic management. Starting in 1978, Chinese economic reform focused on transformation from a centrally-planned economy towards a 1992 consensus to implement a socialist market economy using market mechanisms as key resource allocation devices. (The year 1992 is a critical one since the most dynamic changes toward a market economy are only now likely to be observable.) Of course, our work builds on historical pre-1992 examinations of Joint Ventures in China, such as the excellent study by Pan (1996). A parallel development outside of State-Owned Enterprises involved what might be called "boundary reforms" such as encouragement of collectives, permission for joint ventures, promotion of market competition, freeing of prices and a new system of contracting. Later, there was a movement away from what might be termed "Unitarism" (a term the Chinese use to describe traditional organization of State-Owned Enterprises) towards a system of more "modern" corporate structures.

There is much discussion about how much decentralization has actually been accomplished, but there is no doubt that there has been considerable development in terms of both number of firms and output value (Table 1) of new kinds of enterprises. These developments have generated great interest in whether the new organizational forms–especially Joint Ventures with foreign investors–have had impact on the way Chinese firms are managed and in turn on their performance. In fact, it appears that many Western managers assume such impact will occur. We thus assess more traditionally organized firms (the SOE's) and those of the newer forms (the JV's).

To our knowledge, there has been scant empirical research on management of Chinese firms as it relates to Market Orientation. Interest has developed in China in understanding the values of managers and other individuals who make up these enterprises, as well as their perceptions about their organizations. Chinese scholars have been interested in issues related to both innovation and organizational culture (Subject Study Group 1995). Unfortunately, much of this literature has not been translated from the Chinese and hence is not available to Western scholars. For example, Table 2 (adapted from Zhang and Zhan 1996) shows the values for 16 factor scores summarizing the results on 71 measures in interviews of 177 employees of firms of the sort described in Table 1. Concepts measured include working values of the respondents, measures involving organizational culture, and

TABLE 2. Comparison of Factor Scores from Study of Chinese Organizational Culture

	Type of Firm		
	Large State-Owned Enterprise	Joint Venture	Significantly Different $\alpha = .05$
Factors			
I. Working Values			
Authoritative behavior	58	46	Yes
Desire for achievement	69	69	No
Loyalty and group orientation	64	61	No
Interpersonal dependence	46	54	Yes
Appreciation of leader	64	66	No
Environmental support	69	56	Yes
II. Confucianism Values			
Self-cultivation of moral principles	71	82	Yes
Interpersonal ethics	61	64	No
Self control	49	54	No
Contentment	58	49	Yes
Face saving	55	43	Yes
Value of justice above gains	39	30	No
Maximizing personal benefit	51	48	No
Suspicious of progress	55	38	Yes
III. Corporate Culture			
Flexibility	57	64	Yes
Human management importance	61	60	No

Source: Zhan Degan and Zhang Binglin, (1996), "A Sample Study of Enterprise Culture Structure," *Management World*, Vol. 5, 206.

measures involving traditional Confucian values. We use measures in all three categories in this study. Eight of the sixteen factor scores are significantly different for SOE's and Joint Ventures with foreign firms– a pattern which is also significantly different in all three categories. There are also some interesting and perhaps unexpected results. For example (Part III), the Joint Ventures have more flexible organizations (not surprising), but human management is about equally unimportant for both types of firms. The Joint Ventures have higher scores on ethical scales (Part II), and the SOE's seem more closed to new ideas. Unsurprisingly (Part I), the JV's are less authoritarian, but the leader is appreciated equally in SOE's and JV's.

DATA COLLECTION

Face-to-face interviews were conducted with a representative sample of 100 senior managers of Chinese companies headquartered in Shanghai, using a register of firms assembled and maintained by a major international market research firm for research on business-to-business markets. The interviews were carried out, as they were in all of the countries in our studies, by personnel from the same research firm. All respondents were guaranteed anonymity for themselves and their companies, and were promised a report of the results as an incentive to participate in the study. Inter-rater reliability for the individual items as well as scale reliability and validity were established in the Japanese study described earlier (Deshpandé et al. 1993) and in India (Deshpandé and Farley 1999c) using a complex design of four respondents for each observation–two from the supplier and two from a customer firm.

Shanghai is relevant because the city has been at the forefront of the Chinese economy in transition (Shanghai Economy Yearbook 1996). It is the major Chinese center in terms of broad-based economic growth, and is the one of the major centers for locations of firms in manufacturing and service sectors. Over 40 of the World's largest multinationals have invested in Shanghai, and a total of $35 billion in direct foreign investment has been made in the area. Double-digit growth has recently characterized all categories of industry, and high-tech industry is well represented in the area. The sample reflects the nature of the industrial base in the Shanghai area as it contains 61 SOE's and 36 JV's representing a broad spectrum of industrial, consumer goods, and service businesses. Since, however, Shanghai does represent a special situation, further research is needed to extend results to other parts of China.

For bench-marks in comparison with the Chinese results, we used various results from similar interviews with 160 managers of firms headquartered in Tokyo (Japan is a highly industrialized country) and 100 managers of firms headquartered in Bangkok (Thailand is another Asian economy which is industrializing rapidly). In both Japan and Thailand, the samples were drawn from domestically based firms whose stocks are traded on the local exchange–a sampling method not appropriate to China. The Thai and Chinese studies used a similar questionnaire and single respondents in each firm.

The questionnaire items and description of scale construction for the Corporate Culture and Climate, Market Orientation, Innovation and Performance measures used in all countries in an appropriately translated form are shown in Appendix A. A detailed discussion of scale reliabilities is in Table B.1 in Appendix B. Measured reliabilities of the Chinese scales as indicated by the Cronbach α are about the same as for Thailand. The reliability measures for Corporate Culture are somewhat lower than similar measures from Japan. They are, however, at a level designated by Nunally (1967) as acceptable for exploratory research, appropriate here because of the exploratory nature of the research environment. The measures for Market Orientation and Performance have been shown to be reliable in both Industrial and Emerging economies including China (Deshpandé and Farley 1999b). The measures of Organizational Culture and Climate, and Innovation have been subject to less international comparison.

RESULTS

Analysis of the results involves two steps:

1. The first step involves comparative assessment of the "uniqueness" of Chinese managers and firms with comparable results from other Asian nations. Chinese patterns of personal values are first profiled and compared, and perceptions of elements of national culture are similarly compared. Finally, we compare Chinese profiles of Organizational Culture and Climate, Market Orientation and Innovativeness with similar measures from elsewhere in Asia.

2. Organizational profiles of Chinese firms which perform well are compared to those of Japanese and Thai firms, and the extent to which the results are industry-specific is analyzed. Profiles of State Owned Enterprises and Joint Ventures in China are also compared.

VALUES OF THE SHANGHAI MANAGERS

Be respectful at home, serious at work, faithful in human relations.

The Analycts

The individuals in the sample represent senior managers who will be among the leaders who oversee China's economic and managerial transformation. Like Chinese history, they are steeped in traditions with a heavy Confucian overtone, but they have also been influenced by the events of the past half-century in China. For benchmark purposes, the Chinese responses are compared to those from Thailand, a culture heavily influenced by Buddhist values but less by Confucian ones. (These items were not included on the Japanese questionnaire.) Table 3, which contains the measures on a variety of individual values, is divided into two parts:

What Is Important? These Chinese managers especially value Perseverance and a Sense of Shame (averages above 6 on a 7-point scale measuring importance and Perseverance significantly above the mean for the sample of Thai managers). Saving Face and Respect for Tradition are a bit less important (averages near 5 on the 7-point scale for the Chinese managers and significantly less than the average for Thai

TABLE 3. Values of Individual **Managers** 100 Shanghai-Based Companies

A. WHAT IS IMPORTANT

Perseverance	6.81(a)
Having a sense of shame	6.12
Protecting face	4.85(b)
Respect for tradition	4.72(b)

(1 = Very Unimportant, 7 = Very Important)
(a. Chinese managers significantly higher on average than Thai managers; b. Thais significantly higher)

B. PERSONAL VALUES

I have strong affection for my family	6.59
I interact frequently with family members	6.04
I often compromise my own needs with my family needs	4.82(b)
I give up personal wishes and desire to conform with social norms	4.69(b)
My parents have greatly influenced my way of thinking and behaving	5.36(b)
I behave according to what others expect of me	2.74(b)

(1 = Strongly Disagree, 7 = Strongly Agree)
(a. Chinese managers significantly higher than Thai managers; b. Thais significantly higher)

managers). There are no significant differences between SOE's and JV's on these items, nor are there significant differences over industries. The results thus apply quite broadly.

Confucian Values. Both the Chinese and Thai managers highly value family (the first two items in Table 3B). On matters of conformity and piety, the Thais score significantly higher than the Chinese. This may reflect longer-term cultural differences, and it may also be related to cultural developments during the latter half of the present century as well. In any case, there are clear indications of Chinese uniqueness in these results. These results also apply broadly, as there are no differences related to industry and no differences between SOE's and JV's.

CHINESE NATIONAL CULTURE

If the leaders are courteous, the people are easy to employ.

The Analycts

Measuring perceptions related to one's own culture is a tricky undertaking, and it is particularly useful to have cross-cultural comparisons available.

Cultural Dimensions

In his classic cross-cultural comparisons of managers, Geert Hofstede (1980, 1991, 1994) classified forty countries in terms of the four dimensions described in Table 4. It is insightful to compare his results with this more recent examination of centrally-planned economies undergoing significant change. Hofstede did not include China (or any other centrally-planned economy) in his sample, but he did include aggregate measures for Thailand and Japan. We also analyze Chinese culture by comparing Thai and Chinese managers' assessments of national culture values along these four dimensions using the first two items from each of the Hofstede (1980) dimensions. (Comparable detailed measures are not available on the Japanese managers on these items.) It is important to note that Hofstede concentrates on aspects of national culture which immediately impact managerial behavior.

TABLE 4. Chinese Culture Norms of 96 Chinese Managers Based on Summary Items Drawn from Hofstede (1991)

(Value of 1)	(Value of 7)	Average Chinese Scores	Thai and Japanese position on items in Hofstede(1991)
A. POWER DISTANCE–the extent to which people in a society accept inequality in terms of personal power and often wealth			Thais above average Japanese average
Inequality in society should be minimized	There should be inequality in which everybody has a rightful place	5.18(b)	
All people should be interdependent	Some people should be independent; most should be dependent	5.55(b)	
B. UNCERTAINTY AVOIDANCE–the extent to which people in a society prefer situations which are structured			Thais average Japanese very high
Each day should be taken as it comes	Uncertainty in life should be fought	4.45(a)	
I experience ease and low stress	I experience anxiety and high stress	3.84	
C. INDIVIDUALISM – the extent to which people in a society make decisions based on their own wishes rather than collective considerations			Thais very low Japanese very high
Families or clans protect people in exchange for	People should take care of themselves and their immediate families	4.78(a)	
"We" consciousness dominates	"I" consciousness dominates	3.82(b)	
D. MASCULINITY–the extent to which males in a society share traditionally female roles of nurturing			Thais below average Japanese very high
*Men needn't be assertive but can also take nurturing roles	Men should be assertive	5.07(a)(c)	
(SOE mean 4.88, JV's mean 5.45)			
Sexes should be equal	Men should dominate	2.87(b)	

a. Chinese managers significantly higher than Thai managers
b. Thais significantly higher
c. Significant difference between State-Owned Enterprise and Joint Ventures
* Significant difference between State-Owned Enterprises and Joint Ventures

- Uncertainty Avoidance involves a preference for structured situations and may inhibit entrepreneurialism. The Chinese managers' scores are a bit above those of the Thais, and are about average for the Hofstede sample of 40 countries. Chinese managers, even after decades of central economic planning, are not below average of other countries in this critical dimension. In the original Hofstede work, the Japanese score very high on this dimension.
- Power Distance involves acceptability of unequal personal power (sometimes extending to wealth) in the culture. The Chinese scores are significantly lower than those of the Thais on these items, indicating a more egalitarian culture. The Thais are significantly above average for the Hofstede sample. The Japanese are about average on this dimension (Hofstede 1991).
- Individualism, primarily associated with Western cultures, involves an emphasis on goals and behavior stressing individual performance. Unsurprisingly, the Thais score very low on this dimension, and the Chinese appear to be in the same general neighborhood. The Japanese also score low on this dimension in aggregate.
- Masculinity, perhaps the least clear of the four Hofstede dimensions, really involves the tendency of masculine and feminine roles to differ. Perhaps because of the influence of the past half century, the Chinese managers are somewhat lower than the Thais are, who themselves score in the direction of equality on this dimension. The Japanese have a very high score on this dimension in Hofstede (1991).

Values influenced by Confucian thinking clearly play an important role in terms of general Chinese culture. While the Chinese profiles are unique even among these three Asian countries (in fact, the profiles of most cultures in the Hofstede sample are unique), our Shanghai managers are by no means extreme in terms of the Hofstede cultural dimensions as measured on samples of managers from other Asian countries.

In summary, the value structures and perceptions about culture of comparable samples of Thai and Chinese managers are significantly different. It is probably more interesting to note that, within China, the managers of the Joint Ventures and State-Owned Enterprises have for practical purposes the same profile of values and cultural beliefs. Only one of 18 scales in Tables 1 and 2 (about the number expected by chance) is significantly different. None of the Chinese scales are significantly different for different industries.

CORPORATE CULTURE OF CHINESE AND OTHER ASIAN FIRMS

Ideal people are universal and not clannish.

The Analycts

As has been the case in all of our work on this subject, Chinese Corporate Culture is seen by our sample as more of a mixture of the four corporate culture types in Figure 1 than as mainly prototypical of a particular culture type (Table 5). Since the scales we use to measure corporate cultures are constrained to sum to 400 in all countries, we can make direct comparisons of the Chinese profiles with those of other Asian countries. Before directly comparing Chinese firms with Thai and Japanese organizations, we should observe that Table 5 shows that we should reject the hypothesis of the existence of some sort of "Asian Business Model" of organization, as the profiles for the

TABLE 5. Means of Organization Culture Scores in Three Asian Countries

Organizational Culture Type	China	Thailand	Japan[1]	Culture Type Significantly Different over the Three Countries (p < .05)
Consensual	91.5	108.5	117.0	Yes
Entrepreneurial	109.1	91.9	78.9	Yes
Bureaucratic	111.1	100.5	100.9	Yes
Competitive	88.3	99.0	106.1	Yes
Significant Differences over Countries in Culture Scales Within Country (P < .05)	Yes	Yes	Yes	

[1]Source: Deshpandé, Farley and Webster (1993).

three countries are significantly different across weights assigned to culture types.

The Chinese managers report their organizations as more Bureaucratic than the Thai and Japanese managers, perhaps because of the skills which have been required to operate in a centrally-planned environment for the past 40 years. This conclusion is reinforced by the relatively low value of the means for Competitive cultures. The Chinese are also quite low in terms of Consensual culture–not surprising as Thailand and Japan are quite consensual national cultures. However, the Chinese firms are high on Entrepreneurial scores. This particular pattern of Bureaucracy and Entrepreneurial Culture is unique to the Chinese sample in our cross-national studies. These profiles hold for Chinese industry as a whole, as there are no industry differences in Organizational Cultures in terms of consumer product, industrial or service businesses.

CHINESE STATE OWNED ENTERPRISES AND JOINT VENTURES

As stated earlier, one of the major elements of Chinese economic reform has been the introduction of new organizational forms to complement the older State-Owned Enterprise structure. A great deal of international attention has been focused on these new organizations (Clarke 1997). One hope, sometimes expressed only implicitly, is that, through introduction of appropriate foreign management techniques, Joint Ventures will help move Chinese management to a more market-oriented outlook, with improved organization and ultimately improved performance. It is important to note that the evidence of the effects on performance of these sorts of changes is distinctly mixed. While *de novo* firms have been shown to outperform state firms and privatized firms in Eastern Europe, the latter two show little difference in performance (Konings 1997; Konings and Janssens 1996).

When we examine the elements of our "Universal Market-Focused Model" in China, it appears that Organizational Cultures have been affected by the new forms of organizations (Table 6). Joint Ventures are significantly more Competitive and significantly less Bureaucratic than the SOE's. There is a consistent but very small pattern of difference in Innovativeness, Market Orientation and Organizational Climate as well as in Performance; all of the differences between the

TABLE 6. Profiles of Chinese State-Owned Enterprises and Joint Ventures in Terms of Organizational Culture and Climate, Innovation, Customer Orientation and Performance

	MEANS			Sign of Difference as Hypothesized?	Difference Significant at = .05?
	All	SOE's	JV's		
ORGANIZATIONAL CULTURE					
Consensual	91.5	91.9	91.4	Yes	No
Entrepreneurial	109.1	108.7	109.3	Yes	No
Bureaucratic	111.1	115.0	104.6	Yes	Yes
Competitive	88.3	82.8	94.1	Yes	Yes
INNOVATION	17.7	17.6	17.8	Yes	No
ORGANIZATIONAL CLIMATE	30.5	30.3	30.8	Yes	No
CUSTOMER ORIENTATION	37.4	37.3	37.5	Yes	No
PERFORMANCE	8.2	8.0	8.3	Yes	No

SOE's and the JV's are in the positive direction as we hypothesized. While a sign test of these differences as a set is significant at $\alpha = .05$, the very small differences would no doubt disappoint anyone expecting a "big bang" from the reforms. These results are best viewed as hypothesis generating for further study, as well as for the passage of more time. (Deshpandé and Farley (1999a) report similar results in comparing private and State-Owned Enterprises in Vietnam.)

HOW ORGANIZATIONAL CULTURE, CLIMATE, INNOVATION AND MARKET ORIENTATION RELATE TO BUSINESS PERFORMANCE IN CHINA

Earlier in the paper, we developed the set of hypotheses concerning factors which should relate to firms' performance in the framework of a "Universal Market-Focused Model," which posits positive relationships between Performance and Organizational Cultures and Climates which are relatively open (Entrepreneurial and Competitive cultures coupled with a high level of Market Orientation) as well as to Innovation. When we compare the top quartile of Chinese firms in terms of Performance with the rest of the sample (Table 7), we find the pattern of measures are consistent with the Model.

- All of the differences between the Top Quarter of the performers and the Others conform in sign with those hypothesized earlier in this paper, and a multivariate T test is significant indicating a pattern of differences as a group. Five of the seven differences are individually significant–a particularly strong pattern in view of the reliabilities discussed earlier.
- In terms of individual significant effects, more Bureaucratic firms perform less well, while Innovative, Market-Oriented firms which have more Entrepreneurial and/or Competitive cultures perform better.
- The single most important variable in a multiple discriminant function separating the two performance groups is Market Orientation. This key variable from a marketing prospective has been consistently less important in similar analyses in the Industrial world (Deshpandé et al. 1997). It is possible that a newly developed Market Orientation can be especially effective in a transforming economy, although this proposition requires much more testing. Innovation is second most important in China; this has also proven to be an important factor in high performance in the Industrial world.
- The order of strengths of the partial effects of Organizational Cultures in the discriminant function shows that Bureaucratic Culture has the largest effect–and it is negative. Consensual culture has a smaller but the expected negative effect. Competitive and Entrepreneurial cultures have positive and nearly equal effects.
- Trusting and participative Organizational Climate has very little effect. More study of this factor for possible cultural specificity related to Western management styles is needed.
- Further tests of an alternative explanation of the results showed that there are no specific type of industry with a concentration of good or poor performers. Both can be found among producers of consumer goods, industrial goods and services.

DISCUSSION

If you wish for speed, you won't succeed; if you see small advantage, great things will not be accomplished.

The Analycts

The vastness and diversity of China along with the inherent complexity of the phenomena being studied here prompt us to view this work as a first step towards more systematic exploration of organizational transformation in situations in which market forces are replacing central planning and command structures. Further, there is a real need to track the dynamics of management practices and Organizational Cultures as reforms work their way through the system so that we can be more certain about their real nature.

As a group, the sample of 100 Shanghai firms has a profile quite different from those we have found elsewhere in Asia–a mixture of relatively Bureaucratic but nonetheless Entrepreneurial cultures, with low scores on both Consensual and Competitive cultures. Among the new organizational forms, the Joint Ventures with partners more accustomed to market competition have brought with them more Competitive and less Bureaucratic cultures as expected, but the general

TABLE 7. Profiles of Top Quarter of Chinese Firms in Terms of Performance

	Group Means		Sign of Mean Difference (Good Performers–Others)			
	Top Quarter of Performers	Other Firms	Hypothesized	Actual	Statistically Significant* at $\alpha = .05$?	Correlation of Variable with Discriminant Function of Top Quarter versus Others
ORGANIZATIONAL CULTURE						
Competitive	96.7	86.0	+	+	Yes	.25
Entrepreneurial	117.7	104.7	+	+	Yes	.24
Bureaucratic	98.7	114.5	−	−	Yes	− .34
Consensual	86.8	92.8	−	−	No	− .15
INNOVATIVE-NESS	18.6	17.2	+	+	Yes	.45
CUSTOMER ORIENTATION	39.4	36.8	+	+	Yes	.68
ORGANIZATIONAL CLIMATE	23.9	23.6	+	+	No	.09
PERFORMANCE	16.5	11.2	+	+	Yes	DV

*Overall significant differences between groups based on Multivariate Analysis of Variance of all variables.
DV–Dependent Variable in Discriminant Function

effects (including on performance) are very small. Perhaps the new forms of organizational governance will not have their expected impact, or perhaps more time and experience is needed.

In interpreting these results, it is important to remember that these managers, like others studied with similar methods in other countries, see their organizations much more as a mixture of the four culture types than as prototypical examples chiefly of one type. Thus we are talking about degrees and shadings of differences in Organizational Culture, rather than taxonomically different kinds of organizations.

Nevertheless, the best performers among this representative sample of Chinese firms headquartered in Shanghai share important characteristics of successful firms elsewhere in the more market-oriented world–Innovativeness, a higher degree of Market Orientation and Organizational Cultures which are externally-oriented, flexible and entrepreneurial. Other firms should be able to improve their performance by improvement along one or more of these dimensions. Among the factors which we studied, Market Orientation has the strongest partial effect on Performance of the Chinese firms.

It is important to note that our results are relative and, within China, may be limited to Shanghai. In fact, in comparisons with similar studies in Japan and Thailand, we find the evidence of the same "Universal Market-Focused Model" of success, but we find no evidence of an "Asian Business Model" of organizational culture at the macro level. The sharp differences in the profiles of the means over the three countries indicates that cultural differences may be embodied in the means of measures like the ones we are using. In this case, the Shanghai firms show a unique combination of Bureaucracy and Entrepreneurialism, which offsets low levels of both Consensual and Competitive cultures. (As we noted in the introduction to this paper, our results are consistent with those of Ralston et al. (1997: 202), who conclude that a "global corporate culture concept may be viable in the long term.") However, the Chinese firms still show the expected profile differences around those means for the good performers. We might hypothesize that we would find similar combinations of organizational cultures and relationships with performance in other economies which are quickly emerging from command structures to structures more governed by market mechanisms. To study these developments in greater detail we need to expand our attention to other parts of China and to samples which contain more Independently-Owned Enterprises, Cooperatives and Town-based Enterprises, which may also bring a more market-oriented outlook to Chinese management. Further, change in corporate culture, described earlier as one of the more permanent characteristics of the firm, is not a simple matter and almost certainly requires considerable time to impact on organizational performance.

REFERENCES

Bowman, Douglas, John U. Farley and David C. Schmittlein. 1998. Cross-National Emperial Generalization of a Supply Selection and Usage Model for Global Business Services. West Lafayette, IN: Purdue University.

Buzzell, Robert D. and Bradly T. Gale. 1987. *The Pims Principles: Linking Strategy to Performance*. NY: The Free Press.

Campbell, John P. 1977. On the Nature of Organizational Effectiveness. In P.S. Goodman and J.M. Pennings, eds., *New Perspectives on Organizational Effectiveness*. San Francisco, CA: Jossey-Bass Inc., Publishers.

Cameron, J.P. and Sarah J. Freeman. 1991. Cultural Congruence, Strength and Type: Relationships of Effectiveness. In R.W. Woodman and W.A. Passmore, eds., *Research in Organizational Change and Development*, Vol. 5. Greenwich, CT: JAI Press, Inc.

Capon, Noel, and John U. Farley. 1991. Organizational Culture in U.S. and Australian Firms. Working paper, NY: Columbia University.

Capon, Noel, John U. Farley, and Scott Hoenig. 1997. *Towards a Theory of Financial Performance*. New York: Klewer Publishing Co.

Capon, Noel, John U. Farley and James M. Hulbert. 1988. *Corporate Strategic Planning*. NY: Columbia University Press.

Capon, Noel, John U. Farley, James Hulbert, and Donald R. Lehmann. 1992. Profiles of Product Innovators Among Large U.S. Manufacturers. *Management Science*, 38 (February): 157-69.

Capon, Noel, John U. Farley, James M. Hulbert and David Lei. 1991. An Empirical View of *In Search of Excellence*. *Management Decision*, 29 (4): 12-21.

Clarke, Thomas. 1997. Changing Corporate Governance in China. Working Paper, Shanghai, China: China Europe International Business School.

Deshpandé, Rohit and John U. Farley. 1999a. Culture, Customers and Contemporary Communism: Vietnamese Marketing Management Under Doi Moi. *Asian Journal of Marketing*, forthcoming.

Deshpandé, Rohit, and John U. Farley. 1999b. Reliability in Measuring Market Orientation at Financial Performance in Transition Economies. In: Marketing Issues in Transitional Economies, ed. Rajeev, Batra, Boston, MA: Klaver Academic Publishers. 127-137.

Deshpandé, Rohit and John U. Farley. 1999c. Corporate Culture and Market Orientation: Comparing Indian and Japanese Firms. *Journal of International Marketing*, forthcoming.

Deshpandé, R. and J.U. Farley. 1998. Measuring Marketing Orientation: Generalization and Synthesis. *Journal of Market-Focused Management*, 2 (3): 237-241.

Deshpandé, Rohit, John U. Farley and Frederick E. Webster, Jr. 1993. Corporate Culture, Customer Orientation, and Innovativeness in Japanese Firms: A Quadrad Analysis. *Journal of Marketing*, 57 (January): 22-27.

Deshpandé, Rohit, John U. Farley and Frederick E. Webster, Jr. 1997. *Factors Affecting Organizational Performance: A Five-Country Comparison.* Cambridge, Massachusetts: Marketing Science Institute.

Deshpandé, R., and Frederick E. Webster. 1989. Organizational Culture and Marketing: Defining the Research Agenda. *Journal of Marketing*, 53 (January): 3-15.

Drucker, Peter F. 1954. *The Practice of Management.* New York: Harper and Row Publishers, Inc.

Farley, John U. and Donald R. Lehmann. 1994. Cross-National "Laws" and Differences in Market Response. *Management Science*, 20 (January): 111-122.

Grönhaug, Kjell and Geir Kaufmann. 1988. *Innovation: A Cross-Disciplinary Perspective*, Oslo: Norwegian University Press.

Hofstede, Gert. 1991. *Culture and Organizations: Software of the Mind.* London: McGraw-Hill.

Hofstede, Gert. 1980. *Culture's Consequences: International Differences in Work-Related Values.* Beverly Hills, CA: Sage Publications.

Hofstede, Gert. 1994. Management Scientists are Human. *Management Science*, 20 (January): 4-13.

Kohli, Ajay K. and Bernard J. Jaworski. 1990. Market Orientation: The Construct, Research Propositions, and Managerial Implications. *Journal of Marketing*, 54 (April): 1-18.

Kohli, A.K., B.J. Jaworski, and A. Kumar. 1993. MARKOR: A Measure of Market Orientation. *Journal of Marketing Research*, 30 (November): 467-477.

Konings, Josef. 1997. *Firm Growth and Ownership in Transition Countries.* Working paper, Leuven, Belgium: University of Leuven.

Konings, Josef and Stefan Janssens. 1996. How Do Western Companies Respond to the Opening of Central and East European Countries? Survey Evidence from a Small Open Economy–Belgium. Working paper, Leuven, Belgium: University of Leuven.

Kotabe, M., D.F. Duham, D.K. Smith, Jr. and R.D. Wilson. 1991. The Perceived Veracity of Pims Strategy Principles in Japan: An Empirical Inquiry Journal of Marketing, 55 (January), 26-41.

Levitt, Theodore. 1960. Marketing Myopia. *Harvard Business Review*, 38 (May-June): 45-56.

Mansfield, Edwin et al. 1977. *The Production and Application of New Industrial Technology*, New York: W.W. Norton and Company, Inc.

Narver, John and Stanley F. Slater. 1990. The Effect of a Market Orientation on Business Profitability. *Journal of Marketing*, 54 (October): 20-35.

Newman, Karen L. and Stanley D. Nolen. 1996. "Culture and Congruence: The Fit Between Management Practices and National Culture," *Journal of International Business Studies*, (27), 4th Quarter, 753-779.

Nunally, Jum. 1967. *Psychometric Theory*, New York: McGraw-Hill Book Company.

Ohmae, Kenichi. 1985. *Triad Power: The Coming Shape of Global Competition*, N.Y.: Free Press.

Pan, Yigang. 1996. "Influences on Foreign Equity Ownership Level in Joint Ventures in China," *Journal of International Business Studies*, (27), 1st Quarter, 1-26.

Quinn, Robert E. 1988. *Beyond Rational Management*. San Francisco, CA: Jossey-Bass Inc., Publishers.

Quinn, Robert E. and Michael R. McGrath. 1985. Transformation of Organizational Cultures: A Competing Values Perspective. In Peter Frost et al., eds., *Organizational Culture*, Beverly Hills, CA: Sage Publications, Inc.

Quinn, Robert E. and J. Rohrbaugh. 1983. A Spatial Model of Effectiveness Criteria: Toward a Competing Values Approach to Organizational Analysis. *Management Science*, 29(3): 363-77.

Ralston, David A., David H. Holt, Robert H. Terpstra and Yu Kai-Cheng. 1997. "The Impact of National Culture and Economic Ideology on Managed Work Value: A Study of the U.S., Russia, Japan, and China." *Journal of International Business Studies*, (28), 1st Quarter, 177-207.

Schneider, B. and J. Rentsch. 1988. Managing Climates and Cultures: A Futures Perspective. In *Futures of Organizations*, Jerald Hage (ed.), Lexington, MA: Lexington Press.

Shanghai Economy Yearbook Editional and Publishing Agency. 1996. *Shanghai Economy Yearbook 1996*, Shanghai, China.

Subject Study Group. 1995. Four Different Types of Corporate Culture: Comparison and Research. *Management World*, China, 1: 188-197.

Taguiri, Renata and George H. Letwen, eds. (1968), *Organization Climate: Explorations of a Concept*. Boston, MA: Harvard University.

Webster, Frederick E., Jr. 1988. The Rediscovery of the Marketing Concept. *Business Horizons*, 31 (May-June): 29-39.

Weick, Karl E. 1985. The Significance of Corporate Culture. In P.J. Frost et al., eds., *Organizational Culture*, Beverly Hills, CA: Sage Publications, Inc., 381-9.

Yip, George S., Johny K. Johansson and Johan Roos. 1996. Effects of Nationality on Global Strategy in Major American, European, and Japanese Multinational Companies, Cambridge, MA: Marketing Science Institute.

Zhan, Degan and Zhang Binglin. 1996. A Sample Study of Enterprise Culture Structure. *Management World*, 5: 204-210.

Marketing Science Institute. 1996. *Research Priorities 1996-1998: A Guide to MSI Research Programs and Procedures*. Cambridge, MA. Marketing Science Institute.

APPENDIX A. Measures–Operationalizations

Market Orientation

[The Market Orientation scale was developed and tested in Deshpandé, Farley and Webster 1993. It has been shown to be functionally equivalent to competing scales (Deshpandé and Farley 1998) and reliable in a broad range of settings in industrial and transitional economies (Deshpandé and Farley 1999b).]

The statements below describe norms that operate in businesses. Please indicate your extent of agreement about how well the statements describe the actual norms in your business.

1	2	3	4	5
Strongly		Neither Agree		Strongly
Disagree	Disagree	Nor Disagree	Agree	Agree

Instruction: Answer in the context of your specific product/market or service/market business

1. We have routine or regular measures of customer service.
2. Our product and service development is based on good market and customer information.
3. We know our competitors well.
4. We have a good sense of how our customers value our products and services.
5. We are more customer-focused than our competitors.
6. We compete primarily based on product or service differentiation.
7. The customer's interest should always come first, ahead of the owners.
8. Our products/services are the best in the business.
9. I believe this business exists primarily to serve customers.

[These same items were used in other countries with customers with the first-person pronoun replaced by "the supplier," which was identified at the beginning of the interview.]

Organizational Culture

[The four Organizational Culture scales were computed by adding all four values of the A items for Consensual, of the B items for Entrepreneurial, of the C items for Bureaucracy and of the D items for Competitive type cultures. The results shown in Table 5 can therefore equal more or less than 100, which would be the result only if respondents distributed points equally on each question. The scale was adapted from Cameron and Freeman 1988 and Quinn 1988.]

These questions relate to what your operation is like. Each of these items contains four descriptions of organizations. Please distribute 100 points among the four descriptions depending on how similar the description is to your business. None of the descriptions is any better than any other; they are just different. For each question, please use all 100 points. You may divide the points in any way you wish. Most businesses will be some mixture of these described.

1. Kind of Organization (Please distribute 100 points)

_____ points for A	(A) My organization is a very personal place. It is like an extended family. People seem to share a lot of themselves.
_____ points for B	(B) My organization is a very dynamic and entrepreneurial place. People are willing to stick their neck out and take risks.
_____ points for C	(C) My organization is a very formalized and structural place. Established procedures generally govern what people do.
_____ points for D	(D) My organization is very production oriented. A major concern is with getting the job done, without much personal involvement.

2. Leadership (Please distribute 100 points)

____ points for A	(A) The head of my organization is generally considered to be a mentor, sage, or a father or mother figure.
____ points for B	(B) The head of my organization is generally considered to be an entrepreneur, an innovator, or a risk taker.
____ points for C	(C) The head of my organization is generally considered to be a coordinator, an organizer, or an administrator.
____ points for D	(D) The head of my organization is generally considered to be a producer, a technician, or a hard-driver.

3. What holds the Organization Together (Please distribute 100 points)

____ points for A	(A) The glue that holds my organization together is loyalty and tradition. Commitment to this firm runs high.
____ points for B	(B) The glue that holds my organization together is a commitment to innovation and development. There is an emphasis on being first.
____ points for C	(C) The glue that holds my organization together is formal rules and policies. Maintaining a smooth-running institution is important here.
____ points for D	(D) The glue that holds my organization together is the emphasis on tasks and goal accomplishment. A production orientation is commonly shared.

4. What is Important (Please distribute 100 points)

____ points for A	(A) My organization emphasizes human resources. High cohesion and morale in the firm are important.
____ points for B	(B) My organization emphasizes growth and acquiring new resources. Readiness to meet new challenges is important.
____ points for C	(C) My organization emphasizes permanence and stability. Efficient, smooth operations are important.
____ points for D	(D) My organization emphasizes competitive actions and achievement. Measurable goals are important.

Innovativeness

[The Innovativeness scale was constructed from the items used by Capon, Farley, and Hulbert (1988) to describe organizational innovation and used by Capon, Farley, Lehmann and Hulbert (1992).]

In a new product and service introduction, how often is your company:

	Always				Never
First-to-market with new products and services	1	2	3	4	5
Later entrant in established but still growing markets*	1	2	3	4	5
Entrant in mature, stable markets*	1	2	3	4	5
At the cutting edge of technological innovation	1	2	3	4	5

*Reverse scored in forming the scale

APPENDIX A (continued)

Organizational Climate

[The Organizational Climate scale was measured with items from the non-innovation factors derived from 51 items in Capon, Farley and Hulbert (1988) and used for comparison of U.S. and Australian firms by Capon and Farley (1991).]

We are also interested in your opinions about your organization's decision-making style. We would like to know whether you agree or disagree with the following statements:

1	2	3	4	5
Strongly Disagree	Disagree	Neither Agree Nor Disagree	Agree	Strongly Agree

1. In our organization, there is excellent communication between line managers and staff people.
2. People trust each other in this organization.
3. Decision-making in our organization is participative.
4. A friendly atmosphere prevails among people in our organization.
5. In our organization, people feel they are their own bosses in most matters.

Performance

[Performance is measured using items grounded in Pims procedures (Buzzell and Gale 1987, Kotabe et al. 1991).]

Relative to our businesses' largest competitor, we are:

	(1)	(2)	(3)	(4)	(5)
(a)	Much less profitable	Less profitable	About equally profitable	More profitable	Much more profitable
(b)*	Much larger	Larger	About the same size	Smaller	Much smaller
(c)*	Have a much larger market share	Have a larger market	About the same share	Have a smaller market share	Have a much smaller market share
(d)	Growing much more slowly	Growing more slowly	Growing at about the same rate	Growing faster	Growing much faster

*Reverse scored in construction of the scale.

APPENDIX B. Scale Reliabilities

The fundamental conceptual material on which this study is based was primarily developed with the industrial world in mind. The first application involved scales developed in the U.S. and applied in Japan–again both industrial countries. In the initial application in Japan (Deshpandé et al. 1993), pairs (dyads) of managers were used in all samples to allow analysis of inter-rater reliabilities within firms as well as conventional intra-scale reliabilities measured in terms of Chronabach α's (Table B.1). Inter-rater reliabilities were highly significant. A very high degree of scale reliability was found, where the conventional floor level of .6 (out of 1.0) was met in the case of all but one scale. (Nunally 1967). Similar results were found outside the Industrial World in India (Deshpandé and Farley 1999c).

TABLE B.1. Scale Reliabilities for Three Asian Countries Measured by Chronbach α

	China	Japan	Thailand
		(Deshpandé et al. 1993)	
Organizational Culture			
Consensual	.47	.82	.66
Ad Hoc	.47	.66	.60
Bureaucratic	.51	.42	.41
Competitive	.53	.71	.33
Customer Orientation	.72	.69 (a)	.68
Organizational Climate	.78	.69	.72
Innovativeness	.62	.85	.37
Performance	.80	.71	.82

a. Measured at the supplier

As the research program moved beyond the Industrial world, the question of whether the measurement methods were adequate became important. In Thailand, we found somewhat lower levels of scale reliabilities on Organizational Culture and on Innovation. The pattern of reliabilities of Organizational Culture scales in the Chinese data were to those in Thailand. These levels of reliability are viewed as acceptable for exploratory research of the type represented in this paper. Reliabilities in China of the measures of Customer Orientation, Organizational Climate and Innovativeness and Performance were above .6.

Effects of the Value Chain in International Joint Ventures: The Case of the Electronic and FMCG Sectors

Yanni Yan
John Child

SUMMARY. This paper examines differences in the resource profile and experience of Sino-foreign joint ventures located in the two sectors: non-consumer electronics and fast moving consumer goods [FMCG]. It identifies key dimensions along which the two sectors differ and considers the implications for joint ventures. The impact of sectoral differences suggests that the industrial sector of China into which a foreign company invests is of consequence, especially for the business priorities of Chinese partners and for the ease with which a joint venture can be managed through the foreign partner's corporate network. Foreign partners are likely to find more flexibility, and a greater opportunity to influence joint venture management in the FMCG sector compared

Yanni Yan is affiliated with Department of Marketing, City University of Hong Kong and Department of Accounting, Finance and Management, University of Essex, Wivenhoe Park, Colchester, Essex, CO4 3SQ, United Kingdom (E-mail: yany@essex.ac.uk). John Child is Diageo Professor of Management Studies, University of Cambridge, St. John's College, Cambridge CB2 1TP, United Kingdom (E-mail: JC160@hermes.cam.ac.uk).

Grateful acknowledgement is made of funding provided by the UK Economic & Social Research Council and the Hong Kong Research Grants Council to defray the cost of the research on which this paper draws. The authors also thank Dr. John R. Fawn and Professor Malcolm Warner for their participation in discussions which have contributed toward this paper.

[Haworth co-indexing entry note]: "Effects of the Value Chain in International Joint Ventures: The Case of the Electronic and FMCG Sectors." Yan, Yanni, and John Child. Co-published simultaneously in *Journal of Global Marketing* (International Business Press, an imprint of The Haworth Press, Inc.) Vol. 14, No. 1/2, 2000, pp. 37-56; and: *Greater China in the Global Market* (ed: Yigang Pan) International Business Press, an imprint of The Haworth Press, Inc., 2000, pp. 37-56. Single or multiple copies of this article are available for a fee from The Haworth Document Delivery Service [1-800-342-9678, 9:00 a.m. - 5:00 p.m. (EST). E-mail address: getinfo@haworthpressinc.com].

37

with non-consumer electronic sector. The physical and infrastructural features of the sectors appear to be particularly consequential for managing an investment in China, and they may be more significant than institutional factors. *[Article copies available for a fee from The Haworth Document Delivery Service: 1-800-342-9678. E-mail address: <getinfo@ haworthpressinc.com> Website: <http://www.HaworthPress.com>]*

KEYWORDS. Value chain, joint venture, business in China

INTRODUCTION

Organisations add value through co-ordinating a series of value-creating activities. These activities are perceived to be absolutely essential requirements for success in today's highly competitive global market (Thompson, 1997). The effects of the value chain in unitary organisations have been studied extensively in the west (Miles, 1961). The value chain concept provides an appropriate framework for clarifying how an unitary organisation might maintain substantial discretion over the allocation of its resources, create differentiation and effectively manage its costs (Porter, 1985). The unique structure of International Joint Ventures [IJVs] has given rise to studies of their complexity in terms of understanding how an international investing organisation's resource and competence are used to maintain substantial control over the allocation of the IJV's resources, creation of differentiation and the effective management of its costs (Leonard-Barton, 1992). Many studies explore joint ventures through an analysis of the ownership determinants and the alignment of local versus foreign partners (Blodgett, 1991, Faulkner & Bowman, 1995, Pan, 1996, Child & Yan, 1999). These factors are major determinants in value chain analysis, and data from existing studies can be used to test the validity of extending the application of value chain analysis to the complexity of IJV organisations (Norman & Ramirez, 1993). This study is concerned with the question of how an IJV in particular industry sectors can offer significant strategic advantages through co-ordinating a series of value-creating activities.

There are three general concerns about exploring the effects of value chains in IJVs. The first concern is the contention that competitive advantage can be gained from the investing firms' unique resource and competence, fitting the conditions of that industry (Bartlett, 1986). The value chain of an IJV will be concerned with analysing the bases on which an IJV organisation's core resource and competence can be built. The ability to contribute and manage the value-adding functions in accordance with its industry advantages may provide competitive strength and the success of a joint venture (Yoshino and Rangan, 1995).

The second concern relates to the ability of an IJV to establish and maintain those organisational functions which enhance the industry critical success factors (Hardaker & Ward, 1987). In an unitary organisation, control is exercised by the executives of the company (Miller, 1998). The unique nature of a joint venture stems from the fact that its ownership and control is, to some extent, shared between the few founding partners. The parent companies may have the right to nominate managers who exercise control over specific value-adding functions. Meeting expectations of two or more parents can complicate the control priorities of an IJV (Yan, 1997).

The third concern addresses how competitive advantages can be derived from the structure of the industry in which an IJV is located and from the pursuit of generic strategies–cost leadership, differentiation, or focus (Porter, 1985). The difference in pursuit of generic strategies by different organisations in the same industry can rarely be fully explained by differences in their cost efficiency, the linkages between activities, or their resource and competence base per se (Child & Faulkner, 1998). Competitive advantages can be determined by the way in which resources are deployed to create competence in the organisation's separate activities and the processes of linking these activities together to sustain excellent organisational efficiency (Rumelt, 1991).

With these considerations in mind, this paper is structured as follows. First, the use of value chain analysis in the context of IJVs is described. Secondly, IJV competitive advantages derived from the value chain are examined and compared for the electronics and the fast-moving consumer goods [FMCG] sectors. Hypotheses are formulated concerning of resource-provision by parent companies and the parent company influence on value chain activities. Thirdly, the paper describes the sample of 67 Sino-foreign joint ventures investigated together with the methods employed for testing the hypotheses. Finally, the hypotheses are examined and conclusions drawn.

CONCEPTUALISATION: VALUE CHAIN ACTIVITIES

The concept of value chain provides a useful way of analysing resources and functions within an organisation in the context of how each might individually contribute to competitive advantage (Johnston and Lawrence, 1988). Application of the concept presents a challenge when the value chain activities either have few variables in common within the market sector or the variables in the value chain are not strongly attached to the sector (Preece et al., 1995). When chain activities are only loosely coupled, they will not provide a strong response in generating industry advantages (Rayport and Sviokla, 1995). It is recognised in the corporate governance literature that the ownership impact on the value chain may retain evidence of separateness and identity (Monks and Minow, 1995) and this can be taken to imply loose coupling. On the positive side, partners in joint ventures provide specific resources, skills and knowledge in addition to their equity contribution. These resources should enhance the effectiveness of the control which the provisioning partner possesses through the formal right of ownership. Yan and Gray (1994) regard equity as the provision of a 'capital resource' to a joint venture by its partner companies. The resources that partner firms contribute to joint ventures confer formal control rights through contributions to equity capital, as well as influence deriving from a partner's possession of scarce expertise and resources (French and Raven, 1959). The board of directors is likely to have overall control (Björkman, 1995), but the joint venture general manager's position can affect an IJV's operation, since the general manager is responsible for maintaining relationships with each of the parents, as well as running the venture (Schaan and Beamish, 1988). The parameters by which control priorities are set, given what may be conflicting interests of the parent companies, the IJV board and the general manager, have rarely been operationally measured (Buckley, 1990, Conner, 1991). Thus it can prove difficult to assign values to specific activities for the purposes of value chain analysis (Hall, 1993).

The strategic and competitive advantages offered by a joint venture may lie in the potential synergistic effects of combining the complementary assets of its parent company (Russo and Fouts, 1997). A firm has an area of expertise where its primary activities lie (Preece et al., 1995), and the contribution this makes can be measured using the value chain concept. This applies independently of whether the firm operates up, mid or downstream in the industry chain. A firm's centre of gravity is the part of the chain that is of primary importance to the company and the area where its greatest expertise and capabilities lie its core competencies. Porter (1996) suggests that a company's centre of gravity is usually the point at which the company started. After a firm successfully establishes itself by obtaining a competitive advantage, one of its first strategic intentions is to move forward or backward along the value chain in order to obtain technology, reduce costs, guarantee access to key raw materials, or to guarantee distribution (Gaski, 1984, Bettis and Hamel, 1992).

The value chain is more complex in the case of an IJV as the long-run viability of a joint venture depends on a number of factors which do not apply to an unitary organisation. These include the time span of the joint venture contract, the respective interests of the partners, and the need for complementarity between the different functional competencies provided by the partners. The challenge of achieving a balanced and integrated value chain in a joint venture is especially significant because of the potential conflict of interests between the partners, and the sensitivity of the capital and non-capital resources they supply (Yan et al., 1995).

PROFILE OF VALUE CHAIN ACTIVITIES

The focus of knowledge and competence within the resourcing profile of an IJV may vary by sector. The choice of FMCG and non-consumer electronics sectors in China takes into account several considerations. *First*, the pattern of joint venture investment is influenced by the Chinese economic and political climate. Chinese policy emphasises high-tech and 'pillar' strategic industries, including industrial electronics. At the same time, there has been a rapid market-led development of light consumer industries, such as FMCG. The choice of these two sectors therefore reflects different priorities in mainstream Chinese government policy as it exists in the late 1990s. *Secondly*, both electronics and FMCG contain the largest populations of foreign companies operating in China and therefore provide a statistically sound base of IJVs to study. Thirdly, critical success factors in each industry sector are expected to depend upon support from different value chain activities. In the electronics sector, critical resources for competitiveness are product design and production technology (Pisano et al., 1988). The value chain in this case tilts towards a manufacturer-centred upstream perspective (Pisano et al., 1988). In the FMCG sector, marketing and brand promotion are central (Frazier and Antia, 1995). When key factors for each industry have been correctly identified, they can provide a checklist for the partner of an IJV to proceed with their strategic analysis (Lynch, 1997). This paper focuses on a parent company's provision of resource and involvement in their application. *Finally*, research on foreign direct investment in China suggests that foreign investors concentrate their attention upon the resourcing of specific functions within their IJVs (Yan and Gray, 1996). The foreign parent company's control priorities therefore in each sector may be shown to be significantly different.

Non-Capital Resourcing

Application of the concept of value chain theory to the case of a Sino-foreign joint venture requires the assumption that the provision of both capital and non-capital resources to that joint venture provides a platform for parent control, both through legal ownership rights and the firm's dependency on the expertise, managerial and technological, supplied to it (Yan and Gray, 1996, Child and Yan, 1999). In addition to tangible assets, IJV parent companies may also contribute intangible assets such as brands or management training, which can add value indirectly. Competitiveness comes from the fact these contributions can be provided by the parent company at a lower marginal cost than the joint venture would have to pay to acquire them from the market (Gereffi et al., 1994). Competitiveness also comes from the synergy obtained from the complementary resources provided by the parent companies. The provision of such resources is normally accompanied by a corresponding degree of parental influence in the IJVs operations (Child et al., 1997).

Influence can therefore be taken as an indicator of foreign parent contributions to the IJV's competitiveness in given areas of activity. In electronics, technology and production are likely to be key factors, with product design being a focus of competence. In FMCG, marketing especially brand management, is particularly important. Partners have a weighted influence over areas of the IJV's value chain which is dependent upon the resourcing profile and management support provided. The key factors are the provision of technology, training, and other services (Whitley, 1996). The foreign partners are normally the providers of technology and management expertise to the joint venture while the local partners are the providers of land, building and people

(Yan, 1997). Foreign parent influence are used as indicators of contribution to different IJV activity areas within each industrial sector. It is reasonable to suppose that foreign partners should exert influence over IJV value chain activities for which they supply resources in order to ensure their effective application. These considerations give rise to the following:

Hypothesis 1. The non-capital resourcing profile, provided to the IJV by each partner, will be governed by where most value can be generated in the sector. In the FMCG sector this will be primarily marketing and management services whereas in the electronics sector the emphasis will be on product and production technology.

Value-Adding Functions

The concept of a chain of functional activities within IJVs involves understanding the partner(s) control priorities in the role of each function together with the synergy achieved amongst the value chain specialities (Johnston and Lawrence 1988, Geringer, 1991). The task of meeting the separate goals of the IJV partner(s) in a cohesive manner creates a dilemma as to the kinds of value, structure and process that the IJV should have (Gersick, 1991). An IJV organisation needs to solve the fundamental issue of how to maintain internal cohesion between partners, as the composition of an IJV management structure is associated with the key appointments nominated by the partners (Yan, 1997). It is also anticipated that the synergy derived from IJV functional value-creating activities will mirror the relative extent of the managerial support provided by the joint venture partners where the contributions could be regarded as indicators of their contributions to the value chain. Differentiation in managerial activities throughout a value chain could, for example, be the result of developing an excellent design team in electronics or of being able to source high-quality materials or high-quality production locally in FMCG. The partners to an equity joint venture provide capital which can be applied to investment in plant and other facilities. Capital provision is usually in cash, but Chinese joint ventures often provide it in kind. The provision of capital is enshrined in equity, which conveys certain rights such as seats on the IJV board of directors that can in turn provide a basis for overall control (Bjorkman, 1995). Thus, although the whole capital provision does not contribute directly to the value chain as such, it can provide a foundation for a parent company to exercise managerial influence over part or whole of the IJV value chain especially via the appointment of the its general manager. The above considerations give rise to the following:

Hypothesis 2. The partners seek to control the areas of high value added in an IJV by nominating the occupants of senior management positions. In addition to the post of general manager, the key position in FMCG IJVs is marketing, whereas production and product development appointments are important in the electronics sector.

Partners' Influence

Pfeffer and Salancik (1978) identify the command of critical resources as the basis for exercising power within and between organisations. In an IJV, dependence on key resources is expected to give rise to control of the focal organisation by the partner that provides those resources (Yan and Gray, 1996). External control over organisations can arise from the power of external parties to command those resources which are vital for the successful operation of the organisations (Pfeffer and Salancik, 1978). Internal control over, or access to, resources gives some organisational members more power over the organisation than others (Donaldson, 1985, Pfeffer, 1981). In the electronics sector, for example, the greatest expertise is normally located in purchasing and manufacturing (Pisano et al., 1988). The process of production requires close and continuous vertical links between the IJV and its parent companies which provide the feed of components (Gaski, 1984). The transactional integration between parent companies and their IJVs in electronics may focus on maintaining high technical standard and establishing the presence of global servicing. The management in this sector may be concentrated on technical matters and many components may be provided by parent companies (Child et al., 1997).

In the FMCG sector, analysis of the chain suggests that the greatest value adding expertise is in marketing and retailing (Rayport and Sviokla, 1995). Forward vertical integration takes an organisation closer to its markets and allows more freedom for an organisation to establish contact directly with its customers (Hamel and Prahalad, 1991). The competitive nature of the market and the significance of parent company boards require close and continuous links between the IJVs and their parent companies. These links provide assistance in the local market context by utilisation of the parent company's existing distribution and marketing skills, and brand image. The analysis of downstream supply is concentrated on the partner's existing distribution and business presence in the market place (Rumelt, 1991). The inputs of raw materials in the FMCG, are mainly provided locally, the decision being driven by the determination of transport costs. The management activities are primarily concentrated on marketing support. The above considerations give rise to the following:

Hypothesis 3. Partner influence is derived from non-capital resourcing of the value chain. This will be primarily from brand, marketing and management services provided in the FMCG sector and product and production technology provided in the electronics sector.

Performance

Focusing on the FMCG and electronics sectors, the effective outcomes accrued from the partner's resource input to an IJV may add value or create an inherent distributive dilemma within value chain activities of that IJV (Boris et al., 1995). An IJV's performance can be identified in terms of the potential gain from the partner's resource inputs and the actual benefit from the synergy of the functional specialists shared between an IJV and its partners (Blodgett, 1991). An IJV's performance achievement is constrained by external influences exercised by bodies such as the parent companies and the local government (Yoshino and Rangan, 1995). This will be significant in a transitional economy such as China which is still at the stage of improvement of foreign investment environment and development of relevant institutional policies (Child and Lu, 1996). Managing a joint venture in a given sector has its own specific implications (Rayport and Sviokla, 1995): a series of functions in the chain, such as organisational design, R&D, purchasing, manufacturing, marketing and distribution, directly involve the joint venture with its parent companies. A chain of activities occur where capital, non-capital resources and information move back and forth between the joint venture and its parent companies. The above considerations, taken together with the previous hypotheses, give rise to the following:

Hypothesis 4. The contribution of value chain activities to performance will be based primarily on marketing oriented
investment in the FMCG sector and on product and
production technology investment in the electronics
sector.

METHOD

Sample Characteristics

The sample consists of 67 Sino-foreign joint ventures formed between Chinese and foreign owning companies. The foreign share of IJV
equity ranges between 25 and 95 percent. Thirty-four of the joint ventures are located in the FMCG (branded food, beverage, cosmetics and
tobacco), while 33 are located in the advanced non-consumer electronics sector (computer-related equipment, telecommunications and silicon
chips). The research was conducted in collaboration between staff from
the University of Cambridge and the International Technology and
Economy Institute of the State Council in China. Relatively factual
information on the resourcing profile, the occupation of key managerial
positions, the partner's influences over the chain activities and IJV's
performance were obtained from the interviews with 212 senior foreign
and Chinese respondents in joint ventures.

Operalisation of Variables

The following variables were for testing the hypotheses:

Equity Share: the share of equity held by foreign and Chinese
parent companies.

Non-Capital Resources: the composition of contractual and non-
contractual inputs distinguishing between contributions from foreign
and Chinese partners in the form *of product design, production
technology, management systems, management services, marketing
and training.* Each item of provision and non-provision is scored in a
binary manner (provided = 1; not provided = 0).

Board Membership: The ratio of those IJV directors appointed by
the foreign parent company (ies) to those appointed by the Chinese
parent company(ies).

Managerial Positions: An assessment of whether a person of PRC

Chinese or foreign nationality occupied senior management positions in the IJV. The positions include–general manager, and heads of the finance, HRM, marketing, production, and technical functions.

Partner's Influence over Value Chain Activities: The most senior IJV manager available enumerated, on five-point scales, the degree of influence exercised respectively by the Chinese and foreign parent companies over the areas of value chain activities (1 = very little influence, 5 = dominant). Within the total of 67 joint ventures, 44 of these senior respondents were general managers, 19 were deputy general managers and the rest were functional heads. In 21 IJVs senior Chinese and foreign managers gave separate evaluations of partner's influences over the chain activities, there were no significant differences between these two sets of assessments. This suggests that confidence can be had in the ability of the procedure to compare partners' influences over the chain activities between IJVs in FMCG and electronic sector. The information on *primary activities* covered: inbound logistics include the areas such as (1) receiving and distributing the inputs, setting strategies priorities, and allocating senior managers; (2) operations; (3) outbound logistics covers marketing and sales in international, Asia and domestic markets; (4) financial control; and (5) quality control. The *supporting activities* include: (1) training and development policies; (2) rewards and incentives; (3) technological innovation; and (4) procurement.

Performance Indicators: Subjective assessments were made by the most available senior joint venture manager of the IJV's market share, growth, and profitability. These are scaled between 1 = not satisfied and 5 = highly satisfied. The three subjective measures of IJV performance are significantly inter-correlated and can be aggregated for ease of interpretation ($\alpha = .073$). Financial data on the historical trends of the joint venture over the two years were examined for profitability, growth in profit and growth in sales. These were normally provided and assessed by the most senior available IJV manager and checked when possible against documentary evidence.

RESULTS

Forty out of the 67 IJVs studied had a majority equity share held by foreign parents, almost twice as many in the FMCG sector (N = 26) as in the electronics sector (N = 14). Twelve IJVs had a 50/50 split, six in each sector. In the remaining 15 JVs, where the foreign parent(s) hold a minority equity stake, two are in FMCG and 13 are in electronics. The average capital investment in electronics joint ventures is US$ 31.34 millions and average employment is 506. By contrast, in FMCG the average capital investment is only US$ 11.19 millions and the employment is 307 people on average. The results indicate a higher level of technology and a greater capital commitment to large scale production facilities.

Examination of the differences in partner(s) resource profile by sector reveals a general trend for the non-capital resource supplied in both contractual and non-contractual terms by foreign partners to exceed that contributed by their Chinese counterparts. Table 1 shows a more substantial contrast between the two sectors in the areas of: product design, production technology and management services provided on contractual basis, and training provided on a non-contractual basis. Joint ventures in FMCG tend to rely more on foreign parent provision of these resources, than do the electronics joint ventures. Table 1 indicates generally greater range of resource provision by foreign partners in FMCG, which connected with generally larger equity share. It is especially apparent in contracted technology transfer and management services. A high percentage of materials in a FMCG are sourced locally. The distributions of the resource profile by sector appear less to support the argument that the FMCG products are mainly targeted at the Chinese domestic market and that key inputs can be obtained locally from that market. Hypothesis 1 is not supported.

Table 2 shows the tenure of key appointments by sector. Fifty percent of the IJVs in the FMCG sector have a foreign majority on the board of directors. This compares with the electronics sector where only 24 percent of the IJVs had foreign majority boards. The proportion of Chinese and foreign directors on the joint venture boards quite closely reflects the percentage of the partner equity shareholding ($r = .76$). The ability to dominate the board of directors is likely to be a powerful lever of control, even though most decisions may be made by consensus. Majority equity share bolsters a parent company's influence over managerial occupancies in a joint venture. The great majority (79%) of the IJVs have a foreign general manager (88% in FMCG and 70% in electronics). Foreign tenure of the general manager and marketing manager positions is greater in FMCG than in electronics. In electronics, 53 percent of technical departments are headed by expatriates, but only 42 percent of production,

TABLE 1. IJV Partner(s) Resourcing Profiles by Sector (N = 67 IJVs)

	Percentage of Parent Companies Providing the Resources[1]				
Non-Capital Resources	Electronics (%)		Fast-Moving Consumer Goods (%)		Value of P[2] Between Sectors
	Chinese	*Foreign*	*Chinese*	*Foreign*	
Contractual Input[3]					
Product design	12	73	0	97	.00
Production technology	12	70	0	97	.00
Management services	12	25	15	44	.02
Management systems	15	49	21	62	.24
Training	3	61	0	71	.24
Non-Contractual Inputs[3]					
Product design	18	67	6	71	.27
Production technology	15	58	0	62	.52
Management services	30	64	32	59	.22
Management systems	21	49	24	47	.48
Training	15	55	9	65	.09

[1]Percentages for partners' contractual and non-contractual inputs are derived from frequency testing (electronics: N = 33, FMCG: N = 34).
[2]Probabilities are derived from T-tests which compare the distribution of partner(s) resource profiles by sector. Combined percentages add up to less than 100 percent because either the category of non-capital resource was not used or because it was obtained from a source other than the parent companies.
[3]Inputs or resources that respectively foreign and Chinese parent companies have provided to the joint venture on a contractual or non-contractual basis–covering the same items.

and 33 percent of marketing departments. By contrast, in the FMCG joint ventures, as many as 59 percent of production departments and 56 percent of marketing departments are headed by expatriates. The main value chain contributions by foreign manager in the electronics are in product design whilst the main contributions in the FMCG sector is in process as well as marketing. For FMCG IJVs, the higher proportion of foreign general managers indicate that global integration with foreign parent is considered more important than local adaptation (Yan, 1999). There are more foreign appointments in key positions and more boards with a foreign majority in FMCG ventures. Hypothesis 2 is broadly supported with the qualification that

TABLE 2. Chinese and Foreign Tenure of Key Appointments by Sector (N = 67 Sino-foreign joint ventures unless shown otherwise)

Appointment	Electronics		Fast-Moving Consumer Goods		Value of P[1] Between Sectors
	(%)		(%)		
	Chinese	Foreign	Chinese	Foreign	
Majority on JV board[2]	45.5	24.2	14.7	50.0	.00
General manager	30.3	69.7	11.8	88.2	.06
Deputy general manager[3]	69.7	27.3	73.3	17.6	.25
Technical (N = 51)[4]	46.9	53.1	47.4	52.6	.56
Production	57.6	42.4	41.2	58.8	.19
Marketing	66.7	33.3	44.1	55.9	.07
Finance	66.7	33.3	58.8	41.2	.51
HRM (N = 65)[5]	90.6	9.4	93.9	6.1	.62

[1]Probabilities are derived from T-tests comparing the distribution of Chinese and foreign appointments by each sector.
[2]Percentages where board representation was equal are not shown.
[3]The table excludes six joint ventures which each had one Chinese and one foreign deputy general manager, and another joint venture which had two Chinese and one foreign deputy general manager.
[4]Fifteen joint ventures in fast-moving consumer goods and one in electronics did not have a separate technical or equivalent function.
[5]Two joint ventures did not have separate HRM or personnel functions.

foreign control over processing activities is more prominent in FMCG than was expected.

Table 3 shows the parental influences over the value chain activities by sector and it notes that the differences are statistically significant in the case of inbound logistics, finance control, quality control, training & development, and technology innovation. In both sectors, foreign parents are perceived to exercise above mid-point level influence in comparison with their Chinese partners in every area of the value chain activities. Foreign companies in FMCG are perceived to have greater influence relative to their Chinese partners in the areas of quality control, training and development, procurement, and outbound logistics. The gap across the whole range of issues between the partner(s) tends to be larger in FMCG than the electronics sector. In the FMCG sector, the marketing-related assistance, which many foreign parent companies provide to the IJVs, appears as primary justification for the

TABLE 3. The Chinese and Foreign Parent Company's Influences over the Areas of the Value Chain Activities by Sector (N = 67 Sino-foreign joint ventures)

Value Chain Activities	Average Influence Scores[1]				Value of P[2] Between Sectors
	Electronics (N = 33)		Fast-Moving Consumer Goods (N = 34)		
Primary Activities	Chinese	Foreign	Chinese	Foreign	
Inbound logistics[3]	2.94	3.63	2.59	3.72	.00
Operations	2.89	3.22	2.88	3.88	.14
Outbound logistics[4]	2.33	4.00	2.13	4.11	.33
Finance control	2.44	3.67	2.13	3.88	.07
Quality control	2.11	4.33	1.75	4.25	.00
Supporting Activities					
Training & Development	2.67	3.61	1.88	4.38	.01
Reward & Incentive	2.89	3.00	2.75	3.63	.17
Technology Innovation	1.78	4.44	1.63	4.63	.05
Procurement	2.78	3.56	2.13	3.88	.12

[1]Scored on a scale from 1 = very little influence to 5 = dominant influence.
[2]Probabilities are derived from T-tests, which compare the differences in Chinese and foreign partner's influence over the value chain activities by sector.
[3]Inbound logistics include partner influence on receiving and distributing the inputs.
[4]Outbound logistics are defined as formulating sales and distribution activities in the Chinese domestic market.

degree of control they have over related areas of management. The gap across the whole chain between the partner(s) tends to be wider in the FMCG sector and is more marked in quality control and training and technology development areas. In the electronics sector, foreign companies are perceived to have greater influence in the areas of quality control and technology innovation. Hypothesis 3 is supported.

Table 4 shows inter-correlations between the main indicators of performance and each category of non-capital resourcing, foreign occupancy of key managerial positions and the partners' influence over the chain activities. There are variations in performance within the electronics and FMCG sectors. With the subjective performance indicators, the correlations between the subjective indicator of profitability and the foreign occupancy of production position in electronics is

TABLE 4. IJV's Performance Achieved by Sector (N = 67)

Performance Indicators	Electronics (N = 33)				
	Subjective Measures			Objective Measures	
	Profitability	Growth	Market Share	Profitability [4](N = 39)	Growth in sales[4] (N = 47)
Non-Contractual Resources[1]					
Product Design	.08	.08	.31*	.06	.01
Production Technology	.04	.04	.38*	.22*	.10
Training	.11	.11	.31*	.10	.12
Management Positions[2]					
Marketing	.17	.12	.09	.18	.01
Production	.36*	.10	.04	.12	.10
Influences[3]					
Inbound Logistics	.20	.36*	.12	.06	.25
Outbound Logistics	.29	.31*	.03	.18	.11
	FMCG (N = 34)				
Non-Contractual Resources					
Production Design	.35*	.07	.17	.14	.26
Production Technology	.23	.06	.21	.20	.26
Training	.35*	.14	.21	.07	
Management Positions					
Marketing	.45**	.06	.39*	.05	.30
Production	.07	.13	.14	.05	.24
Influences					
Inbound Logistics	.20	.29	.21	.10	.20
Outbound Logistics	.15	.32*	.30*	.04	.15

[1]Correlations between the non-contractual resource and the performance indicators to joint ventures
[2]Correlations between the managerial positions and the performance indicators to joint ventures
[3]Correlations between the partners' influences over the value chain and the performance indicators to joint ventures
[4]The number of cases are reduced due to incomplete data. Some joint ventures did not supply sales and profit data.

positive and statistically significant ($r = .36$). The results suggest that the higher the technology standards required in a sector, the more likely it is that foreign parents will have to put greater effort into the staffing of technical and production management. The achievement of sales growth is positively associated with foreign parent influence over inbound logistics ($r = .36$) and outbound logistics ($r = .31$). The achievement of market share is more consistently supported by the non-contractual resources such as product design ($r = 31$), production technology ($r = .38$) and training ($r = .31$) invested into joint ventures.

In the FMCG sector, the achievement of profitability is positively associated with foreign provision of non-contractual resources such as product design ($r = .35$) and training ($r = .35$) being invested in joint ventures. The result also indicates that the profitability achieved is highly correlated to foreign headship of marketing ($r = .45$). Correlations between the achievement of sales growth and outbound logistics ($r = .32$) are positive and statistically significant. The high level of market share achieved in the FMCG sector tends to be associated with foreign management of marketing and control over outbound logistics. The expectation that both resourcing and managerial input contributes differently to value creation of joint ventures in each sector is therefore supported. The results suggest that the pattern of the contribution of value chain activities to the performance of joint ventures is centred on primarily on marketing invested in the FMCG sector and on product and production technology in the electronics sector. Hypothesis 4 is partially supported.

CONCLUSION

The application of value chain analysis to IJVs appears to be useful in that the pattern of resource provision each partner is related to critical successful factors in each sector. The study offers insight into the assessment of the resource contributions that each foreign and Chinese partner makes to IJVs in the FMCG and electronics sector. Significant results show that IJVs in the FMCG sector can benefit from the appointment of a foreign expert as marketing manager and from the exercise of a leading influence in that area. In the electronics sector, high technology IJVs have significant relationships between superior performance and resource provision in product design, training, foreign production management and foreign partner influence over the resources provided. The value chain approach and related resourcing perspectives have empirical as well as theoretical power for predicting and explaining the performance of IJVs. Companies wishing to invest in joint ventures need to be clear as to the benefits to be obtained from exerting direct control over the operations of IJVs before establishing the input parameters for them. In other words, the results of this study suggest that control focussed on critical value-chain activities for the sector is more beneficial than an unfocused blanket approach to exercising control. The advantage of adopting a value chain analysis is that it assesses partner contributions in the form of the impact that different contributions have on functional activities. Further studies aimed at predicting and understanding a partner's influence over the IJV's various value chain areas should take this conceptual refinement into account.

REFERENCES

Bartlett, Christopher A. (1986). Building and Managing the Transactional: The New Organisational Challenge in M.E. Porter (ed.) *Competition in Global Industries*. Boston MA: Harvard Business School Press. 367-401.

Bettis, R.A., Bradley, S.P. and Hamel, G. (1992). Outsourcing and Industrial Decline, *Academy of Management Executive*, February, 127-135.

Blodgett, Linda Longfellow (1991). Partner Contributions as Predictors of Equity Share in International Joint Ventures. *Journal of International Business Studies*, 22: 63-78.

Bjorkman, Ingmar (1995). The Board of Directors in Sino-Western Joint Ventures. *Corporate Governance*, 3: 156-166.

Boris Kabanoff, Robert Waldersee, and Marcus Cohen (1995). Expoused Values and Organizational Change Themes. *Academy of Management Journal*, 38: 1075-1104.

Buckley, Peter J. (1990). Problems and Developments in the Core Theory of International Business. *Journal of International Business Studies*, 21: 657-665.

Child, John (1994). *Management in China during the Age of Reform*. Cambridge: Cambridge University Press.

Child, John and Faulkner, David (1998). *Strategies of Co-operation: Managing Alliances, Networks, and Joint Ventures*. Oxford: Oxford University Press.

Child, John and Yuan Lu (1996). Institutional Constraints on Economic Reform: The Case of Investment Decisions in China. *Organisation Science*, 7: 60-77.

Child, John, Yanni Yan and Yuan Lu (1997). Ownership and Control in Sino-foreign Joint Ventures. In Paul W. Beamish and J. Peter Killing (eds.), *Co-operative Strategies: Asian Pacific Perspectives*: 181-225. San Francisco: The New Lexington Press.

Child, John and Yan, Yanni (1999). Investment and Control in International Joint Ventures: The Case of China. *Journal of World Business* (forthcoming).

Conner, Kathleen R. (1991). A Historical Comparison of Resource-based Theory and Five Schools of Thought within Industrial Organisation Economics: Do We Have A New Theory of the Firm? *Journal of Management*, 17: 121-154.

Donaldson, Lex (1985). *In Defence of Organisation Theory: A Reply to the Critics.* Cambridge: Cambridge University Press.

Faulkner, David and Bowman, C. (1995). *The Essence of Competitive Strategy,* Prentice Hall.

French, John R.P. and Bertram Raven (1959). The Bases of Social Power. In D. Cartwright (ed.), *Studies in Social Power.* Ann Arbor, Michigan: University of Michigan Press.

Frazier, Gary L. and Kersi D. Antia (1995). Exchange Relationships and Interfirm Power in Channel of Distribution. *Journal of the Academy of Marketing Science,* 23: 321-326.

Gaski, John F.T., (1984). The Theory of Power and Conflict in Channels of distribution. *Journal of Marketing,* 48:9-9.

Gereffi, G., Korzeniewicz, M. and Korzeniewicz, R. (1994). Introduction: Global Commodity Chain. In Gereffi, G. and Korzeniewicz, M. (eds.), *Commodity Chains and Global Capitalism,* Westport, CT: Praeger.

Geringer, J. Michael (1991). Strategic Determinants of Partner Selection Criteria in International Joint Ventures. *Journal of International Business Studies,* 22: 41-62.

Gersick, C.J. (1991). Revolutionary Change Theories: A Multilevel Exploration of the Punctuated Equilibrium Paradigm. *Academy of Management Review,* 16: 10-36.

Hall, Rochard (1993). A Framework Linking Intangible Resources and Capabilities to Sustainable Competitive Advantage. *Strategic Management Journal,* 14. 607-618.

Hardaker, M. and Ward, B.K. (1987). Getting Things Done, *Harvard Business Review,* Vol. 65, No. 6, 112-20.

Johnston, Russell & Paul R. Lawrence (1988). Beyond Vertical Integration–The Rise of the Value-adding Partnership. *Harvard Business Review,* July-August, 94-101.

Leonard-Barton, D. (1992). Core Capabilities and Core Rigidities: A Paradox in Managing New Product Development. *Strategic Management Journal,* Vol. 13 (Summer), 111-25.

Lynch, Richard (1997). *Corporate Strategy.* Pitman Publishing.

Miller, Alex (1998). *Strategic Management,* Third Edition. Irwin/McGraw-Hill.

Miles, Lawrence (1961). *Techniques of Value Analysis and Engineering.* McGraw-Hill.

Monks, Robert A.G. & Minow, Nell (1995). *Corporate Governance.* Blackwell Business.

Murdick, R.G., Rendern, B. and Russell, R.S. (1990). *Service Operations Management,* Needham Heights, Massachusetts: Allyn & Bacon.

Norman, R., & Ramirez, R. (1993). From Value Chain to Value Constellation: Designing Interactive Strategy, *Harvard Business Review,* July/August, 65-77.

Pan, Yigang (1996). Influences on Foreign Equity Ownership Level in Joint Ventures in China. *Journal of International Business Studies,* First Quarter. 1-25.

Pfeffer, Jeffrey & Gerald R. Salancik (1978). *The External Control of Organisations: A Resource Dependence Perspective.* New York: Harper & Row.

Pisano, Gary, Michael V. Russo & David J. Teece (1988). Joint Ventures and Collaborative Agreements in the telecommunications equipment industry. In D.C. Mowery, editor, *International Collaborative Ventures in US manufacturing*, 23-70. Cambridge, Mass.: Ballinger.

Porter, Michael E. (1985). *Competitive Advantage: Creating and Sustaining Superior Performance*. New York: Free Press.

Porter, Michael E. (1996). What is Strategy. *Harvard Business Review*. (November-December 1996), 73.

Preece, S., Fleisher, C. and Toccacelli, J. (1995). Building a Reputation along the Value Chain at Levi Strauss, *Long Range Planning*, 28, 6.

Rayport, Jeffrey F. & Sviokla, John J. (1995). Exploiting the Virtual value Chain, *Harvard Business Review*, 73: 6 (November-December1995), 75-85.

Rumelt, Richard P. (1991). How Much Does Industry Matter? *Strategic Management Journal*, 12 (March 1991), 167-185.

Russo, Michael V. & Fouts, Paul A. (1997). A Resource-based Perspective on Corporate Environmental Performance and Profitability. *Academy of Management Journal*, 40: 534-559.

Schaan, Jean-Louis and Beamish, Paul W. (1988). Joint Venture General Managers in LDCs. In Farok J. Contractor and Peter Lorange (eds.) *Co-operative Strategies in International Business*. Lexington, MA: D.C. Health.

Thompson, John L. (1997). *Strategic Management: Awareness and Change*. Third Edition. International Thomson Business Press.

Whitley, R. (1996). Business Systems and Global Commodity Chains: Competing or Complementary Forms of Economic Organisation? *Competition and Change*, 1: 411-25.

Yan, Aimin and Barbara Gray (1994). Bargaining Power, Management Control, and Performance in United State China Joint Ventures: A Comparative Case Study. *Academy of Management Journal*, 37: 1478-1517.

Yan, Aimin and Barbara Gray (1996). Linking Management Control and Inter-partner Relationships with Performance in US-Chinese Joint Ventures. In John Child and Yuan Lu (eds.), *Management Issues in China: International Enterprises*. London: Routledge.

Yan, Yanni, John Child and Yuan Lu (1995). Ownership and Control in International Business: An examination of Sino-foreign International Joint Ventures. Paper presented to Academy of Management Annual Meetings, Vancouver.

Yan, Yanni (1997). The Effect of *Ownership on Performance in Sino-Foreign Joint Ventures*. Advances in Chinese Industrial Studies. JAI Press Inc. 5: 219-247.

Yan, Yanni (1999). Managing and Organisational Learning in Chinese Firm. *Asia Pacific Business Review* (forthcoming).

Yoshino, Michael Y. and U.S. Rangan (1995). *Strategic Alliances: An Entrepreneurial Approach to Globalisation*. Boston: Harvard Business School Press.

Entering China Today:
What Choices Do We Have?

Yadong Luo

SUMMARY. The peripherally growing and remarkably dynamic Chinese economy is now encouraging the use of more diverse and creative entry modes for international investors. This article illustrates various entry modes of foreign direct investment available at present to foreign companies entering China. These entry modes include equity joint ventures, wholly foreign owned subsidiaries, contractual joint ventures, umbrella companies, acquisitions, representative offices, branches, build-operate-transfers, licensing and franchising. The merits and limitations of each entry mode are discussed. Some practical advice on entry strategies for international executives active in the Chinese market is also highlighted. *[Article copies available for a fee from The Haworth Document Delivery Service: 1-800-342-9678. E-mail address: <getinfo@haworthpressinc.com> Website: <http://www.HaworthPress.com>]*

KEYWORDS. Entry mode, investment, China

China's astounding economic growth rates over the past years have lured many foreign companies to set up operations there. China's special economic, cultural, and political context is, however, unfamiliar territory to many executives. The rules of the game are often

Yadong Luo is Associate Professor, Department of Management, College of Business Administration, University of Hawaii, 2404 Maile Way, Honolulu, HI 96822 (E-mail: yadong@busadm.cba.hawaii.edu).

[Haworth co-indexing entry note]: "Entering China Today: What Choices Do We Have?" Luo, Yadong. Co-published simultaneously in *Journal of Global Marketing* (International Business Press, an imprint of The Haworth Press, Inc.) Vol. 14, No. 1/2, 2000, pp. 57-82; and: *Greater China in the Global Market* (ed: Yigang Pan) International Business Press, an imprint of The Haworth Press, Inc., 2000, pp. 57-82. Single or multiple copies of this article are available for a fee from The Haworth Document Delivery Service [1-800-342-9678, 9:00 a.m. - 5:00 p.m. (EST). E-mail address: getinfo@haworthpressinc.com].

dissimilar to those in market economies. Choosing the right entry mode is therefore crucial to the success of the joint venture.

For both the new investor beginning to explore the Chinese market and incumbents with multiple investments in China, the choice of entry modes have expanded in recent years. Entry modes available to international trading businesses include conventional import and export, flexible trade (i.e., processing imported materials or foreign samples and assembling imported parts and components), international leasing, and counter-trade (i.e., barter, counter-purchase, offset, switch trading, compensation trade, or buy-backs). For foreign direct investment, entry modes include equity joint ventures, wholly foreign owned subsidiaries, contractual joint ventures, umbrella companies, acquisitions, representative offices, branches, build-operate-transfers, licensing, and franchising. This article is designed to discuss the range of entry modes for foreign direct investment in China.

Two prominent characteristics on entry mode selection have been emerging in the country. First, several new investment vehicles such as umbrella companies, acquisitions of Chinese enterprises, and build-operate-transfers (BOT) have been created and employed. Second, the use of conventional entry modes such as equity joint ventures and wholly foreign-owned subsidiaries is undergoing fundamental structural changes. For example, wholly foreign-owned ventures accounted for less than 1 percent of total contractual value of FDI in 1985; this percentage increased to 43 percent during the first half of 1997. Understanding advantages and disadvantages of each entry mode choice is a prerequisite for foreign firms to formulate their entry strategies.

In general, foreign investors are free to choose from several entry modes. These include: (i) equity joint ventures (EJVs), the most favored mode in the past, accounting for 49.97 percent of the total amount of actual FDI in 1996. An EJV is a limited liability company with equity and management shared in negotiated proportions by foreign and Chinese partners; (ii) wholly foreign-owned enterprises (WFOEs), which represented 29.85 percent of the total value of FDI in 1996. According to China's Law on Wholly Foreign-owned Enterprises, promulgated in April 1986, a WFOE is a foreign company using entirely its own capital, technology, and management while operating in China. The enterprise manages its operations independently and is responsible for all risks, gains, and losses; (iii) contractual (or cooperative) joint ventures (CJVs), which constituted about

20.81 percent of actual FDI in 1994. The CJV refers to a variety of arrangements and a loose association of partners that agree to pursue a joint undertaking (which may include a limited liability company). The Chinese and foreign partner cooperate in joint projects or other business activities according to the terms and conditions stipulated in the venture agreement; and (iv) other options include the establishment of representative offices, branch offices, umbrella companies; the acquisition of existing firms; licensing and franchising, and build-operate-transfer (BOT) operations. A detailed discussion of these entry modes follows.

ENTRY MODE 1: EQUITY JOINT VENTURES

The most common entry for MNCs into the Chinese market has been through EJVs. To set up an EJV, each partner contributes cash, facilities, equipment, materials, intellectual property rights, labor, or land-use rights. According to EJV law, a foreign investor's share must be at least 25 percent of total equity. Generally, there is no upward limit in most deregulated industries. However, in governmentally-controlled or institutionally-restricted sectors, such as automobile and telecommunications, foreign investors are often more confined with respect to equity arrangements. According to the Interim Provisions on the Term of Joint Ventures of Sino-Foreign Equity Joint Ventures, approved by the State Council in September 1990, there is no maximum term of operation for EJVs, although most are granted up to 50 years. This duration can be extended any time depending upon the agreement of the partners. Chinese approval authorities generally encourage these extensions.

As an alternative to either full integration or simple market exchange, the EJV facilitates inter-firm learning and transfer of intangible assets while mitigating incentives for opportunism by creating interdependence between the transacting parties (Luo, 1997). If the benefits derived from joint efforts, minus the transaction costs specific to the formation and operation of an EJV, are greater than the sum of benefits obtained from exploiting firm-specific advantages separately, an EJV creates synergies which enhance economic rents to the partners. These synergies can be the result of risk reduction, economies of scale and scope, production rationalization, convergence of technologies, and improved local acceptance (Beamish and Banks, 1987).

The EJV form provides foreign companies with long-term connections to the Chinese market. The EJV's ability to sell through the local partner's established marketing channels seems especially attractive to manufacturing businesses looking to penetrate the domestic market. The Chinese government normally favors this mode because it often involves significant technology transfer to the Chinese partner. When EJVs enter industries in compliance with governmental plans, they are more likely to receive special access to utilities and critical input than other entry modes such as WFOEs.

EJVs are, however, notoriously hard to sustain even in the relatively stable environments of the United States and Europe (Harrigan, 1985; Osborn & Hagedorn, 1997). Investment in China is even more difficult because the country is vast and varied, its culture and traditions are profoundly different from those of the West, and its social, governmental, and economic systems are particularly complex. Today foreign investors must contend with several additional factors when considering EJVs in China.

First, the marketplace in China is rapidly evolving, fragmenting, and becoming more competitive as more foreign companies set up operations there. Many new entrants are vying for first-mover advantages. Top-level players in some of the most promising industries (e.g., consumer packaged goods, infrastructure, construction, chemicals, pharmaceutical, and electronics) are pursuing aggressive growth strategies with a focus on gaining market share. Some companies are willing to sustain losses in order to establish beachheads in China, be they in the form of manufacturing plants, distribution networks, or consumer awareness of their products.

Second, the distribution system in China is quite chaotic and undergoing fundamental changes. The traditional three-tier (national, provincial, and local) distribution system in China is crumbling, giving way to various parallel channels that charge different fees and provide different services in every geographic area. These changes indicate that getting your product into the Chinese market can be daunting. Expanding the scope of operations can be even more so. Every Chinese company belongs to and operates under some combination of local, provincial, and central government authority, each with its own agenda. Hence, there are many conflicting interpretations of rules and regulations. If your EJV partner tries to do business outside its authorized territory, it is apt to run into trouble.

Third, negotiations on the joint venture contract can be lengthy and complicated, with a tendency to negotiate in a style described by one veteran China trader as "a blend of the Byzantine and evangelical" (Tateisi, 1996). Chinese negotiators often frustrate Western business people unused to their tactics. They may attempt to control meeting locations and schedules, take advantage of perceived weaknesses, use shame tactics, pit competitors against each other, feign anger, rehash old issues, and manipulate expectations. Often negotiation continues even after the signing of the joint venture contract. Therefore, a foreign company should choose effective negotiators, prepare for time-consuming meetings, and develop a sophisticated strategy before starting negotiation.

Fourth, foreign companies often find themselves in a dilemma when the Chinese partners demand technology that is 'state-of-the-art.' Chinese negotiators routinely request the most advanced technology from foreign suppliers during initial negotiations, though they may lack sufficient foreign exchange and an adequate infrastructure to utilize complex technology and trained personnel. To ensure a better chance of success, foreign companies are strongly advised to provide the most appropriate, price-competitive technology.

Finally, it is often difficult to decide the contribution made to the venture by each partner. The Chinese side normally prefers to contribute non-cash items such as land use, existing buildings and construction materials, all of which are easy for the Chinese to overvalue due to the difficulty in assessing prices accurately. In order to avoid such complications, foreign investors should have assessments made by independent professional consulting or accounting firms.

ENTRY MODE 2:
WHOLLY FOREIGN-OWNED ENTERPRISES

The WFOE form offers foreign investors increased flexibility and control. Within the constraints of the Chinese system, WFOEs allow managers to expand as quickly as they want and where they want, without the burden of an uncooperative partner. WFOEs also allow foreign investors to set up and protect their own processes and procedures, which leads to more careful strategic and operational oversight. Moreover, they can be established more quickly than EJVs; local

Chinese authorities are required to respond to initial project proposals within 30 days.

WFOEs offer new hope for a more effective way to work in China. But in any competitive market, turning dreams into reality is challenging. China's complexities double that challenge. However, foreign investors who can let go of the conventional wisdom that joint ventures are the only way to do business in China have a new way to take advantage of the country's vast opportunities. For companies willing to accept the challenge, WFOEs may be ideal.

WFOEs have traditionally been viewed by the Chinese government as offering little in the way of technology transfer or other benefits to the Chinese economy (Vanhonacker, 1997). Although the governmental support of WFOEs still trails behind that of EJVs, the attractiveness of this entry mode to the government has gradually increased. It helps stimulate economic growth, generate foreign exchange earnings, and reduce the unemployment rate. When domestic credit is tight, WFOEs provide China with a means of attracting foreign capital.

WFOEs today operate in many areas where EJVs are currently approved. In some sectors, such as automotive and telecommunications industries, heavy regulations apply, which implies that EJVs are a safer choice. Exceptions always abound in China, however, as Motorola proved in Tianjing and General Motors in Guangzhou. From the Chinese government's perspective, investment form is negotiable; WFOEs are possible even in regulated industries. The real key to the entry mode regulation is not what the rule book says, but instead whether or not a foreign company will bring something of value to the Chinese government.

Some notes of caution should be stated. First, WFOEs must still handle guanxi relations. Many foreign investors need to rely on Chinese agents to make liaisons on their behalf and to help procure land, materials, and services. WFOEs should identify exactly which connections will help and who has them, and then engage with those Chinese individuals and organizations that have access to decision-making authorities to act as advisers.

Second, WFOEs are not allowed to invest and operate in certain industries that are vital to the Chinese economy. Nevertheless, the Chinese regulatory environment is evolving; more industries, including some service sectors, are opening up to foreign investment. Although it will be a gradual opening, China will eventually grant WFOE investment access to increasingly more industries.

Third, as WFOEs operate without the control of a Chinese partner, investment approval authorities often hold them to higher standards, including stricter foreign exchange balance requirements. If a WFOE is profitable, the Chinese government may encourage it to find a Chinese partner, in the hope of getting the foreign party to share it profits and pass along technological and management know-how. Alternatively, a Chinese business may try to form an EJV with another foreign party to produce similar goods in competition with the existing WFOE.

Lastly, WFOEs are more vulnerable to criticism relating to cultural and economic sovereignty. Naturally the Chinese do not want foreign companies taking advantage of their country. WFOE managers should recognize and address this concern. One way to do so is to localize production, that is, to buy as many parts and components as possible from local Chinese suppliers. Another way is to hire Chinese managers. Motorola, for example, employs only Chinese managers, very few of whom hold U.S. passports. Foreign companies can also be active in socially responsible projects, such as financing schools, sports events, the arts, public safety, or other community service projects. WFOEs can also nurture local brands. Coca-Cola, for example, recently transferred the trademark of its new Tian Yu Di fruit drink to a local producer, Tianjin Jinmei Beverage Company. This move was warmly received as an example of the company's sensitivity to the Chinese value of reciprocity.

ENTRY MODE 3: CONTRACTUAL JOINT VENTURES

Unlike an EJV, in which profit distributions and management of the venture are determined by the proportion of total registered capital contributed by each partner, the CJV (as governed by the Law of the People's Republic of China on Sino-Foreign Cooperative Enterprises, adopted by the National People's Congress on April 13, 1988) is an investment vehicle in which profits and other responsibilities are assigned to each party according to the joint venture contract. These are not necessarily in accordance with the percentage of each partner's share of total investment. A CJV is a business partnership in which each party cooperates as a separate legal entity and bears its own liabilities. The two firms entering into a CJV have the option of forming a limited liability entity with legal person status, similar to that of an EJV.

In China, joint exploration projects (e.g., offshore oil exploration consortia) are a special type of CJV. Under these arrangements, the exploration costs are borne by the foreign partner, with development costs later shared by a Chinese entity. Although such explorations allow the foreign firm to manage specific projects, this type of FDI does not necessarily result in the establishment of new limited liability enterprises. Major features of CJVs include:

1. Liability. A CJV is allowed to adopt non-legal person status. The liability of investors in a venture with non-legal person status is unlimited, while the liability of investors in a joint venture with legal person status is limited to the amounts they have invested. Legal person status is automatic for EJVs. CJVs may elect either status. CJV investors in China may be able to use the unlimited liability conferred on non-legal person status in the tax structure for their PRC venture.

2. Capital Requirements. Foreign investors in CJVs with legal person status are required to contribute 25 percent or more of the venture's total registered capital. This requirement does not apply to CJVs that adopt non-legal person status. In practice, 25 percent was generally assumed to be the minimum amount that a foreign investor could contribute to a CJV with non-legal person status.

3. Import Tax Exemptions. Like EJVs, CJVs are exempt from paying transfer taxes and duties on imported of equipment used as part of the foreign partner's investment in the enterprise, provided the equipment is required for the operation of the joint venture and is valued at no more than the total investment amount specified in the CJV contract.

4. Strategic Flexibility. There are no limits on the duration of the contract or prohibitions for withdrawal of registered capital during the contracted term. CJVs have great freedom to structure their assets, organize their production processes, and manage their operations. This flexibility can be highly attractive for a foreign investor interested in property development, resource exploration, and other production projects in which the foreign

party incurs substantial up-front development costs (Randall and Telesio, 1995). A CJV, for example, can build an accelerated return on its share of investment into the contract to allow it to recoup its equity share by the end of the term. Further, CJVs can be developed quickly to take advantage of short-term business opportunities and dissolved when they complete their assigned task.

CJVs differ from EJVs in several following ways. First, profit distributions among parties to a CJV need not be in strict proportion to their registered capital contributions. The foreign party may recover its investment earlier than the Chinese partner upon meeting certain conditions, including reversion of all fixed assets to the Chinese partner. In contrast, the parties to an EJV can distribute profits only in strict proportion to their contributions to the EJV's total registered capital. Moreover, a CJV may distribute profits both in cash and in venture output, while an EJV is restricted to making cash distributions. Second, as noted above, the CJV's ability to adopt non-legal person status also distinguishes it from an EJV. Besides affecting the liability of the joint venture partner, non-legal person status may allow foreign CJV partners to contribute less than 25 percent of the total registered capital of the joint venture. Foreign partners in an EJV must contribute a combined minimum of 25 percent of a venture's registered capital. Lastly, CJVs are not required to survey Chinese sources before importing supplies or raw materials from abroad, while EJVs must give first priority to Chinese suppliers.

Because of their ability to provide foreign investors with returns in excess of their proportional contributions to the venture's total registered capital, CJVs have been the vehicles of choice for build-operate-transfer infrastructure projects. The CJV option is expected to continue to be useful in BOT projects and, as a result of the new regulations, will become a more popular option for other types of ventures as well, especially those in which foreign investors seek a preferential return.

ENTRY MODE 4: UMBRELLA COMPANIES

Many foreign companies are now seeking greater flexibility of operations in China's market. A growing number of firms are interested in establishing fully integrated companies that can combine

sales, procurement, subsidiary investment, manufacturing, and maintenance service for a broad range of products. Foreign investors interested in the concept include those new to China as well as established
firms seeking to unite various existing investments in China under a
parent company. The growing complexity of operations of many
MNCs in China, and the need to more closely coordinate numerous
joint ventures and/or wholly owned subsidiaries, has led several firms
to set up holding companies in recent years. The 'umbrella' enterprise,
also known as 'investment company' (*touzi gongsi*) or 'holding company' (*konggu gongsi*), has emerged for this purpose.

In contrast to joint ventures, which can manufacture and market
only approved product lines, a holding company is able to unite existing investments under one umbrella to combine sales, procurement,
manufacturing and maintenance. It can also help balance foreign exchange reserves between joint ventures, act as a clearing house for
intra-group RMB (Chinese yuan) financing and smooth the establishment of new investments.

Du Pont was an early convert to the holding company format in the
late 1980s, although Philips is credited with being starting the concept–
apparently after the company's CEO met with Li Peng in 1989 and
received the Premier's endorsement. By the end of last year, the Chinese government had approved more than 25 holding companies, both
in wholly owned and joint venture form, involving foreign multinationals. One of the MNCs which recently set up a holding company in
China is CIBA, the Swiss pharmaceutical and chemical giant. The
group's wholly owned umbrella company, CIBA China, employs
approximately 30 people in its Beijing office and has branches in
Shanghai and Qingdao. It was set up in 1993 and is now capitalised at
US$30 million. In total, CIBA boasts 15 equity joint ventures in China,
has a handful of non-equity ventures and one wholly owned subsidiary,
and has US$260 million worth of investments in the country.

The umbrella model is especially useful for companies that are multi-
divisional, where each division adopts different entry modes and is run
independently while the holding company coordinates them. This also
suits the way the company is run worldwide, preferring individual
businesses so as to avoid building up reserves which would limit the
volume of cash that can be cycled on a global basis. With a holding
company in China, profits can be more easily transferred among different strategic business units (SBUs) and taken out of the country.

A foreign investor may consider establishing an umbrella enterprise to achieve some or all of the following objectives: (1) Investment in subsidiary projects; (2) Manufacturing products; (3) Facilitating foreign exchange balance for all China activities; (4) Centralized purchase of production materials for subsidiary projects; (5) Provision of product maintenance service and technical support; (6) Training for subsidiary project personnel and end users of products; (7) Coordination and consolidation of project management. Currently, each foreign-invested enterprise (FIE) has a separate company structure; an umbrella enterprise can centralize management and streamline the subsidiaries as operating units; (8) Marketing subsidiary products. Usually, each manufacturing FIE in China has to set up its own sales capability; an umbrella enterprise can achieve greater efficiency by establishing one marketing entity; and (9) Conversion of representative offices into umbrella or subsidiary branch offices, thus removing many operating restrictions such as the need to hire personnel through labor service companies.

An umbrella company may provide a range of services to its subsidiaries including: (1) Assisting personnel recruitment; (2) Providing technical training, market development, and consulting assistance; (3) Assisting borrowing funds, including providing guaranties; (4) Acting as an agent for subsidiaries in the procurement of machinery and equipment, including office equipment, and raw materials, components, and spare parts necessary for production processes; (5) Acting as an agent for SBUs in the sale of products and providing after-sales service; (6) Balancing foreign exchange among SBUs, with the approval of the foreign exchange administration authorities; and (7) Providing financial support to subsidiaries, with the approval of the People's Bank of China. Without special approval from the Ministry of Foreign Trade and Economic Cooperation (MOFTEC), these services can only be provided to SBUs in which the investment company holds at least a 25 percent equity.

At present, the allowed scope of operations for umbrella enterprises includes manufacturing, investment in subsidiaries, purchase of inputs and raw materials for SBUs, sale of SBU output, and marketing and operational services. An umbrella enterprise cannot act as a general trading company. That is, it cannot import finished product lines and sell them in China. Its business license must state the industries, projects, or products in which it will invest; it does not have an open license to engage in whatever business it wants. If the umbrella enterprise later wishes to engage in an activity not listed in the license, the change must be approved by MOFTEC and the license amended.

Foreign companies wishing to establish an umbrella enterprise usually must have at least two FIEs in China. Internationally known firms are given preference when applying to establish umbrella enterprises. Like all FIEs, an umbrella enterprise has Chinese legal person status.

According to MOFTEC regulations, Chinese partners in prospective joint investment companies must have a minimum total asset value of ¥100 million. Foreign applicants for wholly owned or joint investment companies must meet one of two sets of criteria. In one set, the foreign company must have had a minimum total asset value of US$400 million in the year prior to its application, have established one or more FIEs in which it has contributed at least US$10 million in registered capital, and have obtained approvals for three additional FIE project proposals. Applicants meeting this first set of conditions have the option of establishing an investment company in the name of a wholly owned subsidiary rather than in their own names, which may offer some comfort to foreign investors who want to insulate corporate headquarters from direct exposure to liabilities in China.

The second set of conditions stipulates that the foreign investor must have established a minimum of 10 FIEs in China, engaged in manufacturing or infrastructure construction to which it has contributed at least US$30 million in registered capital. Presently, the investment company itself must have a registered capital of at least US$30 million.

An umbrella company and its various FIEs are each treated by Chinese tax authorities as separate entities; consolidation of revenue and expenditures for tax purposes is not allowed. Subsidiary profits that are remitted to the umbrella enterprise as dividends will not be taxed, however. On the other hand, an umbrella enterprise with no manufacturing of its own will be taxed at 33 percent with no tax holidays. Like all other FIEs, an umbrella enterprise must balance its foreign exchange.

ENTRY MODE 5: ACQUIRING EXISTING FIRMS

The quickest way to expand one's investment in China is to acquire an existing Chinese firm or another foreign company with local ventures. This mode is particularly useful for entering sectors formerly restricted to state-owned enterprises. The Chinese government now permits foreign investors to buy all or part of the ownership interests of a wholly Chinese owned or Sino-foreign joint venture. China lacks sufficient capital, technology, and management knowhow to meet the needs of industries that are not deemed priorities. Foreign acquisition of Chinese firms gives newly privatized and growing Chinese enterprises easier access to much-needed capital for expansion while underutilized assets can be put to profitable use. For these reasons, it is expected that this will remain a long-term governmental policy (Peng, Luo & Sun, 1998).

Since 1992, China has allowed 31 state-owned firms to be listed on international stock exchanges (Rothstein, 1996), which denote the shares by different names according to the bourse: N shares are listed on the New York Stock Exchange, while H and S shares are listed on the Hong Kong and Singapore exchanges, respectively. Foreign investors looking to acquire a piece of Chinese industry can now establish a joint venture company limited by shares (limited company), buy 'B' shares (in hard currency) of one of the 300 or so state-owned enterprises listed on the Shanghai and Shenzhen stock exchanges, or directly acquire a Chinese firm or other joint venture. These firms may be listed on sale in property rights markets that have sprung up throughout China. Foreign investors can also buy into a Chinese business by participating in its conversion into a foreign-invested joint stock company.

For a foreign investor, the main advantage of entering the China market through acquisition is that many state-owned firms, although in the red, have the potential to operate profitably if provided with the right mix of capital, management, and technology (Dong & Hu, 1995). Though the Chinese government has declared that ownership of some 1,000 key state firms will remain in government hands, this still leaves a huge number of enterprises to be cut loose from state support. Foreign companies will have many opportunities to buy into enterprises in different sectors and regions.

Investing in China through acquisitions offers other advantages as well. The investor may participate in management and operations of a target firm, as in the case of EJVs and WFOEs, but the investor does not have to do so. As a result, acquisitions not only allow corporate investors to enter China, but also allow general investors, through holding companies, to gain entry, as in the case of many Hong Kong-based companies. Second, cash flow may be generated in a shorter time than in the case of an EJV or WFOE, since the acquired firm, by definition, does not have to be built from scratch. Finally, acquisition deals may be more attractive than EJVs or WFOEs because acquisitions offer immediate access to resources such as land use, ready-made distribution channels, and skilled labor, even when targeted firms have been losing money.

Foreign investors generally target those enterprises with strong market niches in sectors with potential for growth. Foreigners are most likely to be interested in, and permitted to exercise management control over, medium-sized firms which are collectively-owned enterprises, Sino-foreign joint ventures, or even state-owned, regionally based companies. Many state enterprises have been restructured into limited companies, allowing foreign investors to buy into these firms by purchasing company shares. But restrictions remain. The restructuring of each state firm and its subsequent listing is subject to Chinese government approval. Chinese authorities usually stipulate a ceiling to the extent of foreign ownership interest in state-owned businesses.

A foreign company acquiring a local firm should be familiar with two types of limited companies–those that issue privately held shares and those that issue publicly traded shares. Which form the company takes depends upon the percentage of shares held by the founding parties, who must be legal persons. To set up a private limited company, the firm issues shares which it, or its sponsor, buys back and maintains full ownership. By contrast, in publicly traded limited companies, the founding companies may purchase only 30-35 percent of the venture's shares and the rest is sold to the public at large. If at least 25 percent of a limited company is foreign owned, it is considered a FIE and is therefore accorded preferential treatment. Foreign-funded limited companies require at least ¥30 million in registered capital. Dividends are distributed in proportion to equity shares. Existing joint ventures may be converted into limited companies, pending approval by MOFTEC and the original approval authority.

Investors buying a stake in a Chinese company must first evaluate various risks. Gaining government approval for the transfer of ownership and clearance of property titles is often a difficult hurdle. Foreign investors should be careful to obtain accurate information when buying into a Chinese entity, particularly concerning existing liabilities.

Analysis of investment risk should also take into consideration the locality, including the workings of the local bureaucracy, transportation links, and other infrastructure issues, since regional rivalries and an aged and inadequate infrastructure often hamper the efficient movement of goods, information, services, and labor throughout many parts of China.

Foreign companies who choose to invest in Chinese companies by buying shares alone should not be under the illusion that they will have a significant voice in running the company. Because foreign investors in a large Chinese enterprise are limited to a minority shareholding position, either in practice or by law in some sectors, they lack the ability to challenge decisions made by the Chinese shareholders on the board of directors. The Company Law in China lacks any provision for minority shareholders to challenge the decisions of the board, as they are able to do in the United States.

While the transformation of China's state businesses can happen on paper overnight, the culture of state domination remains strong, thwarting the implementation of efficient business practices. In China, a fundamental ambiguity remains between 'shareholding' and 'control.' Many Chinese shareholders are typically agents of the state or state-owned enterprises, making it less likely that they will prioritize maximization of profits. The term 'red capitalist' refers to the majority of Chinese shareholders who claim to be committed to the bottom line but are reluctant to reduce the numerous welfare benefits of Chinese employees or lay off redundant workers.

ENTRY MODE 6: REPRESENTATIVE OFFICES

Although technically not considered a FIE, a representative office is a quick and relatively simple way to become acquainted with the Chinese market. It is widely used by many foreign companies which are new to China. This helps foreign companies test the waters before taking the plunge of formatting a FIE within China's complex economy.

Representative offices allow firms to establish contacts with key industrial ministries and begin to build their company's reputation in China. By law, representative offices are prohibited from engaging in direct, profit-making business activities in China. They are allowed to undertake non-commercial activities including business communication, product promotion, market research, contract administration, and negotiations, on behalf of the head office. Equally important, they can also liaise with potential Chinese trading partners, as well as to various Chinese commercial and government offices, and can lay the foundation for further investment by promoting the foreign company's name and reputation. Corporate giants like Bechtel Corp. and Apple Computer Inc. had representative offices in China for at least 10 years before building legal-person status FIEs.

The most apparent advantages the representative office has over other entry modes are its simplicity and flexibility (Rothstein, 1996). Unlike an EJV or WFOE, a representative office gives a foreign company a formal presence in China without the complications of an unfamiliar local partner or a substantial financial commitment. A representative office, unlike other investment vehicles, has no minimum registered capital requirements. Many foreign businesses find the establishment of representative offices, although not cheap, an excellent way to become familiar with Chinese business environment before making a major commitment.

One flexible feature of representative offices is the lack of restrictions on the line of business in which the company can engage. Other entry modes, by contrast, can only participate in sectors and industries designated by governmental authorities. For example, the government discourages foreign participation in media communications, except for representative offices. Foreign companies in restricted industries such as insurance, banking, trading, also have found that the establishment of representative offices offers them a platform from which to try to convince Chinese government officials to open these sectors for foreign activity.

As the representative office operates independently, it can proceed with liaison, market research and consulting activities in whatever fashion it sees fit. Closing down a representative office is also relatively easy compared to terminating a joint venture. It is also relatively easy for representative offices to hire talented Chinese college graduates or managers who see employment at a representative office as a way to gain exposure to the world of international business, or even as a springboard to working at the head office in the future. Such benefits make the representative office an ideal means to explore further investments in China, establish a presence in other regions of China, or arrange future investment projects.

This entry mode, however, has several disadvantages. Though establishing a representative office is comparatively easy, a host of regulatory and start-up costs make them quite expensive to maintain. In addition to high labor costs paid to local employees, representative offices must usually pay high rents, as they tend to be located in major cities where office spaces in chronic short supply. Of the total 24,402 representative offices which were operating in China as of 1994, 3,802 were located in Beijing, 3,294 in Shanghai, and 6,918 in Guangzhou. Far fewer have been established in interior locations. Moreover, a representative office cannot issue invoices or receive payment directly for its services to Chinese customers. It has also to pay duties on all imported office equipment. At present, the imposed tariffs on computers, photocopiers, fax machines, video and audio equipment, air conditioners, and other office items, can be as high as 100 percent. Furthermore, a representative office can officially hire local employees only through one of the four approved management service companies, namely Foreign Enterprise Service Co., China International Enterprise Cooperations Corp., China International Intellectech Corp., and China International Talent Development Center. These service companies withhold a maximum of 50 percent of gross pay of local Chinese working in foreign representative offices. Many representative offices have to pay a substantial bonus directly to the employees in order to compensate for the low net pay resulting from the management service company's withholdings.

Many foreign companies continue to use representative offices as their company's China headquarters even after they have established other types of ventures in China. On balance, the merits of this entry mode make it an invaluable way to sample the fruits of China's current economic dynamism and growth.

ENTRY MODE 7: OTHER OPTIONS

Branch

One of the newest options for expanding investment is the establishment of branch offices that can undertake business transactions. The 1994 Company Law allows foreign companies to open branches that engage in production and operating activities. A FIE can also open a branch office in another region of the country to expand its operations in China.

Up until now, only a handful of foreign banks and law firms have been approved to open branch offices. These offices are limited to specified cities and their scope of business is highly regulated. Branch offices may ultimately offer a relatively simple means for establishing or expanding a presence in China, but the fact that they do not have legal-person status means the foreign parent company is liable if civil charges are brought against the branch. To shield the parent company from unlimited damages, foreign companies interested in establishing branch offices in China should designate an offshore subsidiary as the parent.

Build-Operate-Transfer (BOT)

Build-operate-transfer (BOT) is a newly emerging mode of entry into the Chinese market. It is especially useful in the power generation sector and for other large-scale infrastructure projects. For instance, negotiation on one of the first BOT power projects was recently completed. According to officials in Southeastern Guangxi, the final contract for the Laibin B power plant will be signed soon with Electricite de France, Britain's National Power International, and Barclays Bank. Recently, China's State Planning Committee has ratified ten more BOT projects calling for foreign operations: (1) the Summer Palace light rail in Beijing; (2) the Zilanda hydropower plant; (3) the Tuoketro B power station in Inner Mongolia; (4) the State highway 104 in Shandong; (5) the Shenyang elevated expressway in Liaoning; (6) the Wuhan light rail line in Hubei; (7) the Yinglongshan power plant in Zhejiang; (8) the Second Nanjing Yangtse River Bridge in Jiangsu; (9) the Shenyang-Beijing Expressway in Liaoning; and (10) the Shenyang second ring road in Liaoning.

BOT is a guarantee-fee method of cooperation by which an investor identifies a project in a host country, assumes sole responsibility in investing in the construction and operation of the project, and, after recovering investment and obtaining compensation, returns the project to the local organization in the host country. It is a relatively new means of international capital investment, applied usually in projects where building infrastructure facilities calls for a huge investment and great length of time. It is popular in developing countries short on capital and technology. The first BOT project, implemented in China on a trial basis, was the Beijing-Tongxian Expressway, by Beijing civil construction departments and an American company. Construction started in September 1994, with 20 months as the projected time for completion. The approved term of the BOT is 20 years, after which the expressway will be returned to China.

Due in part to difficulties working out financing and equity arrangements, the BOT approach is often used together with other entry modes. Foreign businesses may set up BOT project firms by means of either equity or cooperative joint ventures with Chinese partners or wholly foreign-owned ventures. Because of their ability to provide foreign investors with returns in excess of their proportional contributions to the venture's total registered capital, CJVs have been the vehicles of choice for BOT infrastructure projects.

Franchising and Licensing

Two forms of contractual arrangements most often used in international expansion are franchising and licensing. Both involve a contract between parties in different countries, but franchise contracts cover more aspects of the operation and are typically of a longer duration than licensing. A licensor in one country makes limited rights and/or resources available to the licensee in a foreign country. The rights and/or resources may include patents, trademarks, technology, managerial skills, and so on. These allow the licensee to produce and market a product similar to the one the licensor has already been producing in its home country, without requiring the licensor actually to create a new operation abroad. For instance, licensees in China and other countries have contracts to produce and sell toys and clothing bearing pictures of Mickey Mouse and other Walt Disney characters.

Licensing is a popular method for profiting from a foreign market without committing sizable funds. Since the foreign producer is typically 100 percent locally owned, political risk is minimized. Income from licensing, however, is lower than that from other FDI entry modes, although the return on the marginal investment can be higher. Other potential disadvantages include loss of quality control; establishment of a competitor in a foreign market; improvements of the technology by the local licensee, which then enters the home market; and loss of the opportunity to make a direct investment in the licensee's market.

Most licensing agreements by MNCs have been with their own

affiliates or joint ventures in China. Licensing fees have been a way to spread the corporate research and development costs among all SBUs. They are also a means of repatriating profits in a form typically more acceptable to the Chinese government than dividends.

Compared to licensing, a franchise usually includes a broader package of rights and resources. Production equipment, managerial systems, operating procedures, access to advertising and promotional materials, loans and financing may all be part of a franchise. McDonald and KFC are examples of foreign companies with franchises in China. This arrangement can lead to the creation of a new business in which the franchise is designed to stand in perpetuity (Chen, 1996).

It is important for foreign licensors or franchisors to familiarize themselves with the legal framework for international licensing and franchising in China. Currently, the Regulations on the Administration of Technology Import Contracts (RATIC), promulgated by the State Council in May 1985, are the most comprehensive. In addition, foreign companies should confirm the identity, legal status, and authority of the potential Chinese recipients. The simplest verification is a review of their business license and, if possible, articles of association. A foreign supplier should also make sure that the relevant planning authorities in China have authorized the proposed project. Moreover, foreign suppliers must be aware that Chinese law tends to encourage the conversion of a licensing contract into an installment sale plan, by forbidding restriction on the licensee's continued use of the knowhow, trademark, or technology received from the foreign firm after expiration of the contract. The RATIC also mandates that license contracts shall generally not exceed 10 years.

SOME ADVICE TO INTERNATIONAL EXECUTIVES

Factors for Consideration

Foreign companies can structure their entry into China in many different ways. Some will be more suitable than others depending upon specific situation and business objectives (Beamish, 1993). A foreign company that is not familiar with the Chinese business environment may want to engage a dependable distributor to sell its goods in China. Those firms that want to minimize investment of capital and resources at the initial stage may find a contract manufacturing arrangement suitable. Some may want to first test the market and establish a relationship with their current and potential customers by setting up a representative office. Those who are knowledgeable about China may want to ask themselves whether they need a partner at all (Shenkar, 1990). Under certain circumstances, they can set up a wholly foreign-owned enterprise and put in their own management team, then hire locally to staff their Chinese company.

Various other forms of doing business in China are also available. Foreign firms should make sure they know all possible options before they determine the best one. Some options, particularly expanding or buying into an existing FIE or setting up a new one, are attractive because existing legislation and experience make them transparent, feasible, and relatively predictable (Osland and Cavusgil, 1996). Other methods, such as buying into a Chinese enterprise other than an FIE or seeking to establish a branch of the foreign company, may lead investors into uncharted waters. Investors must select among these various options in an environment marked by bureaucratic struggles both within the central government and between the national and local governments.

Inevitably, there are tradeoffs in choosing one entry mode over another. Once a foreign investor decides to pursue an FDI project in China, its choice of entry mode will depend on a wide range of factors. In brief, the selection of entry modes in China depends upon the following four groups of factors: (1) firm-specific factors such as strategic objectives, degree of global integration, firm size and experience, and its distinctive competencies such as technological and managerial know-how; (2) host country-specific factors including contextual risk, cultural distance, market potential, market knowledge, infrastructure conditions, intellectual property right systems, and government policy and treatment toward FDI; (3) industry-specific factors such as entry barriers, industrial policies of the Chinese government, structural uncertainty, degree of competition from both local and other foreign firms, and collaboration of suppliers, distributors, and related industries; and (4) project-specific factors such as contractual risk, project size, amount of investment needed, project orientation (technological, local market, export, or infrastructure-oriented), and availability of appropriate local partners. Figure 1 schematically shows an integrated framework for entry mode selection in China.

It is particularly worthwhile noting that the strategic objective of a project influences the entry mode selection. If the project is export-oriented, for instance, a WFOE might be a better choice (Pan, 1996). By manufacturing in the location where factor conditions are optimal and then exporting to the rest of the world, a foreign company may be able to realize substantial location economies and a positive experience curve (Luo, 1998). This arrangement also gives the company the tight control over marketing that might be required to coordinate a globally dispersed value chain as well as better transfer pricing for avoiding various taxes or tariffs. Thus, foreign companies pursuing global strategies may prefer to establish WFOEs.

FIGURE 1. An Integrated Model of Entry Mode Selection into the Chinese Market

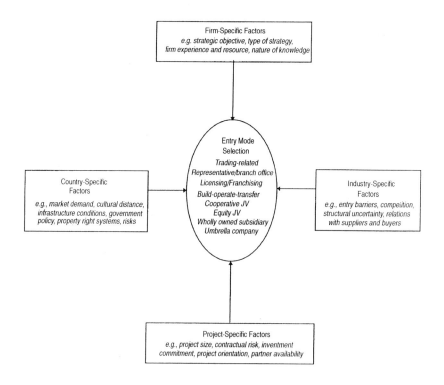

Special value should be also attached to the nature of an investor's distinctive competency. In particular, it is imperative to distinguish between technological know-how and managerial know-how. If a company's competitive advantage derives from its control of proprietary technological know-how, licensing and joint venture arrangements are not advisable because of the risk of losing control of that technology. A WFOE might be a better choice in this situation. The licensing or joint venture mode can be used for these companies only if the arrangement is structured in such a way as to reduce the risk of a company's technology being expropriated by licensees or joint venture partners (Shan, 1991). Companies can arrange to prevent leakage of their most sensitive technologies by only allowing their partners access to production processes that do not expose some kinds of knowledge. Contractual safeguards can also be written into a joint venture contract. Cross-licensing agreements between parties can also protect a foreign investor's technological knowhow, if both parties agree in advance to exchange skills and technologies. Comparatively, the risk of losing control of management skills to franchisees or joint venture partners is not that great. This is one of the reasons that many service companies favor a combination of franchising and subsidiaries to control franchisees in China.

Foreign companies in China tend to start with low risk/low control options and then advance to higher levels of risk and control as they gain experience and build confidence (Yan and Gray, 1994). Initial market entry often starts with import/export or counter-trade. Representative offices, licensing, and franchising may also be considered as trial steps. EJVs or CJVs may be established as investment vehicles with intermediate risks. These modes are still dominant in China because they included partnerships with players already experienced in the targeted market. They also reduce risk through cost sharing. Thus, they represent an appropriate entry strategy for early market development tactics.

To secure a stronger presence in China, acquisitions, BOT, WFOEs, or umbrella companies may be required. Indeed, many consider these approaches more risky. They are likely to come at later stages in the development of an international diversification strategy in China. These modes, however, enable foreign investors to better control local operations and, more importantly, become more profitable from the economic boom and market growth (Teagarden, 1990). Foreign investors may employ some or all of these alternatives in sequential fashion or use different modes simultaneously with different products or in different regions of China.

Combining Options

Selecting between an EJV and a WFOE is not necessarily an either-or decision. Sometimes a Chinese partner does have a strong distribution network or operates in a restricted sector that is attractive to a foreign investor. In such situations, foreign companies can, for instance, surround their WFOE production operation with EJVs that market and sell their products in China. Motorola in Tianjin does exactly that. Since 1993, Motorola has been laying the groundwork for the biggest U.S. manufacturing venture in China. Its $300-million-plus commitment to China focuses on pagers, simple integrated circuits, cellular phones, and, eventually, automotive electronics. The production site in the Tianjin Economic Development Zone is a WFOE; marketing and sales of products will be done through various EJVs with local partners.

Another approach is to consider an EJV and a WFOE in sequence. A foreign investor can get initial entry as part of an EJV for a fixed period which is normally stipulated in the duration clause of the joint venture contract. At the end of the stipulated term, it can take over the assets from the Chinese partner and continue to run the operation as a WFOE. This is an attractive alternative if the added value of the Chinese partner is significant but limited to the early stages of the venture. Some EJVs have integrated this option in the termination clause of the joint venture contract.

It is also possible to structure a WFOE under the legal umbrella of an EJV. In other words, the project would be an EJV as a legal entity but would be run and operated as a WFOE. Many foreign partners that have increased their equity stakes in existing ventures are going in that direction. In some cases, they turn their Chinese partner into a silent partner with a minority stake.

China is by far the biggest and most impressive economy of the developing countries. When one considers that it also has a population of 1.3 billion people, approximately a quarter of the population of the earth, the potential of its future market is clear. A number of factors exist which make the selection of entry mode difficult and risky. Economically, there are a myriad of neo-mercantilism rules and regulations which both restrict and control the flow of FDI within the territory (Luo and Peng, 1999). Realistically, putting aside the actual content of Chinese law, it is important to note that there are few legal guarantees for foreign companies, a fact which by itself increases the risks of investing in China. These environmental factors surely have a critical influence on the choice of entry mode for foreign companies.

These fears, however, are likely to diminish following China's admission into the World Trade Organization, an eventuality which is currently being delayed by the United States. The Chinese economy will continue to lurch forward as the authorities maintain their pragmatic and ad-hoc attitude toward market reform and foreign investment. The uncertainties inherent in transforming economies are a source of challenges as well as opportunities. In China, as elsewhere, those investors best prepared to circumvent the former and exploit the latter are apt to survive and prosper. In fact, the growing complexity of operations of many MNCs in China, and the need to better explore market opportunities and more closely coordinate numerous strategic business units in China, has led many firms to set up an inter-SBUs network in China whereby different entry modes are flexibly adopted and strategically integrated.

REFERENCES

Beamish, P. W. (1993). The characteristics of joint ventures in the People's Republic of China. *Journal of International Marketing*, 1: 29-48.

Beamish, P. W. & Banks, J. C. (1987). Equity joint ventures and the theory of the multinational enterprise. *Journal of International Business Studies*, 18: 1-16.

Bulletin of the Ministry of Foreign Trade and Economic Cooperation, the People's Republic of China, Serial No. 40: 1-9, 1997.

Chen, M. (1996). Technological transfer to China: Major rules and issues. *International Journal of Technology Management*, 10: 747-756.

Dong, J. L. & Hu, J. (1995). Mergers and acquisitions in China. *Federal Reserve Bank of Atlanta Economic Review*, November/December: 15-29.

Harrigan, K. R. (1985). *Strategies for joint ventures*. Lexington, MA: D. C. Heath.

Luo, Y. 1998. Timing of investment and international expansion performance in China. *Journal of International Business Studies*, 29: 391-408.

Luo, Y. 1997. Partner selection and venturing success: The case of joint ventures in China. *Organization Science*, 8(6): 648-662.

Luo, Y. & M. W. Peng. 1999. Learning to compete in a transition economy: Experience, environment, and performance. *Journal of International Business Studies*, 30(2): 278-307.

Osland, G. E. & Cavusgil, S. T. (1996). Performance issues in U.S.-China joint ventures. *California Management Review*, 38: 106-130.

Osborn, R. N. & Hagedorn, J. (1997). The institutionalization and evolution dynamics of interorgnizational alliances and networks. *Academy of Management Journal*, 40(2): 261-278.

Pan, Y. (1996). Influences on foreign equity ownership level in joint ventures in China. *Journal of International Business Studies*, 27: 1-26.

Peng, M. W., Luo, Y. & Sun, L. (1998). Firm growth via mergers and acquisitions in China. In L. Kelley and Y. Luo (eds.), *Towards the Year 2000: Emerging Business Issues in China*, 73-102, Sage Publishing Co., Thousand Oaks, CA.

Randall, D. & Telesio, P. (1995). Planning ahead. *China Business Review*, January-February: 14-18.

Rothstein, J. (1996). Easing your way into China. *China Business Review*, January-February: 30-32.

Shan, W. (1991). Environmental risks and joint venture sharing arrangements. *Journal of International Business Studies*, 22: 555-578.

Shenkar, O. (1990). International joint ventures' problems in China: Risks and remedies. *Long Range Planning*, 23: 82-90.

Tateisi, N. (1996). How to invest in China? *The Columbia Journal of World Business*, Summer: 66-75.

Teagarden, M. B. (1990). *Sino-U.S. joint venture effectiveness*. Unpublished PhD dissertation, University of Southern California, Los Angeles, CA.

Vanhonacker, W. (1997). Entering China: An unconventional approach. *Harvard Business Review*, March-April: 130-140.

Yan, A. & Gray, B. (1994). Bargaining power, management control, and performance in United States-China joint ventures: A comparative case study. *Academy of Management Journal*, 37: 1478-1517.

Choice of Market Entry Mode in Emerging Markets: Influences on Entry Strategy in China

Huang Lin

SUMMARY. This study explores the antecedents of market entry strategy in emerging markets and examines the market environmental, transaction-specific, competitive strategic factors and organizational capability that influence the choice of market entry mode. Empirical results based on a survey of Japanese companies support the combined relevance of their factors on choice of market entry mode in an emerging market. Although most of the mode of entry research assumes that the firm has the option to choose any entry mode in a given market, this study examines the impact of the factors in the internationalization process of firms. The results suggest that experiential knowledge has an immense impact on the choice of entry mode in China, an emerging market with high environmental uncertainty, but also high market potential. The empirical findings also show the important influences of risk-absorption capability and risk-dispersion mechanism on the choice of entry mode into the Chinese market. *[Article copies available for a fee from The Haworth Document Delivery Service: 1-800-342-9678. E-mail address: <getinfo@haworthpressinc.com> Website: <http://www.HaworthPress.com>]*

Huang Lin is Associate Professor of Marketing, Graduate School of Business Administration, Kobe University, Rokko Kobe, Japan 657-8051. His primary research interest is global marketing management, including strategy and behavior of MNCs in Japan, China and the Pacific Rim region. His research interest is also on the issues related to system reform in China, behavior of Chinese companies and development of market system. His research has appeared in journals, such as: the Japan Marketing Journal, JETRO: China Economy, and the Journal of Japan-China Association on Economy and Trade, among others (E-mail: koulin@kobe-u.ac.jp).

[Haworth co-indexing entry note]: "Choice of Market Entry Mode in Emerging Markets: Influences on Entry Strategy in China." Lin, Huang. Co-published simultaneously in *Journal of Global Marketing* (International Business Press, an imprint of The Haworth Press, Inc.) Vol. 14, No. 1/2, 2000, pp. 83-109; and: *Greater China in the Global Market* (ed: Yigang Pan) International Business Press, an imprint of The Haworth Press, Inc., 2000, pp. 83-109. Single or multiple copies of this article are available for a fee from The Haworth Document Delivery Service [1-800-342-9678, 9:00 a.m. - 5:00 p.m. (EST). E-mail address: getinfo@haworthpressinc.com].

KEYWORDS. Market entry mode, market environmental, transaction-specific, competitive strategic factors, organizational capability, experiential knowledge, process of internationalization

INTRODUCTION

Foreign market entry strategies involve decisions on the choice of a target market (country), entry mode, marketing plan and control system [Root 1994]. The decision on which entry mode to use for a foreign market has a major impact on the success of entry and performance of international operations [Davidson 1982, Killing 1982]. The diversity of uncertainties faced by firms in foreign markets necessitates the balancing of control and flexibility in market entry decisions. The four most common modes of foreign market entry are exporting, licensing, equity joint venture (EJV) and wholly owned subsidiary (WOS). At one extreme, the firm can integrate forward and perform all the production, marketing or R&D functions itself by establishing a subsidiary. At the other extreme, a firm may choose not to perform any of these functions in a foreign market, but to use independent distributors to export, alleviating investment in assets in the host country. A firm may also use intermediate options such as international EJV. Because these modes of entry involve resource commitments, control and risk at varying levels, the initial choice of a particular mode is difficult to change without considerable loss of time and money. The choice of entry mode is therefore a very important strategic decision as well as a critical determinant of the likely success of the foreign operation.

Previous attempts to provide a unified framework within which different factors can be placed, the relationships between them were analyzed and made by a few researchers [Anderson and Gatignon 1986, Hill et al. 1990, Agarwal and Ramaswami 1992, Aulakh and Kotabe 1997, Tse et al. 1997]. Much of the existing literature on the choice of entry mode is focused on many seemingly unrelated factors, including: market potential, country risk, location familiarity, competitive conditions, transaction-specific, strategic and organizational factors. The eclectic approach to foreign entry mode proposed by Hill et al. [1990] identifies the exogenous environmental, strategic and transaction-specific factors relevant for choice of entry mode. It is in order to better capture the diverse objectives and constraints of firms making this decision. Anderson and Gatignon [1986] are based on the transaction cost framework, a dominant paradigm to explain choice of entry mode. Researchers have recently stressed the need to complement the efficiency considerations of the transaction cost explanations, that focusing on each entry decision *in isolation* with strategic issues concerning global competition. A multinational envisages the strategic relationships between its operations across borders, and may be willing to sacrifice the cost advantages in order to improve the competitive position in the global network and global competition.

Another dominant paradigm used to explain choice of entry mode is based on Dunning's ownership, locational, and internalization framework [Dunning 1988]. The internalization perspective, closely related to transaction cost, is concerned with the minimization of transaction cost and market failure.

Researchers have recently stressed the need to complement the transaction cost or internalization explanations with the organizational capability perspective. The organizational capability perspective asserts the firm's ability to acquire and exploit the resources depending on time and space [Barney 1991]. Internationalization of a firm is a process in which the firm gradually increases their international involvement, acquiring, integrating and using the knowledge about foreign markets and operations. The outcomes of past history and international experience restrict the firms to perform operations in different markets by themselves [Johanson and Vahlne 1977, Madhok 1996]. Each entry decision can not be explained *in isolation* with the internationalization process and experiential capabilities of a firm.

The most of mode of entry research assumes that the firm has the option to choose any entry mode in a given market [Aulakh and Kotabe 1997]. The choice of entry mode becomes even more complex for firms operating in emerging markets, where they face high external uncertainty and internal constraints. An emerging market is a market that is growing and shows very potential, also usually becomes a new focus for global competition.

There are two major research objectives in this study. First, this study examines market environmental, transaction-specific, competitive strategic factors and organizational capability that influence the choice of international market entry mode. This study stresses that firms have no option to choose all entry modes in a given market, and examines the impact of the factors in the internationalization process of the firm. The choice between exporting and local production, contractual entry and investment entry, EJV and WOS are all strategic alternatives. The choices are constrained by the market environmental factors and the resource capabilities and outcomes of past history of internationalization. The second objective of this study is to explore the systematic relationship between the factors and the choice of EJV and WOS based on a survey of Japanese firms which have invested in China. The remainder of the paper is organized into three parts. The first part reviews the relevant literature to identify the factors especially related to the choice of EJV and WOS, and develop the hypotheses. The second part describes the methods used for data collection, details the operational measures and research method. The last section provides the results and discusses implications and limitations.

LITERATURE REVIEW AND HYPOTHESES

Entry Mode. Although much has been written recently about choice of entry mode, past studies have often considered the entry mode in several characteristics, such as level of resource commitments, level of control and extent of inter-organizational dependence [Contractor and Lorange 1987, Hill et al. 1990].

Most mode of entry research assumes that the entering firm has the option to choose any entry mode in a given market and at a given time. The primary area of focus is the degree of international channel integration [Anderson and Coughlan 1988, Klein et al. 1992, Aulakh and Kotabe 1997], choice of licensing, EJV and WOS [Anderson and Gatignon 1986, Agarwal and Ramaswami 1992, Kim and Hwang 1992], and choice of equity ownership level [Gatignon and Anderson 1988, Gomes-Casseres 1989, Hennart 1991, Pan 1996]. While the conceptualization of ownership has changed in recent years, researchers have explicitly considered the EJVs that formed by multiple partners, or alliance formation between foreign firms with a local partner [Shan 1991, Pan and Tse 1996, Tse et al. 1997, Makino and Beamish 1998].

The continuous vector of hierarchical option to market mode is based on the transaction cost paradigm. These considerations ignore the internationalization process of firms and over-simplify the environmental factors and internal constraints as a unidimensional construct.

Historical research suggests that the exporting mode was the main internationalization strategy of Japanese companies until 1985. Most of the Japanese MNCs chose joint venturing as their investment entry mode in the 1970s. Contrasted with Japanese MNCs, American MNCs chose WOS as their entry mode [Yoshihara 1997, Stopford and Wells 1972].

The internationalization process perspective asserts exporting and local production, contractual entry and investment entry, EJV and WOS are strategic alternatives. The historical dimension of a firm's activities is critical, since its past experiences and resources influence subsequent actions.

The internationalization process is also one of increasing commitment to foreign markets. Increasing levels of involvement in foreign markets relate to a firm's accumulation of experiential knowledge and local knowledge [Anand and Delios 1997]. The high growth of international JVs justifies them as an effective strategy for internationalization.

Faced with rapid technological changes, increasing market risk and global competition, firms are motivated to entry with multiple partners. In this paper, we pay significant attention to the difference between the foreign firms only with EJV and the foreign firms with WOS in emerging markets. This research examines the factors that increase the firm's commitment and control under an uncertain and changing environment.

Transaction-Specific Factors: A transaction cost or internalization explanation for choice of entry mode involves the question of how a firm should organize its boundary activities with other firms in a foreign market. The underlying dimensions of transaction cost paradigm are the behavioral assumptions of self-interest, opportunism, and bounded rationality of parties involved in a situation of bilateral governance. A firm chooses how to transact according to the criterion of minimizing the sum of production and transaction costs [Williamson 1975]. Transaction cost perspective is based on transaction characteristics such as asset specificity, the degree to which assets are specialized to support trade for only a few parties, external and internal uncertainty, and the frequency of transactions. The focus of internalization is on the market for know-how and this theory can be considered to be a transaction cost theory of the multinational corporation [Buckley and Casson 1976, Rugman 1980]. The internalization perspective reasons that market mechanisms for the transfer of know-how fail when the know-how is of a tacit nature. In the 1980s, research on the choice of entry mode has predominantly been from the transaction cost paradigm [Madhok 1996].

The external uncertainty is considered as conditions that make optimal contracting unrealistic. Thus, when faced with external uncertainty, opportunistic behavior of partner, and asset specificity, firms are better off internalizing the transaction by a WOS to allow the absorption of uncertainty. Thus, we expect that:

> H1: As the asset specificity increases, the entering firm is more likely to choose WOS.

Market Environmental Factors. A number of exogenous environmental factors impact a firm's choice of entry mode. Existing research of international marketing suggest that the market environmental factors are external to the company and may be regarded as parameters of the entry mode decision. Foremost among these are the demand and competition conditions, market risk, location familiarity, and marketing infrastructure that exist in the host market. The home country factors also influence the choice of entry mode [Root 1994]. Most research on international marketing looked at the heterogeneity of markets and emphasized the diversity of cultural, political, legal and economic environments [Robinson 1978, Cateora and Keavency 1987]. The environmental factors influence the choice of entry mode through its impact upon resource commitments and strategic flexibility. Existing empirical study supports this general relationship [Goodnow and Hanz 1972].

The uncertainty of future demand conditions is likely to be greater in emerging markets and embryonic industries in the host country [Harrigan 1985, Vernon 1966]. Heterogeneity of a market is the perceived distance of culture, economic systems, business practices and management styles between the host and home country. A number of previous studies have argued that the greater the location unfamiliarity, the more likely it is that a firm will be difficult to acquire the market knowledge and favor low resource commitment mode [Stopford and Wells 1972, Johanson and Vahlne 1977].

Market risk as another type of external uncertainty is likely to be great in emerging markets. A number of previous studies have focused on country risk, which refers to the perceived discontinuity or unpredictability of the political and economic environment of a host country [Gatignon and Anderson 1988, Kim and Hwang 1992, Tallman 1988]. Country risk is an important source of external uncertainty in foreign countries. Another type of market risk in emerging markets is operation risk or business risk, which refers to the perceived discontinuity or unpredictability of the changes of business environment and rules of the game. Firms facing high market risk retain flexibility and shift risk to local firms or other parties. Firms facing a manifestation of country risk will develop the risk-absorption capability to retain control in the emerging market. Thus, heterogeneity and diversity of the international market environmental factors influence the choice of entry mode. External uncertainty is a multidimensional construct.

In emerging markets, the marketing infrastructure conditions as well as government policies toward foreign investment are important to the choice of entry mode. Marketing infrastructure refers to the conditions of the investment climate, such as the local labor market and sourcing market, taxation, transportation, and legal factors.

Previous studies have argued that EJVs with local firms are an effective means of overcoming the location-specific disadvantages. With the local partner's knowledge and resources, the foreign firms can overcome the environmental disadvantages [Anand and Delios 1997]. Thus, it is hypothesized that:

> H2: The greater the market risk in emerging market, the entering firm is more likely to choose EJV.
>
> H3: The greater the heterogeneity of the market in emerging market, the entering firm is more likely to choose EJV.
>
> H4: The greater the intervention of the local government, the entering firm is more likely to choose EJV.
>
> H5: The greater the marketing infrastructure of location in emerging market, the entering firm is more likely to choose WOS.

Competitive Strategic Factors. The competitive strategic perspective involves configuring the firm's value chain in such a way that value added at each stage is maximized [Hout et al. 1982]. Thus, the objective of entering an emerging market may be to specialize in manufacturing only part of the product line, or certain components of the end-product, or exchanging parts and products within the MNCs' global network. Achieving coordination within the context of an interdependent global network requires a high degree of control over the operations in the foreign markets. Each entry decision may be obedient to the strategic issues concerning the governance and coordination within the global network. Along with the efficiency objective proposed by the transaction cost perspective, the strategic perspective also focuses on the effectiveness of integration and collaborations.

Firms may be expanding in emerging markets to proactively achieve a global market position and head off global rivals and potential competitors. This perspective goes back to the view that foreign investment by MNCs attempts to create market imperfections in order to achieve monopolistic power and create entry barriers for other global competitors [Kogut 1988]. Thus, the strategic motivations for establishing a foreign business unit can range from setting up an outpost for future expansion, to developing a global sourcing site, or to attack competitors. Those strategic aims are set at the corporate level for the overall corporate efficiency maximization.

The demand in an emerging market can be defined as the actual demand of existing customers and the potential demand of local market. A firm can generally be expected to be more knowledgeable regarding its demand when it enters an emerging market to develop a global sourcing site, or serves its domestic customers who have already invested in that market. Therefore, this refers to firms preferring to maintain control over their operations and choose an entry mode with high involvement level and resource commitment [Erramilli and Rao 1990]. The competitive structure and high production cost in the home country encourages entry modes involving local production and influence the strategic objectives at the corporate level [Root 1994].

Though a firm may decide to enter a foreign market in the interests of remaining competitive on a global basis, the form of entry itself is shaped by the competition conditions of the market and the intensity of global competition. An emerging market is one where rapidly changing macro-economic, social, demographic and regulatory factors produce a situation of intense competition. Limits of adaptability to changing market and competition circumstances leads firms to favor entry modes involving low resource commitments when competitive pressures in the host market are intense. Collaboration is a more flexible form of entry and exit as well as a useful means to improve competitive positioning [Harrigan 1988]. In an emerging market, timing of entering is a critical issue driving to choose EJV or other forms of collaborations. Firms are motivated to form EJV or alliances with other firms to reduce risks, share the knowledge and resources, enhance global mobility, and strengthen global competitiveness [Auster 1987]. Taken together, a firm can be theorized to favor EJV when competition in the emerging market is intense.

These opposing effects of market environmental factors on the entry mode choice are due to the consideration of external uncertainty as a unidimensional construct and ignoring the constraints by the transaction cost and competitive strategy theorists [Balakrishnan and Wernerfelt 1986]. Accordingly, the argument for collaboration driven by competitive pressures tends to ignore the potential friction with a partner, however the consideration of internalization is not really concerned with the dynamics and global competition. It is a widely accepted premise that international JVs represent an inherently unstable and problematic organizational form [Franko 1971, Porter, 1990 Yan 1998].

On the other hand, the two perspectives have argued that increasingly transfer and exploitation of the know-how and core input factors of a firm such as marketing, manufacturing, or R&D can increase a firm's commitment and control over the operations in foreign markets.

> H6: The greater the competitive pressures in emerging markets, the entering firm is more likely to choose EJV.
> H7: The greater the influences of home country factors, the entering firm is more likely to choose WOS.
> H8: The greater the intention to service the existing customers, the entering firm is more likely to choose WOS.
> H9: The greater the intention to develop global sourcing site, the entering firm is more likely to choose WOS.

Organizational Capability Factors. The market knowledge and international experience of firms influence their ability and willingness to invest resources. Firms are initially risk averse when entering new markets, and therefore not willing to invest substantial resources in unfamiliar foreign markets. As firms get knowledge for a foreign market, the better perceptions of market risk, competitive pressures and returns, and therefore becoming more confident and aggressive, manifested into a willingness to commit more resources. The basic mechanism to explain the process of internationalization of firms is knowledge about foreign markets and operations. Market knowledge relates to market environmental factors, such as present and future demand, competition conditions, and marketing infrastructure. The more important is experiential knowledge, which provides the framework for perceiving the risk and returns, and formulating market opportunities. Establishing and performing the operations in foreign markets require both general knowledge and market-specific knowledge [Johanson and Vahlne 1977].

A foreign market is perceived as an unfamiliar market to the firm, the accumulation of market-specific knowledge may require the time and cost as an incremental process. Also, the stock of international experience is frequently not feasible for the new entry. The heterogeneity and diversity of market environments in which a firm operates may be a key asset of the firm since it provides the firm with a superior knowledge base [Ghoshal 1987]. In the accumulation process of knowledge and experience, firms may develop new capabilities to adapt the risky and competitive environment in an emerging market. Because the experiential knowledge is market-specific and cannot be transferred between firms or business units, accumulating experiential knowledge is costly. Lack of local market knowledge has a strong impact on the commitment to an emerging market [Eriksson et al. 1997].

Based on experience-related considerations, the change of organizational capabilities and impact of environment factors in the internationalization process of the firm are proposed in Figure 1. Accordingly, it is hypothesized that:

> H2a: The greater the market risk in emerging markets, the entering firm with the risk-absorption capability is more likely to choose WOS.
> H6a: The greater the competitive pressures in emerging markets, the entering firm with the marketing power is more likely to choose WOS.

From the organizational capability perspective, the internal constraints of capabilities are a critical determinant of the decision of entry mode. Existing stock of a firm's resources, capabilities, and the requirements of the operational context both direct and limit its choice of entry mode. The internationalization is essentially a path-dependent incremental process where the pattern of resource commitment and involvement by a firm is a function of its past market knowledge and international experience. Capability accumulation is a dynamic pro-

FIGURE 1. Environment Factors, Internationalization Process and Organizational Capabilities

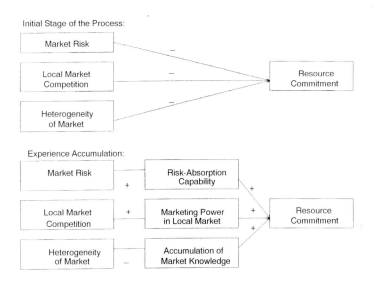

cess which refers to the information and knowledge management of the firm. The true source of competitive advantage arises not from the visible elements of the know-how but from the supporting structure or complementary capabilities [Dunning 1988, Madhok 1997].

The value of market-specific knowledge is enhanced through new combinations and is deployed in order to exploit market opportunities. Previous research on the EJV in emerging markets addresses how the government of a host country affects the investment strategies [Beamish 1984, Osland and Cavusgil 1996, Lou 1997]. The relationship with the host government is an important resource to operate in the emerging market. Thus, it is hypothesized that:

H10: The greater the stock of a firm's knowledge of exporting to the market, the entering firm is more likely to choose EJV.

H11: The greater the stock of a firm's knowledge of doing business in the market, the entering firm is more likely to choose WOS.

H12: The greater the stock of a firm's market-specific knowledge of the market, the entering firm is more likely to choose WOS.

H13: The greater importance of the relationship with host government, the entering firm is more likely to choose EJV.

International EJV provides the structural mechanisms for fostering more intimate interaction for the interchange of knowledge. A successful joint venture provides for complementary contribution of resources and capabilities by the major parties involved. A more successful joint venture creates synergies through the partners pooling their resources, capabilities, and strengths [Harrigan 1985, Dymsza 1988]. Combining the production process, know-how, and management system of an entering firm with the national partner's local capital, management, existing plant, marketing expertise, and knowledge of the market environment, the EJV results in a more efficient and productive enterprise than WOS. Previous research provided that foreign majority ownership is not common in LDCs and China, and that shared control reveals better performance [Beamish 1984, 1993, Pan 1996, Luo 1997]. Thus, it is hypothesized that:

H14: The greater the resources and capabilities of the partner, the entering firm is more likely to choose EJV.
H15: For the objective of manufacturing operations, the entering firm is more likely to choose EJV.

Concept Model. The preceding discussion on transaction cost analysis, market environmental, competitive strategic considerations, and organization capabilities perspective on the choice of entry mode implies that they provide complementary and overlapping explanations of the market entry strategy in foreign markets.

While the transaction cost analysis is useful to understand problems in bilateral bargaining related to individual transaction, competitive strategic considerations provide a meaningful approach to examine the effectiveness of each market entry in light of interdependent operations of the firm across markets at the corporate level. The international marketing analysis is useful to understand the complex and multiple dimensions of the market environment that influences the motivations of the entering firm and constrain its decisions and activities. The organizational capability perspective provides a substantial approach in understanding the firm's knowledge, experience and resources relevant to the market entry strategies. Based on these perspectives, five sets of factors are proposed in Figure 2. In next section, the data collection and method are described. The operational measures are also developed.

METHOD AND RESULTS

Entry Modes in China. China opened its door to foreign investment in 1979. As the world's largest potential market and currently its fastest growing economy, China is the second largest foreign direct investment (FDI) recipient in the world, surpassed only by the US from 1993 [OECD: *Financial Market Trends, 1994*]. Now China is a typical emerging market in the world which is unstable, and it is changing in the institutions, systems and rules of the game. The Chinese market is also the focus of global competitions.

Foreign investors are free to operate for either WOS or EJV as an entry mode to make direct investment to almost all the industries in China. FDI in China is often from Hong Kong, Taiwan and other ethnically related countries. The number of contracts and actual FDI utilization in China from the USA and Japan always ranks No. 3 or No. 4. The foreign-invested enterprises have played a principal part in

FIGURE 2. Conceptual Model

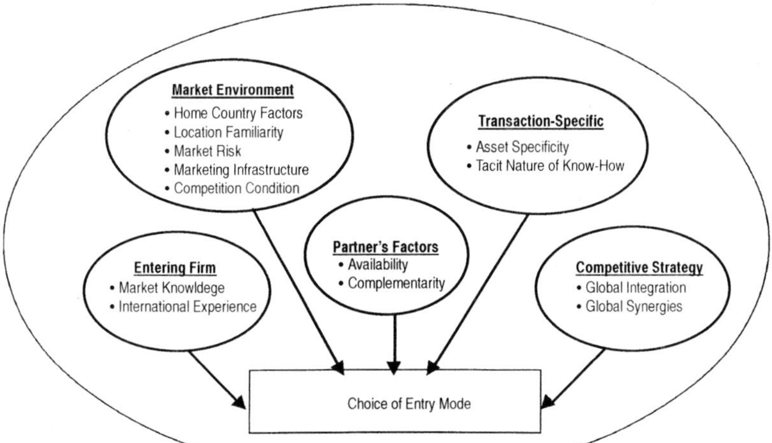

the Chinese economy. The industrial output of the foreign-invested enterprises has reached 19%, and import/export volume of the foreign-invested enterprises has reached 40% of the nation's total. About 16 million Chinese people are currently employed in the foreign-invested enterprises (MOFERT: *Foreign investment in China 1996*).

Entry modes in China are classified into four main forms by the Chinese government. These modes include:

a. EJV, which accounts for more than 50% of the total amount of actual FDI;
b. WOS, which represents about 25% of total FDI;
c. Contractual or cooperative joint ventures, which refers to a variety of arrangements and are about 20% of total FDI;
d. Joint exploration projects (e.g., offshore oil exploration consortia), compensation trade, international leasing, and processing and assembling.

Although the percentage of WOS in total FDI has been growing in the recent years, EJV remains a dominant entry mode selected by foreign investors.

Data Collection. The database of 1003 affiliates of Japanese firms established before 1994 shows that the percentage of a minority EJV, a 50% foreign equity, a majority EJV and a WOS was 23%, 20%, 36% and 21% respectively (Toyo Keizai: *Japanese overseas investments in China 1995*). Since no published data are available for a firm's specific market entry strategies and decisions, following previous studies on foreign market entry, a survey method of data collection was considered appropriate (e.g., Klein et al. 1990, Agarwal and Ramaswami 1992, Kim and Hwang 1992, Aulakh and Kotabe 1997). The sampling frame for the data collection was the Toyo Keizai: *Japanese overseas investments in China 1995*. A total of 635 firms that have more than one EJV or WOS were selected from the database. A survey questionnaire was developed and pre-tested with Chinese business managers of the firms located in Tokyo and Osaka area. The refined questionnaire was mailed to the presidents of 635 firms in July 1995, along with a personalized cover letter explained the nature of the study. After one follow-up, 251 usable questionnaires were received for a response rate of 40%. Half of the respondents held upper-management positions (Presidents, Vice-presidents and Directors) and 40% of the respondents are area managers of foreign business or Chinese business. Out of the responded firms, 64% have manufacturing affiliates in China.

Dependent Variable. The unit of analysis is the firms which have EJV or WOS in China. Fifty percent of the responded firms have only one affiliate in China. The percentage of the firms having two or more affiliates in China was 20% and 30% respectively. Thirty percent of the responded firms have selected EJV and WOS as the entry mode into China and 80% of the firms having subsidiaries in China have also established EJV. The data of the survey contains 30 firms which have only subsidiary. However, 24 of these firms established their WOS after 1992 and have a long experience of compensation trading, or processing and assembling with the Chinese firms in textiles, apparels and food processing industry.

The other survey on Japanese affiliates in China shows that the average scale of the Japanese WOS and EJV was 634 and 300 employees, respectively. While the 39% of Japanese EJV planned to maintain or decrease the level of their activities in the Chinese market, 82% of the Japanese WOS have planned to expand their investment in China [Huang 1997]. The firms having WOS have involved a high level of resource commitment and have a strong willingness to invest in China than the firms only having EJV in China. Therefore, the dependent variable of the study is the choice of EJV and WOS. In the analysis, there are two categories: the firm which has WOS (= 0) and the firm which has only EJV (= 1) in China. The study assumes that the firms have no option but to choose EJV in China in a specific stage of the internationalization process, while other firms have the option to select any entry mode. This study examines the impact of the independent (effect) variables on this process. In this study, the probability of a firm choosing an EJV instead of WOS is modeled as a function of the hypothesized effects as follows:

Probability (Choosing EJV over WOS) = $1/[1+\exp^{(-Y)}]$,
Where $Y = b_0 + b_1X_1 + b_2X_2 + \ldots \ldots + b_kX_k$.

$X_1, X_2, \ldots X_k$ are the hypothesized effect variables. The $b_0, b_1, b_2, \ldots b_k$ are estimated using maximum likelihood [Logistic Regression, SPSS 1993].

Operational Measures. The operational measures of all independent variables were adapted for the existing research, and new ones were developed for the purpose of this study. The measurement of variables is the five-point scale (e.g., 1 = no importance . . . 5 = major importance).

Market Risk. A five-point scale measuring the respondent's perception of unpredictability of a great political/social change which would cause a lot of damage to their business in China within 5 years, was developed for the measuring the country risk. A seven-item scale measuring the respondent's perception of business risk in China is also adapted [Kim and Hwang 1992, Aulakh and Kotabe 1997]. The items are shortage of information, inflation, foreign exchange balance, legal protection of intellectual properties, political uncertainty, effectiveness of legal system, and social security/welfare system. This composite scale has reliability greater than .70 (coefficient *alpha* = .82), but it has a strong correlation with the variable of heterogeneity of the market (correlation coefficient = .60). For avoiding the major multi-collinearity problems, the variable of business risk was deleted in the initial model.

Competition Conditions. The intensity of competition was measured by the number of competing players, or four-firm-concentration ratio in the previous researches. A high growing emerging market is usually a focus of global competitions and new target markets to enter. Thus, the number of players is not an appropriate measure of competition conditions. A five-point scale was used for measuring the respondent's perception of intensity of competition in the Chinese market.

Heterogeneity of Market. The location unfamiliarity or heterogeneity of a foreign market compared with the home country is a composite construct. The existing measure is the perceived differences between the home and host country with respect to political systems and economic/legal conditions [Kim and Hwang 1992]. The business risk is resulted from those differences. For a firm that has invested in China, heterogeneity of market is more related to the perceived differences between the home and host country with respect to culture, management mentality and government bureaucratic system. Therefore, a three-item scale was developed to measure the heterogeneity of market (coefficient *alpha* = .60). The basic research suggests that in the early stages of research reliabilities, .50 or .60 suffice, but reliabilities greater than .70 is recommended [Nunnally 1978, Churchill 1979].

Home Country Factors. Existing measures for this construct are not available; therefore, a four-item scale was developed. The related items are the lack of domestic labor, the limit of cost reduction, unpredictable exchange-rate, and sudden increase of imports (coefficient *alpha* = .77).

Market Infrastructures. The conditions of market infrastructure in China was measured the city of location, a 0-1 city dummy variable. Almost every city can be classified into two categories: the city has the Economic and Technological Development Zone (ETDZ) and the other cities. One prominent piece of FDI legislation in China is the Provision to Encourage Foreign Investment, often called "22 articles," initiated by China's State Council in October 1986. It authorizes local governments to establish ETDZ in their own jurisdictions to attract foreign investment.

Fourteen open cities near a harbor were opened and were designed to attract FDI in export-oriented and technologically advanced projects. Foreign-invested enterprises located in these cities benefit from preferential treatment in tax, customs duties, and land rent. The governments of those cities have also improved the market infrastructure in a number of areas, such as transportation, energy, water, and telecommunication [Luo 1997]. Thus, the firm which has affiliates located in the open cities was assigned 1, and the firm which has affiliates located in other cities was assigned 0.

In China, foreign investors are facing the intervention of the central and local governments in a number areas, such as industry selection, location, project type, equity distribution, and timing of investment. To measure this influence on the choice of entry mode, a single-item scale about the host government pressure on the partner selection was developed.

Entering Firm Factors. Previous research measured the international experience of the firm on a single-item scale: the approximate dollar value of foreign sales as a percentage of total worldwide sales. While this scale is an operational measure of the international experience in the corporate level, it is not an appropriate measure of market-specific knowledge or experiential knowledge. Thus, the initial year of trading and investing in China, number of affiliates, favorable past relationship with the local firms and host governments were used to measure the experience and knowledge accumulation. The initial year of trading and investing in China has strong correlation (correlation coefficient > .50). Thus, accumulation of experiential knowledge is measured by the number of affiliate. The initial year of investing was deleted. A two-item scale, the invitation of host government and the connection with the host governments, was developed to measure the favorable past relationship with host governments (coefficient *alpha* = .72).

Strategic Factors. The existing scales of strategic factors in the corporate level are not appropriate measures for the Chinese market. Thus two composite scales were developed. The intentions of investment strategies of the Japanese firms can be divided into following the existing customers and developing a global sourcing site [Huang 1995]. A three-item scale was developed that incorporates the potential Chinese market size, demand of foreign firms in China, and investing in China by their customers for the former (coefficient *alpha* = .63). A two-item scale, low labor cost and good export base, was developed for the latter (coefficient *alpha* = .68).

Transaction-Specific Factors. Asset specificity refers to the extent of firm-specific assets to support a transaction. Based on this definition, a five-item scale was developed. The five items are the importance of transfer of excellent products/services, well-known company name/brands, marketing capabilities, the most efficient facilities, and advanced technology (coefficient *alpha* = .77). The number of human resources dispatched to China was used to measure the tacit nature of the firm-specific assets. This variable has a strong correlation with the number of affiliates in China (correlation coefficient > .50), and was deleted in the initial model.

Partner's Factor. A four-item scale, the partner's technology capabilities/management resource, existing marketing network, convenient facilities, and satisfactory location, was used to measure the complementarity of resource and capability (coefficient *alpha* = .69). The availability of joint venturing partner was influenced by the intervention of host government on the partner selection and the knowledge and relationship with the local firms. Moreover, a type of business dummy variable was developed (the firm that has the manufacturing business in China was assigned 1) to measure the effect of local production.

Analyses. The independent variables, number of items, mean, standard deviation, correlation matrix and coefficient of reliability is given in Table 1. The influence direction of the hypothesized effect variables is also given in the last column. From the response structure of the variables used in this study, the multi-item scales show reasonable internal consistency, all having reliabilities (coefficient *alpha*) greater

TABLE 1. Response Structure of Variables

Expected

	Sign VARIABLE	No. of Items	Mean	S.D.	1	2	3	4	5	6	7	8	9	10	11	12	13	14	15	*
1	Country Risk	1	2.87	1.102	(N.A.)															—
2	Intensity of Competition	1	4.05	.918	.02	(N.A.)														—
3	Heterogeneity of Market	3	12.29	1.966	−.01	.09	(.60)													+
4	Home Country Factor	4	14.02	3.779	.02	.13	.13	(.77)												—
5	Intervention of Local Gov.	1	4.28	.851	.10	.14	.18	.09	(N.A.)											+
6	Initial Year of Trading	1	76.85	15.127	.11	.02	.00	−.01	−.01	(N.A.)										+
7	Number of Affiliates	1	3.86	6.845	−.20b	.14	.05	.14	.06	−.22b	(N.A.)									—
8	Past Relationship with Local	1	3.81	1.018	.20b	.07	.01	.01	−.04	−.08	.16	(N.A.)								+
9	Relationship with Host Gov.	2	6.76	1.741	−.12	−.14	.20b	.06	.23b	.04	.01	−.01	(.72)							+
10	Existing Customer Oriented	3	10.94	2.641	−.14	.01	−.08	−.05	.13	−.14	.23b	.13	.06	(.63)						—
11	Export-Oriented FDI	2	7.83	2.004	.05	.05	−.01	.50a	.07	.05	.10	.11	−.05	−.01	(.68)					+
12	Partner's Factor	4	14.53	3.170	−.05	.14	.29a	.15	.12	−.00	.04	.12	.01	.01	.12	(.69)				+
13	Firm-Specific Assets	5	18.27	3.458	−.22b	.07	.14	.12	.00	−.04	.06	−.03	−.04	.11	.09	.16	(.77)			—
14	Type of Business Dummy	1	.79	.412	−.10	−.11	.00	.39a	.12	−.03	−.02	−.05	.13	−.25a	.22b	.09	.06	(N.A.)		+
15	City Dummy	1	.59	.494	.01	−.19b	−.01	−.14	−.07	.18	−.25a	−.14	.05	−.15	−.27b	−.13	−.25a	−.21	(N.A.)	—

Zero-Order Product Moment Correlations

*: + = Encourages Equity Joint Venture. − = Encourages Wholly Owned Subsidiary.
**: n = 112, a: p < .01; b: p < .05.
***: Numbers in parentheses on the diagonal are the reliability estimates (Cronbach's alpha).

than .60. The validity considerations of the fifteen independent variables were assessed through a factor analysis. A fifteen-factor solution accounts for approximately 79.8% of the variance. After establishing internal consistency and validity of the multi-item scales, the respective items were summed to create composite scales. Although the variable of home country factors is correlated with the strategic intention to develop a global sourcing site (correlation coefficient = .50), the correlation matrix of independent variables gives no indication of major multicollinearity problems.

Logistic regressions and multiple discriminant analysis are the most often used method in studies on the choice of entry mode. In order to gain a better understanding of the impacts of the antecedent variables on the choice of EJV and WOS in China, two analyses were performed.

Estimation Results. The results of the logistic regression and multiple discriminant analysis are shown in Table 2. The estimated logistic regression coefficients at the initial model and the final model, and the standardized coefficients of discriminant function are shown in the table. Out of 15 terms in the initial model, 11 terms were deleted, and the effect variable in the final model were country risk, home country factors, number of affiliates in China, and the relationship with the host government. After deleting the variable of home country factors in the initial model, the variable of strategic intention to develop a global sourcing site was negatively related to the choice of EJV in China (b = -0.28, p < .10).

The overall initial model is significant (x^2 (15 d.f.) = 41.87, p < .001) and correctly classifies 81.3% of the observations. Although the variable of the relationship with local firms are found to be negatively related to the choice of EJV in China, the negative and positive sign of other independent variables are found to support to the hypothesized direction of influence. Four relationships are supported in the initial model and final model. As hypothesized, country risk of China, number of affiliates in China and home country factors are found to be negatively related to the choice of EJV in China, thus supporting H2a, H7, and H11. The relationship with host government is positively related to the choice of EJV in China.

The standardized coefficients given in Table 2 are found to support the significant relationships of country risk, number of affiliates in China, and the relationship with host government with the choice of

TABLE 2. Logistic Regression Estimation and Discriminant Analysis Results

VARIABLE	Logistic Regression Estimation		Discriminant Analysis
	Coefficient of Initial Model	Final Model	Standardized Coefficients
1 Country Risk	−.489c	−.416c	.407
2 Intensity of Competition	−.399		.090
3 Heterogeneity of Market	.016		−.042
4 Home Country Factor	−.133	−.132c	.254
5 Intervention of Local Government	.042		.021
6 Initial Year of Trading	.014		−.146
7 Number of Affiliates	−.307b	−.340a	.642
8 Past relationship with Local	−.116		.102
9 Relationship with Host Government	.294c	.311b	−.409
10 Existing Customer Oriented	−.118		.204
11 Export-oriented FDI	−.188		.247
12 Partner's Factor	.046		−.138
13 Firm-Specific Assets	−.059		.181
14 Type of Business Dummy	.531		−.130
15 City Dummy	−.121	2.895b	−.066
	6.674c		
Log Likelihood	−49.40	−52.82	Eigenvalue .400
Goodness of Fit	99.49	114.66	Canonical correlation .535
Chi-square	41.87	35.03	Wilks' Lambda .714
Degrees of freedom	15	4	Chi-square 34.50
Significance, p <	.001	.001	Degrees of freedom 15
Correct classification	81.3%	80.4%	Significance, p < .01
n	112	112	n 112

Significance of Wald test, a: p < .01, b: p < .05, c: p < .10.

103

EJV in China, based on the cut-off of ±.40 for the coefficients. The results suggest that firms with a higher level of experience and risk-absorption capability to do business in China, and with a weak relationship with the host government have the option to choose EJV and WOS.

The significant coefficients for country risk and number of affiliates in China supported that the organization capabilities, such as experiential knowledge and market-specific knowledge, have an immense impact on the choice of entry mode in China. The greater the stock of a firm's experience of doing business and market-specific knowledge, the firm is more likely to choose WOS. The market-specific resource, such as the good connection or relationship with host government influences the firm's decision to choose the EJV. In an emerging market where foreign investors face much government intervention in a number of areas of investment, the good relationship with host government is an important resource.

CONCLUSIONS AND DISCUSSION

When the market risk is high, the entering firm may be well advised to limit its resource commitments and increase its ability to exit from the market quickly without taking a substantial loss should the market environment worsen. The level of resource commitment consistent with a joint venture will usually be lower than establishing a WOS in foreign markets. Furthermore, EJV is a mode to retain flexibility and shift risk to the local firm, who may have capabilities to influence host government policy [Hill et al. 1990]. Regardless of the results of previous studies, the results of this study given in Table 2 point to the negative influence of country risk in the choice of EJV. This interesting finding suggest that firm's uncertainty absorption capability and risk dispersion mechanisms influence the decisions of market entry, irrespective of the level of market risk.

A firm is initially risk averse when entering an unfamiliar foreign market, and therefore not willing to invest substantial resources in EJV or WOS. Despite the level of the country risk of an emerging market, a firm will develop the capabilities to absorb the uncertainty through accumulating the experience and market-specific knowledge. The firm will also develop the risk dispersion mechanism and exploit its rent-yielding firm-specific advantage in a high-risk and high-return market. Thus, the risk absorption capabilities and risk dispersion mechanisms are important supporting structures, or complementary firm-specific assets. The results of this study suggest that the accumulation of experience and market-specific knowledge is a major influence on the choice of entry mode in a dynamic process.

Based on the survey data, the countermeasures to meet the country risk in China were described. 46% of respondents perceived the possibility of a great political/social change in China as 50-50. The response of "very strong and strong" possibility and "a slight and no" possibility are about 25%, respectively. There is not significant difference between the group of firms which have WOS and which only have EJV. Firms having WOS in China set up an upper limit of investment in China, or withdraw the investment in a short time to meet and the country risk in China, while firms only having EJV lay a stress on keeping good connections with local officials.

The results suggest that decisions of entry into emerging markets are influenced by firms' uncertainty absorption mechanisms, irrespective of asset specificity. These findings, along with the previous studies' result [Rangan et al. 1993, Aulakh and Kotabe, 1997], suggest that the relationships between exogenous environmental factors and entry mode are much more complex than the propositions of the transaction cost explanation or the competitive strategic perspective.

In terms of specific implications, the dependent variable of this study is a categorical variable based on corporate level, while most of the previous studies focused on each entry decision based on transaction level. Support for the hypotheses regarding the home country factors on choice of entry mode into an emerging market has important implications. First, the finding suggests that Japanese firms having WOS in China were driven by strategic motivations based on the home country factors. Second, when they enter the Chinese market by EJV, Japanese firms were driven by the favorable past relationship with the host government.

Finally, the results also suggest that the strong positive correlation between experiential knowledge accumulation and choice of WOS in the Chinese market. The Japanese firms acquired the market-knowledge through establishing affiliates in China, and accumulated the experience through performing the operations in the Chinese market. The results of this study can be seen as generally consistent with the organizational capability perspective.

Although the results of this study outline a rich agenda for further study, it is of course subject to limitations. We need to know more about the incremental process of accumulation of market-specific knowledge. The sample consists only of Japanese firms having EJV or WOS in China. Thus we also need more accurate measures for the variables the affect choice of entry mode into the Chinese market, especially if they are to be used in the USA and EU MNCs context. Firms are facing a manifestation of uncertainty and risk of the emerging markets. Thus future research is needed to explicitly examine the uncertainty absorption capability and risk dispersion mechanisms. Lastly, the short history of FDI into China from MNCs and the research design used here do not allow us to analyze a number of issues, such as the relationship between entry modes and performance in an emerging market. The importance of this relationship has been highlighted in recent research [Chowdhury 1992; Luo 1997].

REFERENCES

Agarwal, S. and S. Ramaswami, 1992, "Choice of foreign market entry mode: Impact of ownership, location, and internalization factors," *Journal of international business Studies*, 23(1): 1-27.

Anand, J. and A. Delios, 1997, "Location specificity and the transferability of downstream assets to foreign subsidiaries," *Journal of international business Studies*, 28 (3): 571-603.

Anderson, E. and H. Coughlan, 1987, "International marketing entry and expansion via independent or integrated channels of distribution," *Journal of Marketing*, 51(1): 71-82.

_____ and H. Gatignon, 1986, "Modes of foreign entry: A transaction cost analysis and propositions," *Journal of international business Studies*, 17(3): 1-26.

Aulakh, P. M. and M. Kotabe, 1997, "Antecedents and Performance Implications of Channel Integration in Foreign Markets," *Journal of international business Studies*, 28(1): 145-175.

Auster, Ellen R. 1987, "International corporate linkages: Dynamic forms in changing environments," *Columbia journal of world business*, 33(2): 3-6.

Balakrishnan, S. and B. Wernerfelt, 1986, "Technical change, competition and vertical integration," *Strategic Management Journal*, Vol. 7 (July-August), pp. 347-359.

Barney, J.B. 1991, "Firm resources and sustained competitive advantage," *Journal of Management*, 17, pp. 99-120.

Beamish, P. W. 1984, *Multinational Joint Ventures in Developing Countries*. London: Routledge.

_____, 1985, "The characteristics of joint ventures in developed and developing countries," *Columbia Journal of World Business*, 20: 13-19.

_____, 1993, "The characteristics of joint ventures in the People's Republic of China," *Journal of international Marketing*, 1(2): 29-48.

Buckley, P. J. and M. Casson, 1976, *The future of the Multinational Enterprise*, NY: Holmes.

Cantwell, J. 1991, "The theory of technological competence and its application to international production," in McFetridge, D. (ed.), *Foreign Investment, Technology and Economic Growth*, pp. 33-67. University of Calgary Press.

Cateora, P.R. and S. Keavency 1987. *Marketing: An international perspective*, Richard D. Irwin, Inc.

Chowdhury, J. 1992, "Performance of international joint ventures and wholly owned foreign subsidiaries: A comparative perspective," *Management International Review*, 32(2): 115-133.

Cohen, W. M. and D. A. Levinthal, 1990, "Absorptive Capacity: A New Perspective on Learning and Innovation," *Administrative Science Quarterly*, 35(1): 128-152.

Contractor, F. and P. Lorange, eds. 1987, *Cooperative strategies in international business*, MA: D. C. Heath.

Davidson, W. H. 1982, *Global Strategic Management*. NY: John Wiley.

Dymsza, W. A. 1988, "Successes and failures of joint ventures in developing countries," in Contractor, F. and Lorange, P. (eds.), op. cit.

Eriksson, K. et al. 1997, "Experiential knowledge and cost in the internationalizaion process," *Journal of international business Studies*, 28(2): pp. 337-60.

Erramilli, M.K. and C.P. Rao, 1993, "Service firms' international entry-mode choice: A modified transaction-cost analysis approach," *Journal of Marketing*, 57(3): 19-38.

Franko, L. G. 1971, *Joint venture survival in multinational corporations*, New York, NY: Praeger.

Gatignon, H. and E. Anderson, 1988, "The multinational corporation's degree of control over foreign subsidiaries: An empirical test of a transaction cost explanation," *Journal of Law, Economics, and Organization*, 4(Fall): 305-336.

Ghoshal, S. 1987 "Global Strategy: An Organizing Framework," *Strategic Management Journal*, Vol. 8, pp. 425-440.

Goodnow, J. D. and J. E. Hanz, 1972, "Environmental Determinants of Overseas Market Entry Strategies," *Journal of international business Studies*, 3(1): 33-50.

Harrigan, K.R. 1985, *Strategies for joint ventures*. MA: D.C. Heath.

_____, 1988, "Joint ventures and competitive strategy," *Strategic Management Journal*, Vol.12 (Special Issue), pp. 141-158.

Hennart, J. F. 1991, "The transaction costs theory of joint ventures: An empirical study of Japanese subsidiaries in the United States," *Management Science*, Vol. 37(4), pp. 483-497.

Hill C. W.L., P. Hwang and W. C. Kim, 1990, "An eclectic theory of the Choice of international entry mode," *Strategic Management Journal*, Vol. 11(2), pp. 117-128.

Hout, T., M. E. Porter and E. Rudden, 1982, "How global companies win out," *Harvard Business Review*, 60 September-October, 98-108.

Huang, L. 1992, "Global marketing innovation: Marketing practices of foreign firms in Japan," in Kojima K. ed. *Innovation and Business Dynamics in Japan and*

Korea, Kobe Economic and Business Research Series No. 11, pp. 75-95, Kobe University.

_____, 1997, Entry Strategies for the Chinese Market and Performance (in Japanese), *Journal of Economics & Business Administration (Kobe University)*, Vol. 176(1), 61-75.

Inkpen, A. 1992, *Management of international joint ventures: A organizational learning perspective*. New York: Routledge.

Johanson, J. & Jan-Erik Vahlne, 1977. "The international process of the firm–A model of knowledge development and increasing foreign market commitment," *Journal of international business Studies*, 8(1): 22-32.

Lou, Y. 1997, "Performance Implications of International Strategy: An empirical study of foreign-invested enterprises in China," *Group & Organization Management*, Vol. 22(1), pp. 87-116.

Kim, W C. and P. Hwang, 1992, "Global strategy and multinationals' entry mode choice," *Journal of international business Studies*, 23(1): 29-53.

Klein, S., G.L. Frazier and V.J. Roth, 1990, "A transaction cost analysis model of channel integration in international markets," *Journal of Marketing Research*, 27(May): 196-208.

Kobrin, Stephen J. 1991, "An empirical analysis of the determinants of global integration," *Strategic Management Journal*, Vol. 12, pp. 17-19.

Kogut, B. 1988, "Joint ventures: Theoretical and empirical perspectives," *Strategic Management Journal*, Vol. 9, pp. 319-332.

_____ 1989, "A note on global strategies," *Strategic Management Journal*, Vol. 10, pp. 383-389.

Madhok, A. 1997, "Cost, value and foreign market entry mode: The transaction and the firm," *Strategic Management Journal*, Vol. 18, pp. 39-61.

Makino, S. and A. Delios 1996, "Local knowledge´transfer and performance: Implications for alliance formation in Asia," *Journal of international business Studies*, (Special Issue): 905-927.

Makino, S. and P. W. Beamish 1998, "Performance and Survival of joint ventures with non-conventional ownership structures," *Journal of international business Studies*, 29(4): pp. 797-818.

Nelson, R. and S. Winter 1982. *An Evolutionary Theory of Economic Change*, MA: Harvard University Press.

Pan Y. 1996, "Influences on Foreign Equity Ownership Level in Joint Ventures China," *Journal of international business Studies*, 27(1): pp. 1-26.

Pan, Y. & David K. Tse 1996, "Cooperative strategies of foreign firms in an overseas country," *Journal of international business Studies*, 27(5): pp. 926-46.

Porter, M. E. 1990, *The competitive advantage of nations*. New York: Free Press.

Root, Franklin R. 1982. *Foreign Market Entry Strategies*, AMACOM.

_____, 1994. *Entry strategies for international market*, New York: Lexington Books.

Rugman, A.M. 1980, "Internalization as a general theory of foreign direct investment: A reappraisal of the literature," *Weltwirtschaftliches Archiv*. 116: pp. 365-379.

Stopford, J. M. and L. T. Wells 1972, *Managing the multinational enterprise*. New York: Basic Books.

Tse, David K. et al. 1997, "How MNCs choose entry modes and from alliances: The China experience," *Journal of international business Studies*, 28(4): pp. 779-805.

Vaupel, J. W. and J. P. Chrhan 1973, *The world's multinational enterprises*. Harvard University Press.

Wernerfelt, B. 1995."The resource-based view of the firm: Ten years after," *Strategic Management Journal*, Vol. 16, pp. 174-175.

Yoshihara, H. 1992, *Miracle of Fuji-Xerox* (in Japanese), Toyokeizai.

———, 1997, *International Business Management* (in Japanese), Yuhigaku ARMA.

Foreign Direct Investment in China:
The Importance of Market Entry Timing

Xiaolian Li

SUMMARY. China has attracted the second largest amount of foreign direct investment in the world each year since 1993. Hundreds of thousands of foreign-invested enterprises are in operation in China. However, what drive the success or cause the failure of foreign investments is still not well understood. This paper critically examines one success factor, i.e., the importance of timing of marketing entry into China. It begins with a brief review of the literature on first-mover advantages and the recent empirical research. It then attempts to theorize on why timing of market entry matters in the context of foreign direct investment. Apart from drawing upon the four recent studies in this area, this paper focuses on the auto industry in China and the case of Volkswagen to illustrate the importance of early entry into an overseas market. It calls for foreign investors to seize the first-wave opportunities when the door is opened a certain sector. It pays in the long run both in terms of the market share position and profitability. *[Article copies available for a fee from The Haworth Document Delivery Service: 1-800-342-9678. E-mail address: <getinfo@haworthpressinc.com> Website: <http://www.HaworthPress.com>]*

KEYWORDS. Foreign direct investment, timing of entry, China

INTRODUCTION

China has been very successful in attracting foreign direct investment since it opened its door in the late 1970s. Foreign investments in

Xiaolian Li is a graduate research student, School of Business, the University of Hong Kong, Pokfulam Road, Hong Kong (E-mail: lian@business.hku.hk).

The author acknowledges the kind assistance from Yigang Pan.

[Haworth co-indexing entry note]: "Foreign Direct Investment in China: The Importance of Market Entry Timing." Li, Xiaolian. Co-published simultaneously in *Journal of Global Marketing* (International Business Press, an imprint of The Haworth Press, Inc.) Vol. 14, No. 1/2, 2000, pp. 111-127; and: *Greater China in the Global Market* (ed: Yigang Pan) International Business Press, an imprint of The Haworth Press, Inc., 2000, pp. 111-127. Single or multiple copies of this article are available for a fee from The Haworth Document Delivery Service [1-800-342-9678, 9:00 a.m. - 5:00 p.m. (EST). E-mail address: getinfo@haworthpressinc.com].

China have expanded dramatically to reach an annual total of US$34 billion in 1994 and 1995, US$42.6 billion in 1996, and US$45.3 billion in 1997. China was the second largest recipient of foreign direct investment in the world after the United States since 1993. By the end of 1996, 284,000 foreign enterprises have been approved by the Chinese authorities, of which 140,000 have been in operation (China Statistical Yearbook 1997). Foreign enterprises are playing an increasing important role in the Chinese economy. They now employ more than 17.5 million people, which account for about 10 percent of the country's non-rural labor force. They now account for 47.3 percent of China's total foreign trade volume, i.e., US$137.1 billion in China's total trade volume of US$289.9 billion in China's total trade volume of US$289.9 billion in 1996. The export and import trade of China have also undergone a similar fast pace growth. Ten years ago in 1989, China exported US$195.25 and imported US$201.85. By 1996, its export had increased to US$1255.0 and import to US$1152.9. Evidently, China has become a hot spot for competition for firms all over the world. They come to China via a variety of entry modes, such as export, non-equity arrangement, equity joint venture or wholly owned operation.

With hundreds of billions of dollars at stake, many investors are seeking to understanding what the success factors in China are. The literature on successful cases of foreign investments in China is increasing rapidly [Beamish 1993; Child 1994; Pan, Li, and Tse 1999; Vanhoacker 1997; Yan and Grey 1994]. Apparently, the success of a foreign-invested enterprise hinges on any factors, one of which is the timing of market entry [Pan and Chi 1999]. The paper attempts to give an in-depth examination and to provide a more comprehensive understanding on why order of market entry is important in the context of foreign direct investment.

This paper begins with a brief review of the literature on first mover advantages and the four recent empirical studies related to the timing of entry in China. It then extends the first-mover principles to the context of foreign direct investment. Factors that contribute to the first-mover advantages that are not salient in a domestic context, but are unique to foreign direct investment are identified. Finally, this paper will resort to the auto industry in China as well as the case of Volkswagen to illustrate the importance of early entry into an overseas market. The fundamental argument of this paper is that it pays to be an early-mover in a foreign market in the long run.

EARLY MOVER ADVANTAGES

Order of market entry has been of interest to researchers [Chang 1995; Lambkin 1998; Lieberman and Montogomery 1990; Mitchell 1991; Pan, Li and Tse 1999]. When there are initial asymmetries in timing, the early-movers have genetic advantages over later comers. Early movers gain an advantage over later comers. Early movers gain an advantage over the later comers in many aspects, including economic, preemptive, technological, and behavioral factors [DeCastro and Chrisman 1995].

With respect to the economic factors, early-movers are often more cost competitive due to the advantages in the economy of scale and existing assets in areas such human resources, marketing, distribution, and customer reputation [Lambkin 1988].

As for the preemption advantages, early movers are in the position to choose among the best available locations and partners; early-movers are able to patent their products and services and fill product differentiation niches before their competitors even have a chance. The availability of retail space is often seen as a preemptive tactics used by the existing players to discourage the entry of new players [Bain 1956; Lillien and Yoon 1990]. Early players have the opportunity to craft the shape of an industry by initiation certain industry standard by which the late comers would find it hard to change [Chang 1995].

In regard to technological factors, the standard learning-curve model posits that unit production costs fall with cumulative output. If the early-movers can maintain leadership and maintain their market share dominance, they can enjoy a sustainable cost advantage. More importantly, Early lead in patent or R&D can help to put them in a winning position [Lillien and Yoon 1990; Robinson, Fornell and Sullivan 1992].

With respect to behavioral factors, studies have shown that early movers often enjoy a higher degree of customer preference and loyalty than late entrants [Carpenter and Nakamoto 1989]. A significant proportion of customers are risk adverse and would stick to an existing product until an overwhelming evidence shows the superiority of a competing product. Such customers are more likely to stick to the products offered by the early-movers and it rests on the shoulders of the late entrants to prove that it is worthwhile to the customers to switch to their products [DeCastro and Chrisman 1995]. Also, host country government policy changes over time due to economic and social needs. A development or investment once highly encouraged and favored is no longer preferred. The Government objectively helps block out the later comers.

These propositions were made and tested in the Western context. Recent studies have re-investigated these propositions in the context of foreign investment in China [Luo 1997; Pan, Li and Tse 1999]. This paper provides a brief review of work done by Luo (1997), Pan, Li and Tse (1999), Pan and Chi (1998), and Pan and Chi (1999).

RECENT EMPIRICAL STUDIES

In a study of foreign firms in Jiansu province in China, Luo [1998] found that early-movers (97 firms started in 1980-81) had an average sales growth of 26.78% while late-entrants (24 firms started in 1989-90) had 15.28%. Early-entrants had a higher asset turnover than late-entrants. However, the late-entrants had a higher return on investment than early-entrants. Apart from a very small sample, his results are based on one industry (textiles) and one province (Jiangsu), which raises the question of generalizability of his findings.

A recent study by Pan and Chi [1997] offers stronger evidence that is based on a larger and more representative sample. Their study was based on a sample of 962 foreign enterprises. In their sample, the earliest time that an enterprise started production was December 1980, and the latest time was June 1993.

Pan and Chi [1997] found that foreign enterprises that entered China at an earlier time were more profitable that those that entered at a later time. Specifically, 59.62% of foreign enterprises that entered China prior to 1984, and 58.77% of those that entered during the 1984-89 period were profitable. However, only 44.27% of those that entered after 1989 were profitable. Further, those that entered China the earliest were most profitable, because 48.08% of the first-wave firms earned at least 3% or higher profit, while only 43.64% of the second-wave and 32.3% of the third-wave fell in the same category.

In Pan and Chi (1999), similar patterns of results were found when they used the multivariate analysis, thus ensuring the robustness of the findings (see Table 1).

The most comprehensive study came from Pan, Li and Tse [1999]. It was based on the 1995 Chinese industrial census. The total number of enterprises (both foreign and local) in their data set was 450,233. Together, these enterprises accounted for 91% of the total industrial output in China in 1995. There were 41,958 foreign enterprises, accounting for 17% of total industrial sales revenue in 1995. Due to selection of industry sectors, their final sample had a total of 23,518 foreign enterprises in China.

The average market shares of foreign enterprises are 0.385%. As expected, early-entrants have an average of 2.024% of the market shares, which is much higher than the average for all foreign enterprises. The followers have smaller market shares. The average market shares are 1.285% for the followers in the first three years, 0.781% for those in the second three years, 0.439% for those in the third three years, 0.226% for those in the fourth three years, and 0.111% for those in the last two years. The descriptive results support the hypothesis that early entry foreign enterprises have larger market shares than the early followers, and early followers have larger market shares than late followers (see Table 2).

TABLE 1. Timing of Market Entry into China

Profit level	Firm's timing of entry in China			
	1978-1984	1985-1989	1990-1993	Overall
> 15%	9.62	12.06	6.61	9.36
8-15%	13.46	12.94	10.13	11.64
3-8%	25.00	18.64	15.64	17.57
< 3%	11.54	15.13	11.89	13.41
No profit	7.69	6.80	12.33	9.46
Minor loss	9.62	9.21	18.72	13.72
Heavy loss	7.69	7.24	8.59	7.90
Out of business	15.38	17.98	16.08	16.94
Column total	100%	100%	100%	100%
N	52	456	454	962

Note: Based on the paper written by Pan and Chi 1998.

TABLE 2. Timing of Market Entry into China

Independent variables		Market share (%)	ROA (%)	N
Overall average		0.385 (2.07)	0.65 (0.133)	23518
Order of entry				
Early entrants		2.024 (7.66)	3.10 (0.120)	688
Followers:	1st 3 years	1.285 (4.91)	3.17 (0.130)	810
	2nd 3 years	0.781 (2.60)	1.89 (0.126)	2446
	3rd 3 years	0.439 (1.59)	0.54 (0.135)	5416
	4th 3 years	0.226 (0.75)	0.42 (0.131)	6606
	5th 2 years	0.111 (0.69)	0.03 (0.135)	7552

Note: The data based on 1995 Chinese Industrial Census, Pan, Li, and Tse 1998.

Early entry foreign enterprises have a ROA of 3.10%, which is much higher than the overall average of 0.65%. Increasing, the average ROA for the followers in the first three years is quite similar, at 3.17%. However, the average ROA for later followers are much smaller at 1.89% for those in the fourth three years, and 0.03% for those in the last two years. The descriptive results shows that early entry foreign enterprises have higher profitability than late followers. In their multivariate analysis, the results of early mover on market share and profitability came out quite strongly [Pan, Li and Tse 1999].

These four studies provide quite a strong pattern of evidence supporting the early mover advantages for foreign firms in China. While it is gratifying that the findings are strong and seem to be in line with those reported in the literature, these recent studies have not been about to provide adequate conceptual explanations on why the principles of early-mover advantages apply to the foreign direct investment. More importantly, it remains unclear to what extent the uniqueness of host country, that is China, play a role.

A CONCEPTUAL MODEL:
TIMING OF ENTRY OF FDI IN CHINA

In this section, a conceptual model is provided that explains why we see the principles of early movers at work in China. These factors are not only unique to the foreign direct investment context in general, but they also help us gain a better understanding on the order of entry effect on performance in emerging countries.

Gate-Keeper Role of Host Country Government. The government of most countries, developing or developed, sees it as an important function to protect the home industries from foreign competition [Ohmae 1989]. It opens up an industrial sector when it feels the domestic firms can compete in the face of foreign players. At times, external forces may force the host country government to open up sectors before it is ready to do so on its own. In the case of China, the Chinese government opens up its market to foreign firms on a gradual basis. It controls the timing and pace of inflow of foreign investment in each of the product sector. Under this circumstance, foreign firms that could get into the door early enjoy the monopolistic opportunity to develop the market, promote the product, and tap into a variety of strategies to preempt the future entry of competitors. In 1995, the Chinese government awarded the contract to build minivans to Mercedes, even though Chrysler has a much enviable reputation with its minivans. Industry critics see this as an important competitive move of Mercedes against Chrysler in the China market, mostly because the Chinese government made it known that it did not plan to allow new major foreign operations in the auto sector in the near future [Business Week, July 31, 1995, p. 50].

By getting into the market early, foreign firms have a free hand establishing their products, markets customers, business partners, suppliers and even industry standards [Lambkin 1988; Lilien and Yoon 1990]. Again, take the example of auto industry (Tables 3 and 4). The Chinese government approved three joint ventures in automobile sectors in the 1980s, namely Volkswagen in Shanghai, AMC/Chrysler in Beijing, Peugeot in Guangzhou. In 1993, these three ventures ranked the first, second, and fourth largest foreign invested ventures in China in terms of total sales in 1993, and reached a combined sales of US$2.84 billion [Luo 1997]. According to People's Daily (February 20, 1996), the top 30 foreign-invested manufacturing firms were all established before 1984 [Luo 1997].

Strategic Choice of Local Partner. In many product sectors, the host country government in the developing countries discourages the wholly owned operation by foreign firms. Equity joint ventures is thus the only option available to foreign firms looking for a direct involvement

TABLE 3. Volkswagen in China

Key Statistics and Information

1978	Minister of Machinery of China visited the headquarters of Volkswagen
1979	Negotiation began with Shanghai Auto Works
1983	Test assembly of Santana at Shanghai Auto Works
1984	Agreement on Shanghai Volkswagen Auto Joint Venture
1985	Shanghai Volkswagen Auto Joint Venture began operation with registered capital of 350 million Yan
1987	Shanghai municipal government set up an office to assist localization of Volkswagen parts
1991	Santana sales reached 35,000 units
	Develop Santana 2000
	Agreement between First Auto Works and Volkswagen to produce 150,000 Jetta
1994	Santana sales reached 115,000 units
	Santana 2000 certified
1995	Santana sales reached 160,000 units
	Santana 2000 was launched in the market
	Santana localization reached 85%
	Agreement to form First Auto Works Volkswagen Joint Venture
	Sales revenue reached RMB 18.5 billion
1985-95	Cumulative sales revenue reached RMB 60.8 billion
1985-95	Cumulative gross profit was RMB 14.3 billion
1985-95	Cumulative net profit was RMB 5.1 billion
1996	Volkswagen took 54.5 per cent of the Chinese car market
1997	Volkswagen Sales volume was RMB 26.3 billion, in lead of the top 500 joint venture enterprises in China

Note: The Economist Intelligence Unit 1996 Wang, Zhile [1995]. *Investment of Transnational Corporations*, China Economics Press. www.industrywatch.com

in the actual investment. The choice of a suitable local partner is a vital issue because of the lack of quality local partners. If the host country is under the transformation from a planned economy to a market economy to a market economy, like China and Eastern European countries, few local firms have the same caliber as their Western counterparts in terms of technology, resources, or management and marketing know-how. Nonetheless, there are comparatively better ones. The ability of early movers to pick and choose these local partners is particularly significant. It ensures a better match and a higher level of complementarity between foreign and local partners.

TABLE 4. Sedan Sector in China in 1995

Top 10 firms by revenues	Start year	Ownership	Revenues in million RMB	Profit in million RMB	Number of employees
Volkswagen Shanghai	1985	foreign	18,431	2,480	9,437
Tianjin Auto	1984	state-own	10,400	0	1,515
Beijing Jeep	1984	foreign	5,746	353	8,067
Tianjin Mini Auto	1988	state-own	3,929	572	3,479
FAW-Volkswagen	1991	foreign	2,417	8	3,046
Quangzhou Peugeot	1985	foreign	1,098	− 321	3,134
Yi Qi Shunde	1992	collective	548	8	222
Quangdong Wemry	1989	state-own	289	11	501
Chongqing Suzuki	1993	foreign	269	− 65	594
Pu Dong Vi Qi assembly	1993	domestic JV	154	− 1	40

Note: Page 915 of China's Industrial Markets Yearbook 1997, City University of Hong Kong Press.

What is more important is that which often precludes the partnership of same kind with late comers.

Volkswagen entered China in 1984 via a joint venture with Shanghai Automotive Industry Corporation (SAIC). SAIC is the biggest, most efficient and consequently most profitable auto group in China. In 1997, the company's sales volume was 26.3 billion yuan out of the total volume of 601.04 billion yuan earned by the top 500 joint venture enterprises in China. The Shanghai Volkswagen Co Ltd has, for the seventh consecutive year, maintained its position as the most successful overseas-funded industrial enterprise in China [Xinhua news agency, 1998]. This decision of Volkswagen to form partnership with SAIC began with the visit of the Minister of Machinery of China to the headquarters of Volkswagen in Germany in 1978, which was followed with frequent negotiations that led to the final agreement in 1984. In the eyes of Volkswagen, SAIC is not only the best managed auto firm in China, but it also sits in Shanghai, the most economically vibrant city in China. It enables Volkswagen to draw upon the best human resources and the best suppliers to achieve a high level of content localization to be cost competitive.

This ability of Volkswagen to lock in SAIC prevents other foreign auto firms to enter the sedan market in Shanghai for a period of time of at least 15 years. Therefore, the early-movers take the first cut at the investment location, access to key natural resources, market exclusivity, and even local human resources [Child 1994; Osland and Cavusgil 1996]. When Honda wanted to build cars in China, it had to take over the joint venture in South China where Peugeot decided to withdraw.

Strategic Choice of Local Market. The choice of appropriate location is important for many developing countries for several reasons. The gap in income and living standards is often much bigger in the developing countries. The transportation and production logistics also differ from one geographic location to another. Local market protectionism can rampant. Therefore, being able to locate one's operation closer to the target customers is of vital significance.

Volkswagen's choice of SAIC is of strategic importance also in terms of geographic location in Shanghai. Shanghai is the most populous and affluent city in China. It is the hub of Central China serving the whole Yangtze River Delta and upstream Yangtze River region. Because of the close economic ties Shanghai has with the Central China, its products have always enjoyed a high reputation and are much less to be excluded based on local protectionism. In contrast, Chrysler's joint venture is located in Beijing, a capital town, and Peugeot's joint venture is located in Guangzhou, a city smaller in size and less well known for its heavy industry.

With Shanghai as it base, Volkwagen Shanghai was able to sell about 160,000 Santanas in 1995, and had taken a lion's share of sedan market, accounted for about 40% of the domestically-made cars sold in China. The profitability of Volkswagen Shanghai was also among the highest in the sector.

Better Incentives and Local Government Support. Foreign firms that entered China at an earlier time received better incentives and support from the host country governments at various levels than later-entrants. China re-opened its door to foreign investors in the late 1970s. In the first years, there was a high degree of skepticism about investing in China. Only 2531 foreign enterprises were approved in the first five years of 1979-83 [Johnstone 1997]. For those foreign investors that entered China then, they had shown a great deal of trust in the open-door policy of the Chinese government. In return, they were rewarded with incentives and concessions in terms of taxes, land use, supplies of energy and materials, and market access that were not readily available to late-entrants [Beamish 1993]. The early-movers were granted more flexible standards in terms of size of investment, requirements for environment protection, and so forth [Osland and Casvusgil 1996; Vanhonacker 1997]. These differences enhance the early-mover advantages and contribute to a higher degree of performance success in China.

In the case of Volkswagen, the city government of Shanghai set up an office to assist Volkswagen's joint venture in July 1987. Soon, this office brought more than 100 local parts producers together and assisted them in working with Volkswagen to explore localization of parts. In 1988, a core group of local parts producers formed a common network to aid Volkswagen for reaching its target level of localization. In order to solve the lack of financial resources for research and development, the government allowed a fee of RMB 28,000 to be collected for each vehicle sold to form a fund to assist local parts manufacturing. This practice faded out in 1994. By then, a total of RMB 5 billion contributed to the success of Volkswagen in Shanghai [Wang 1995].

The Chinese government has gradually faded out policies of incentives in favor of foreign investors. For instance, the State Council announced that tariff and import taxes will be levied on imported equipment and raw and semi-finished materials in accordance with the legal tax rates for newly approved foreign-funded enterprises. Foreign enterprises set up before December 31, 1997 will, within the specified grace period, continue to enjoy the preferential terms on the reduction and exemption of tariff and import taxes. The policy has not been fully implemented due to the negative response from foreign investors. Nonetheless, the State Council in February 1998 decided that all office, communication, and transportation equipment used by foreign enterprises are not subject to import tariff. After GM got the approval to produce "Regal" sedan in Shanghai, it spent a lot of time negotiating with Chinese authorities to waive import duties on imported equipment.

A new policy issued by the State Planning Commission on February 19, 1994 and approved by State Council July 3, 1994 states that the State will promote the development of two or three large automotive groups, six or seven key auto plants and eight to ten major motorcycle plants. In the longer term, to 2010, the State will promote further consolidation towards having only three or four auto groups and three or four motorcycle groups. The State will support companies meeting certain criteria and priority projects. This policy further proves that the early-movers in China seize strategic opportunities that came once in a long while. Those foreign firms that could not get in at an earlier time had a lot to lose.

Less Stringent Requirements. Foreign firms that entered China at an earlier time had less stringent requirement on environment protection, product safety labor management, and thus, the overall costs of operation were lower than the later entrants.

The first Santana produced by Volkswagen Shanghai was a vehicle brought from Volkswagen Brazil. It was a car of 1980s. It did not have the latest design and comfort. But it met with the needs of China before 1995. Importantly, it met with environment and safety requirements of that time. Now there is an increasing public awareness that has prompted auto manufacturers to upgrade the quality of the vehicle. Major cities in China are now enforcing the use of unleaded gas, as well as plans to require air bags and ABS systems in the near future. Volkswagen introduced Santana 2000 around 1995 and was prepared for the tougher environmental and safety expectations.

Competing Against Weak Local Firms. Foreign firms that entered China at an earlier time competed against a weaker domestic industry, and thus, had a higher chance of success. Take China's auto sector as an example. The whole domestic industry remained at the level of 1950s when three auto joint ventures were approved in mid-1980s. The Chinese manufacturers lacked capital and technology. The production equipment was basically what was left over by the Russians. Research and development abilities were weak. Product innovation was non-existent. The "Liberation" brand truck produced by the First Automotive Plant in Changcun did not change its appearance in thirty years. Automotive sector has become a pillar sector in China. From mid-1980s, the auto sector has increased at a double-digit rate to a total of 1.55 million vehicles by 1997. Only 48,000 vehicles were imported.

Foreign firms that entered this sector early met with a weak local competition. They came with capital, technology, manufacturing process and equipment, product, and management know-how.

In contrast, there was only one foreign enterprise in the top ten manufacturers in the refrigerator sector in China in 1995. That foreign enterprise was started in 1994. By then, the Chinese manufacturers had dominated the refrigerator market. Top ten brands had a 91.58% of total sales in China by 1997, indicating a high level of competition intensity and brand consolidation.

Longer Learning Curve. Foreign firms that entered China at an earlier time had a longer time to learn and adjust to the Chinese market than the later-entrants, and thus, would perform better.

Direct investment in China can be seen as buying an option through which foreign firms gain the rights to future choices and flexibilities in China [Bowman and Hurry 1993]. In other words, initial FDI can be a platform for obtaining rights to future opportunities. Most large multinational corporations now have dozens of investment projects in China. The earlier they jumped into the China market, the more experienced they are today. Foreign firms learn about the political system, market system, distribution, logistics and so on. Also, foreign firms acquire and accumulate knowledge about how to function as an organization in China.

Early-movers have a longer period of time to carry out the learning and adjustment. As pointed out in point 3, they can do it at a time when the local Chinese competition was rather weak, thus enhancing the success likelihood [Chang 1995].

Foreign firms that entered China at an earlier time had a longer time to develop corporate and brand position than later-entrants. The bulk of sedans were purchased by government institutions. In 1996, government sector bought 64% of all domestically produced sedans, and 50% in 1997. Companies, especially taxi firms, bought 21% in 1996, and 29% in 1997. Individuals bought 15% in 1996 and 21% in 1997.

It is important for firms to have a strong corporate and brand position to sell successfully to the government and institutions. A strong consumer perception, acceptance, and strong distribution network are important. The ability to work with local governments to overcome local protectionism is vital. All this takes time. An early-mover has the time advantage over the late comer. Volkswagen has established a nation-wide brand recognition and distribution system.

In general, the competitors' hesitating and waiting created an asymmetry in time for Volkswagen. Volkswagen takes advantage of the asymmetry because from its experience in investment in Brazil and Mexico, it realizes that early-mover can enjoy unique advantages, such as participating in market establishment and development; setting production pace in line with gradual demand increases. The early-mover position of Volkswagen has led a modern way for China's auto market [Wang 1995]. Volkswagen has already moved into fulfilling the second stage of its strategy, producing new models, enlarging production capacity, and broadening production line, while later comers, such as Honda have just started establishing itself in the China's auto market.

Evidently, there are risks and uncertainties associated with an early entry. It is imperative that the early-movers be prepared to deal with them effectively. There are many early-movers that did not survive. Recently, Peugeot decided to sell its joint venture in Guangzhou to Honda, thus giving up on its early-mover advantage in China.

While it is not the focus of this article, it is nonetheless worth listing the kinds of risks and uncertainties that an early-mover in China might encounter. First type of risks comes from uncertainties that an early-mover in China might encounter. First type of risks comes from the political uncertainty. The 1989 Tiananmen Square student movement was a case in point. Second type of risks is associated with the cyclical nature of Chinese economy. The Chinese economy had gone through growth, inflation, tightening up, stagnation, and growth at a cycle of around 4-6 years. Third type of risks is specific to certain industries and sectors that are subject to national industry policies. For instance, the Chinese government has designated in the 1990s several key industries as pillar industries. Sectors that do not fall into this category do not receive as favorable support as those pillar sectors do. Fourth type of risks incorporates various operational difficulties, which may be hard to cope with on a daily basis [see Vanhonacker and Pan 1997]. Evidently, early-movers have to cope with these risks and uncertainties effectively in order to reap the early-mover advantages.

CONCLUSION

Timing of market entry affects market share and profitability performance. The empirical results show that foreign firms that entered early are now more profitable than those entered late. While the previous empirical papers did not provide adequate conceptual explanations on this phenomenon, this paper proposes a model that incorporates seven factors that are unique to the order of entry in foreign direct investment context. They are: gate-keeper role of host country government; strategic choice of local partner; strategic choice of local market; better incentives and local government support; less stringent requirements; competing against weak local firms; and longer learning curve. Throughout the paper; the auto industry and Volkswagen's success in China is used as case examples to illustrate this conceptual model.

The importance of order entry impact on performance has at least two practical managerial implications. Firstly, if a foreign enterprise has entered China quite early, but has not been more profitable than its later competitors, it needs to identify why it has not been able to achieve the pioneer advantages it is supposed to. It has not taken full advantages of its potentials. Secondly, if a foreign enterprise has entered China quite early, but has not been more profitable than its later competitors, it needs to identify why it has not been able to achieve the pioneer advantages it is supposed to. It has not taken full advantages of its potentials. Secondly, if a foreign enterprise is a later-entrant, it has to find out what advantages it has in China. How long their privileges will last? What are the niche opportunities not captured by the early-movers? Are there any changes in the market environment that will erode early-movers' market positions? It should pay close attention to the host country policies.

What to expect as China continues its economic and social reform? Undoubtedly, China will push forward its reform. The government will rely more and more on market mechanisms instead of on administrative means. This will produce numerous positive impacts on how foreign firms operate in China. They will eventually be able to compete on a level-playing field with other domestic and foreign firms.

Ironically, this may turn out to be a bit "undesirable" for some foreign firm in some industry sects. When the local government is authoritarian and uses its power, things get done fast. In the past, the government wants foreign investment, and they deliver quickly what foreign firms want. Roads are expanded, power plants are built and so on, while the oppositions are pushed aside. As market forces and rule of law take the center stage, the power of local government will be reduced. It is possible that things will take no longer to get done, and various due processes will follow suit. It is our hope that policy makers in China will strive to maintain the "will do" attitude and create an even more attractive environment for foreign investors in China in the years to come.

REFERENCES

Bain, Joe S. 1954. Conditions of entry and the emergence of monopoly. *Monopoly and Competition and Their Regulation*, E.H. Chamberlin, ed. London: Macmillan & Co, Ltd. 215-241.

Beamish, Paul W. 1993. The characteristics of joint ventures in the People's Republic of China. *Journal of International Marketing*, 1(2): 29-48.

Bowman, Edward H. & Dileep Hurry. 1993. Strategy through the option lens: An integrated view of resource investments and the incremental-choice process. *Academy of Management Review*, 18(4): 760-782.

Carpenter, Gregory S. & Kent Nakamoto. 1989. Consumer preference formation and pioneering advantage. *Journal of Marketing Research*, 26: 285-98.

Chang, Sea Jin. 1995. International expansion strategy of Japanese firms: Capability building through sequential entry. *Academy of Management Journal*, 38(2): 383-407.

Child, John. 1994. *Management in China During the Age of Reform*. Cambridge, England: Cambridge University Press.

De Castro, Julio O. & James J. Chrisman. 1995. Order of market entry, competitive strategy, and financial performance. *Journal of Business Research*, 33: 165-177.

Lambkin, Mary. 1988. Order of entry and performance in new market. *Strategic Management Journal*, 9: 127-140.

Lieberman, Marvin B. & David B. Montgomery. 1988. First mover advantages. *Strategic Management Journal*, 9: 41-58.

Lillien, Gary L. & Eusang Yoon. 1990. The timing of new entry: An exploratory study of new industrial products. *Management Science*, 36(5): 568-585.

Luo, Yadong. 1998. Timing of investment and international expansion performance in China. *Journal of International Business Studies*, 29(2), 391-408.

Madhok, Anoop. 1997. Cost, value and foreign market entry mode: The transaction and the firm. *Strategic Management Journal*, 18:39-61.

Mitchell, Will. 1991. Dual clocks: Entry order influences on incumbent and newcomer market share and survival when specialized assets retain their value. *Strategic Management Journal*, 12: 85-100.

Ohmae, Kenichi. 1989. The global logic of strategic alliances. *Harvard Business Review*, March-April,

Osland, Gregory E. & S. Tamer Cavusgil. 1996. Performance issues in U. S.-China joint ventures. *California Management Review*, 38(2):106-130.

Pan, Yigang. 1997. The formation of Japanese and U.S. equity joint ventures in China. *Strategic Management Journal*, 18: 247-254.

Pan, Yigang & Peter S.K. Chi. 1998. The promises and challenges of direct foreign investments in China. *Business & the Contemporary World*, 10(1): 87-105.

Pan, Yigang & Peter S.K. Chi. 1999. Financial performance and survival of multinational corporations in China. *Strategic Management Journal*, 20(4): 359-374.

Pan, Yigang & Xiaolian Li. 1998. Do timing and modes of entry in China matter to market share position and profitability? in *Marketing Issues in Transitional Economies*. ed. Rajeeu Batra, Boston, MA: Kluwer Academic Publishers. 211-223.

Pan, Yigang, Shaomin Li, & David K. Tse. 1999. The impact of order and mode of market entry on profitability and market share. *Journal of International Business Studies*, 30(1): 81-104.

Robinson, William T., Claes Fomell, & Mary Sullivan. 1992. Are market pioneers intrinsically stronger than later entrants? *Strategic Management Journal*, 13: 609-624.

Tse, David K., Yigang Pan & Kevin Y. Au. 1997. How "Cs choose entry modes and form alliances: The China experience. *Journal of International Business Studies*, 28(4): 779-805.

Vanhonacker, Wilried R. 1997. Entering China: An unconventional approach. *Harvard Business Review*, March-April, 130-140.

Vanhonacker, Wilfried R. & Yigang Pan. 1997. Impact of national culture, business scope, and geographic location on joint venture operations in China. *Journal of International Marketing*, 5(3): 11-30.

Wang, Zhile. 1995. *Investment of Transnational Corporations*, Beijing: China Economics Press.

Xinhua News Agency. 1998. Volkswagen and Motorola Lead Top 500 Joint Venture in China, BBC Monitoring Asia Pacific-Economic.

Yan, Aiinin & Barbara Gray. 1994. Bargaining power, management control, and performance in United States China joint ventures: A comparative case study. *Academy of Management Journal*, 37(6): 1478-1517.

The Impact of Guanxi
on Export Performance:
A Study of New Zealand Firms
Exporting to China

Doren D. Chadee
Benjamin Y. Zhang

SUMMARY. Broadly defined as interpersonal relationship in Chinese society, guanxi embodies several intricate and unique Chinese cultural values. Although more and more western business people are becoming increasingly aware of the importance of guanxi in doing business in China, its potential impacts on the performance of business are still not well understood by western business people. This paper uses path analysis to assess the impacts of guanxi on export performance of a sample of New Zealand firms exporting to China. The results show that guanxi variables significantly facilitate trade partnering, business negotiating, and problem solving and generally contributes positively to the overall export performance of firms. *[Article copies available for a fee from The Haworth Document Delivery Service: 1-800-342-9678. E-mail address: <getinfo @haworthpressinc.com> Website: <http://www.HaworthPress.com>]*

KEYWORDS. Guanxi, China, export performance, New Zealand

Doren D. Chadee and Benjamin Y. Zhang are affiliated with the Department of International Business, The University of Auckland, Auckland, New Zealand.

Address correspondence to: Dr. Doren D. Chadee, Department of International Business, The University of Auckland, P.O. Box 92019, Auckland, New Zealand (E-mail: D.Chadee@Auckland.AC.NZ).

[Haworth co-indexing entry note]: "The Impact of Guanxi on Export Performance: A Study of New Zealand Firms Exporting to China." Chadee, Doren D., and Benjamin Y. Zhang. Co-published simultaneously in *Journal of Global Marketing* (International Business Press, an imprint of The Haworth Press, Inc.) Vol. 14, No. 1/2, 2000, pp. 129-149; and: *Greater China in the Global Market* (ed: Yigang Pan) International Business Press, an imprint of The Haworth Press, Inc., 2000, pp. 129-149. Single or multiple copies of this article are available for a fee from The Haworth Document Delivery Service [1-800-342-9678, 9:00 a.m. - 5:00 p.m. (EST). E-mail address: getinfo@haworthpressinc.com].

129

INTRODUCTION

The primary objective of this study is to assess how guanxi affects the performance of firms exporting to China. The motivation for this study comes from the fact that China's economy has experienced phenomenal growth over the past two decades (Luo, 1997; He & Li, 1996). Rapid economic growth together with the government's willingness to make China an integral part of the world economy has meant that vast business opportunities are available to western businesses particularly with foreign direct investment (FDI), import and export activities.

Recent growth in trade and investment in China has meant greater interactions between western business people and their Chinese counterparts in a country that was largely closed to foreigners only two decades ago. Despite phenomenal growth and abundant opportunities that the Chinese market offers, recent evidence suggests that doing business in China can be more difficult than is anticipated by foreign businessmen (Davies et al., 1995). Foreign companies frequently experience apprehension and discouragement while conducting business with their Chinese counterparts (Lindsay & Dempsey, 1983). Although the Chinese government has gradually removed many barriers encountered by overseas companies willing to do business in China, there are still many "hidden" barriers which affect foreign businesses and as a result, western companies have not been fully responsive to the available opportunities (Wood & Young, 1994).

One important intangible barrier in doing business in China is *guanxi*. Although western business people are generally aware of the importance of guanxi, many still do not fully understand the meaning of it and the subtle forms that it can take. According to the *Modern Chinese Dictionary* (1977), guanxi is defined as: (1) connections of certain nature between people and people or between people and things; (2) a state of mutual functions and mutual impacts among things; and (3) links or involvement. Hence, broadly translated, guanxi refers to personal and interpersonal relationships or connections among people and places high values on network, trust, commitment, favor, mutuality, reciprocity and long-term benefits (Luo, 1997; Shi, 1997; Yeung & Tung, 1996; Hwang, 1987). Within the business context, guanxi can manifest itself in several ways. These include: (a) the use of close friends and associates (network) as intermediaries in assisting with general business activities (Shi, 1997, Yeung and Tung, 1996); (b) socialization for the purpose of developing and nurturing business connections (Shi 1997); (c) developing a high degree of mutual trust between business partners (Shi, 1997; Wilson, 1995; Yeung and Tung, 1996) and; (d) using government officials to bypass or facilitate legal and administrative hurdles–a practice commonly known as the back door (Ambler, 1995; Brunner et al., 1989). Thus, the elements of guanxi suggest that as China becomes more and more integrated into the world economy through trade and investment, a sound understanding of guanxi by foreign business people is critical for successfully conducting business there.

Because of its operationalized features, guanxi's counterpart in the western business literature is relationship marketing (Alston, 1989; Ambler, 1995). Relationship marketing refers to the process of establishing, maintaining and enhancing inter-organizational relationships with customers and other business partners for transactions (Shi, 1997; Morgan & Hunt, 1994). We will not attempt to review the literature on relationship marketing because this has been conducted comprehensively elsewhere (e.g., see Wilson, 1995; Barnes, 1995; Ambler, 1995; Sheth & Parvatiyar, 1995; Gronroos, 1995; Mogan & Hunt, 1994; Anderson et al., 1994; Webster, 1992; Wilson & Moller, 1991; Anderson & Narus, 1990; O'Neal, 1989; Dwyer et al., 1987; Berry & Gresham, 1986; Jackson, 1985). Interestingly, the majority of studies on relationship marketing have focused on the domestic activities of firms with only few investigations of businesses across national boundaries in culturally-diverse settings. Similarly, only few attempts have been made to study the role of guanxi from the perspective of western business people doing business in China (Luo, 1997; Yeung & Tung, 1996; Chen, 1995; Ambler, 1995; Alston, 1989; Hwang, 1987). Despite the importance of guanxi, a review of the literature shows that to date no comprehensive attempt has been made to empirically assess the impact of guanxi on export performance. Thus, this study fills an important gap in the literature by developing and estimating an empirical model of the impacts of guanxi on the performance of New Zealand firms exporting to China.

LITERATURE REVIEW

Export Performance

Research on export performance abounds in the literature and has focused mostly on methodological and measurement issues related to the determinants of export performance. In recent years, the rapid internationalization of the world economy has led to renewed interests in export performance research (Bodur, 1994; Donthu & Kim, 1993). There is no universally accepted definition of export performance in the literature (Cavusgil & Zhou, 1994) because a firm's interpretation of export performance usually depends on its main reason for exporting. Nevertheless, export performance may be defined as the extent to which a firm's objective, both economic and strategic, with respect to exporting a product into a foreign market, are achieved through planning and execution of export marketing strategies (Cavusgil & Zhou, 1994).

A variety of measures have been used to evaluate export performance at the firm level (Bodur, 1994), including economic measures such as export sales, export growth, profit from exports, export as a percentage of total sales at the firm level (Cavusgil & Zhou, 1994; Evangelista, 1994). Other measures for export performance include propensity to export (Bilkey, 1985; Reid, 1986); export involvement (Diamantopoulos & Ingilis, 1988); overcoming barriers to export (Bauerschmidt et al., 1985); acceptance of product by export distributor (Angelmar & Pras, 1984); exporter internationalization (Piercy, 1981); attitude toward export (Brady & Bearden, 1979); export stage (Cavusgil, 1984); export profitability (Cavusgil & Zhou, 1994; Madsen, 1989; Dominguez & Sequeira, 1991); export productivity (Diamantopoulos & Schlegemilch, 1994), international commitment (Dalli, 1994) and, export intention (Yang et al., 1992). Subjective variables such as management's evaluations and perceptions of export activities have also been utilized in previous research (Aaby & Slater, 1989; Cavusgil, 1990) as well as satisfaction with export activities (Bonoma & Clark, 1988; Seifert & Ford, 1989; Evangelista, 1994). Although the subjective measures of export performance are increasingly taken into account, the most commonly used measurement of export performance is still expressed in objective terms (Brown & Yau, 1995; Cavusgil & Zhou, 1994).

A common approach used to investigate the determinants of export performance has involved modeling export performance as a function of both external and internal environments facing businesses (Evangelista, 1994). Internal factors include firm characteristics, firm competencies, export marketing strategy (Aaby & Slater, 1989; Cavusgil & Zhou, 1994; Evangelista, 1994), and management characteristics

(Madsen, 1989; Holzmuller & Kasper, 1991). By contrast, the external environment refers to those factors over which firms have no control and may include macro economic, political, cultural, legal, social, financial and physical elements in both home and host countries in which firms operate (Evangelista, 1994; Bodur, 1994). Although the external environmental forces are beyond management's control (Donthu & Kim, 1993), adequate understanding of these allow firms to formulate appropriate strategies in order to take advantage of emerging opportunities as well as avoiding adverse influences from affecting them (Sheth, 1992; Cavusgil & Zhou, 1994). Culture, in particular, is an important external factor facing businesses operating overseas (Hofstede, 1983). Previous research has shown that it may be significant in explaining the process of buying and selling behavior (Tornroos & Moller, 1993). However, only few research to date has investigated the influence of the unique characteristics of culture on export performance.

Guanxi and Performance

As pointed out earlier, one of the most striking features of doing business in China relates to the importance of personal relationships–guanxi (Luo, 1997). Although the Chinese society has experienced tremendous changes over the past few decades, traditional socio-cultural values, such as guanxi, have retained their influence on the social behavior of the Chinese (Chen, 1995). Within the business context, guanxi is of such great importance that it has been compared to a "second currency" which permeates the economic sphere, and constitutes a key and "secret" to corporate success in China (Kao, 1993). Transnational investors can gain an edge over their competitors in the Chinese market by building and maintaining their own guanxi network because guanxi constitutes an effective and efficient marketing tool. Guanxi-related variables, such as sales force, marketing and credit-granting have been found to be significantly and positively related to firm's performance (Luo, 1997; Shi, 1997). Thus, people who understand the subtle meanings of guanxi, such as Chinese from Hong Kong, Taiwan and Singapore, are generally more successful in China (Lou, 1997).

Guanxi has also been ranked as the single most important key success factor in a study of 19 MNC from five different western countries operating in China (Yeung & Tung, 1996). Guanxi has been found to be most instrumental in the initial stages of entering the Chinese market (Shi, 1997) by facilitating entry into a market where legislation can be ambiguous. Guanxi can greatly facilitate business negotiations (Leung & Wong, 1993; Leung, Wong & Wong, 1996; Leung & Yeung, 1995) and help firms in their marketing activities (McGuinness et al., 1991; Shi, 1997). Similarly, the results of a large scale survey by Davies et al. (1995) confirm that personal connections with local Chinese is a critical success factor in their business. Generally, guanxi is most useful in the execution of routine and frequent transactions (payment and transport), followed by access to information and administrative approvals (Shi, 1997). In summary, guanxi network forms part of a firm's core competency and competitive advantage which can enhance its overall performance (Luo, 1997). The literature review suggests that to date research has provided valuable conceptual and managerial insights into guanxi's influence on business performance of foreign companies in China but only limited attempts have been made to empirically assess the impact of guanxi on firm's performance from the perspective of the western business partner. This is the subject of the next section.

CONCEPTUAL MODEL AND HYPOTHESES

The main objective of this paper is to gauge the influence of guanxi on the export performance of firms exporting to China. Following the literature, a conceptual framework showing the linkages between Guanxi and export performance is developed. More specifically, the present study focuses on how guanxi variables influence a firm's export performance through its selling activities (see Figure 1).

For the purposes of this study, guanxi is represented by the following four variables describing common business practices: (1) *Intermediary* refers to the use of a go-between, such as a Chinese business agent, to act as a business facilitator (Shi, 1997; Yeung & Tung, 1996; Keijzer, 1992); (2) *Social investment* refers to the financial cost and time spent by management in socializing with clients in order to develop and tailor business ties (Shi, 1997; Leung, Wong & Wong, 1996; Davies et al., 1995; Yang, 1994); (3) *Back door* refers to the use of Chinese government officials to assist with doing business in China (Ambler, 1995; Brunner et al., 1989) and; (4) *Mutual trust* refers to the degree of mutual trustworthiness between the seller and the buyer in a

FIGURE 1. Conceptual GX-EP Framework

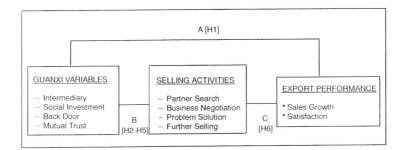

business deal (Shi, 1997; Wilson, 1995; Yeung & Tung, 1996; Morgan & Hunt, 1994).

The process of selling to the Chinese client is treated as the mediating variable and consists of four business activities: (1) *partner search* involves locating clients in China; (2) *business negotiation* refers to the negotiation process involved in signing contracts and filling orders; (3) *problem solution* refers to the ability to resolve minor disputes between the trade partners and; (4) *further selling* refers to the ability of winning new contracts and sales. Shi (1997) has empirically examined guanxi's influence on the organizational buying process of the information technology and consulting industry. Davies et al. (1995) have identified the benefits that accrue to the establishment of guanxi on the procurement of resources, information acquisition, bureaucracy and transaction smoothing. Brunner et al. (1989) have conceptually described the role of guanxi in the negotiation process with Chinese business counterparts. Leung, Wong and Wong (1996) and Leung and Yeung (1995) have empirically assessed the impact of guanxi on negotiation, source of information and resources, and transaction arrangement. In the present study, partner search, business negotiation, problem solution and further selling constitute the main elements involved in the selling activities of exporters.

The dependent variable, export performance, consists of two subjective measures that have been widely used previously, namely exporter's expectation with their export sales growth and their overall satisfaction with export activities in China (Evangelista, 1994; Seifert & Ford, 1989; Bonoma & Clark, 1988).

Hypotheses

Previous studies suggest that Guanxi is an important factor in conducting business in China although no concensus exist (Leung & Wong, 1993, 1995; Lee & Lo, 1988; Stewart & Keown, 1989; Cambell & Adlington, 1988). It is hypothesized in the present framework that export performance is positively influenced by a foreign firm's guanxi relations with the Chinese counterparts. More specifically, export performance is expected to be positively influenced by each of the four guanxi variables namely, intermediary; social investment; back door; and mutual trust. Hence the following hypothesis:

H1: *Export performance is positively influenced by (a) intermediary; (b) social investment; (c) back door; and (d) mutual trust.*

Yeung and Tung (1996) argue that guanxi is most effective at the initial stage of setting up a business in China. Shi (1997) confirms this by pointing out that good guanxi assists firms to win business, particularly during the initial stage. Yang (1994) has described guanxi building as the transformation process whereby two discrete individuals construct a basis of familiarity to enable the subsequent development of relations. An effective way of being included and accepted in a particular social network is to use an intermediary or go-between who can make the appropriate introduction and provide support for the conduct and sincerity of either party (Yeung & Tung, 1996). Thus, it is postulated that the use of intermediary positively assist foreign firms in their search for appropriate trade partners.

H2: *Intermediary positively influence partner search.*

Social activities such as gift giving, organising banquets, providing overseas business trips for Chinese partners and entertaining with family members of Chinese clients are common means of building and maintaining close relations with Chinese partners (Shi, 1997; Yeung & Tung, 1996; Leung et al., 1996; Yang, 1994). Entertaining family members and non-business activities create social and emotional bonds between the business agents and can be beneficial to trade partner selection and negotiation processes. They can also assist with problem solving. Thus, social investment by foreign firms is expected to enhance their partner search, business negotiation and problem solving.

H3: *Social investment positively influence (a) partner search; (b) business negotiation; and (c) problem solution.*

Guanxi can be helpful in working through the complex bureaucratic red tape of China in securing information, approval of contracts, administrative approvals, competitive prices, policy interpretation, material acquisition and in general, to get things done more smoothly (Davies et al., 1995; Brunner et al., 1989). Additionally, good rapport with Chinese authorities are seen as a strength with importance and dignity, which in turn favorably influence the process of searching for a partner and resolving problems. Hence the following hypothesis:

H4: *Back door is positively influence (a) partner search; and (b) problem solution.*

Even though short-term favors and immediate rewards can initiate the cycle of guanxi development, they may not be the basis for long-term guanxi (Yeung & Tung, 1996). To maintain a permanent and irreplaceable guanxi relation, creation of trust between the parties with sincerity is essential for long-term mutual benefits. Trust is a critical variable in relationship research (Wilson, 1995) and trust leads directly to cooperative behaviors that are conducive to relationship marketing success (Morgan & Hunt, 1994). Hence, mutual trust between the seller and buyer is expected to facilitate business activities.

H5: *Mutual trust positively influence (a) partner search; (b) business negotiation; (c) problem solution; and (d) further selling.*

In the current model, the selling activities refer to the degree of ease that exporters experience with respect to the four selling activities when doing business in China. Thus, the greater the degree of ease in executing each of the selling activities, the better the overall performance of the firm is expected to be.

H6: *(a) Partner search; (b) business negotiation; (c) problem solution; and (d) further selling positively influence export performance.*

MODEL ESTIMATION AND RESULTS

Data

The data for analytical purposes come from a mail survey of New Zealand firms exporting to China carried out in 1998. A comprehensive questionnaire was developed and pilot tested before being mailed to a population of 201 firms actively exporting to China provided by the New Zealand Trade and Development Board, a government export promotion agency. The questionnaire was addressed to the export marketing manager or the next best person with export and overseas responsibilities. Following the initial mail out and a subsequent follow-up, a total of 68 questionnaires were returned within the specific time frame. Of these 62 questionnaires were retained for the purpose of analysis giving an effective response rate of 33.8 percent. Six questionnaires which were not filled out completely were deemed inappropriate for analysis.

An analysis of the sample characteristics indicate that the sample did not include any Chinese owned firm. Approximately 82.3 percent are New Zealand owned companies with the rest being subsidiaries of overseas companies. Most firms in the sample are experienced exporters with 63 percent exporting to China for 3 to 10 years and 18 percent for more than 10 years. In terms of type of products exported to China, 43.5 percent were primary goods exporters (such as wood, wool, meat, fish, dairy and coal), 34 percent are exporters of industrial goods and 10 percent export processed food and 8 percent export other consumer goods exporters. Only 5 percent were classified as services exporters.

Measurement

In the questionnaire, respondents were asked to rate the guanxi, mediating and performance variables on a 5 point Likert-type bipolar scale anchored at both ends. Table 1 summarizes the guanxi, mediating and dependent variables together with their measurement scales, reliability estimates, item-to-total correlation and scale anchors. In all cases, an equally weighted mean across the different items was used. The guanxi variable intermediary, for example was operationalized by three items: frequency of using friends, Chinese business agents or local agents to facilitate exports to China, all measured on a five point

TABLE 1. Operational Measures of Independent and Dependent Variables

Variable Definition/ Scale	Item-to-Total Correlation
X1: Intermediary *(α = 0.80), mean of three items anchored by never = 1 and always = 5.*	
1. use close friends as go between	0.80
2. use Chinese business agents as go between	0.77
3. use NZ business agent to assist with China business	0.70
X2: Socialization *(α = 0.74), mean of two items anchored by not important = 1 and very important = 5.*	
1. give gifts to Chinese clients/government officials	0.75
2. entertain clients/govt. officials at dinner banquets	0.73
X4: Back Door *(α = 0.78), mean of two items anchored by never = 1 and always = 5.*	
1. use contacts with government officials in China	0.62
2. use close relationship with contact in local government	0.78
X5: Mutual Trust *(α = 0.81), mean of two items anchored by not important = 1 and very important = 5.*	
1. develop mutual trust with Chinese partner	0.73
2. maintain long term mutual trust with Chinese partner	0.77
Y1: Partner search *(α = 0.72), mean of two items anchored by never = 1 and always = 5.*	
1. identifying suitable business partners is easy	0.82
2. collecting industry information for partner selection is easy	0.63
Y2: Business negotiation *(α = 0.85), mean of two items anchored by not at all = 1 and all the time = 5.*	
1. it is easy to negotiate with existing clients	0.71
2. it is easy to negotiate with new clients	0.64
Y3: Problem solving *(α = 0.80), mean of two items anchored by never = 1 and always = 5.*	
1. payments are collected promptly following sales	0.69
2. minor disputes with clients are easily resolved	0.51
Y4: Further selling *(α = 0.71), mean of two items anchored by not easy = 1 and always easy = 5.*	
1. secure additional orders from existing clients	0.76
2. secure new orders from new clients	0.56
Y5: Export performance *(α = 0.82), mean of two items anchored by below expectation = 1 and above expectation = 5.*	
1. satisfaction with doing business in China	0.80
2. growth in export revenue in China	0.78

scale where never = 1 to all the time = 5. The second guanxi variable, social investment was operationalized by two observable variables: (a) socialization, a two item scale explaining the importance of giving gifts to clients and government officials and the use of dinner banquets to entertain clients measured as not important = 1 to very important = 5; (b) business trip is a single item measure of the importance of sponsoring overseas trips for the Chinese client measured on a similar scale as above. Two items were used to operationalize back door. The first is the frequency of using government officers and the second is the frequency of using friends and relatives with contacts in government for the purposes of doing business; both measured on a five point scale where never = 1 and always = 5. The last guanxi variable, mutual trust, consists of two items namely the importance of creating trust with clients and the importance of maintaining trust over the long term, both measured on as not important = 1 to very important = 5.

A list of ten selling activities (e.g., partner search, contract negotiation, collecting payments) was first pilot tested and then subjected to a principal components analysis with promax rotation. Eight items reflective of four factors were retained for the purposes of the present study. The four selling factors are partner search, business negotiation, problem solving and further selling. Each factor was computed by taking the mean of the relevant items. Respondents were asked to state the degree of ease with which each of the selling activities are executed while exporting to China (see Table 1). The dependent variable, export performance, was measured using two items namely exporter's satisfaction with sales growth and their overall satisfaction with doing business in China, both measured from below expectation = 1 to above expectation = 5 (see Table 1 for correlation matrix and summary statistics).

Estimation and Results

Path analysis, with LISREL program (Mueller, 1996; Joreskog & Sorbom, 1989) is used to test hypotheses H1 to H6. The path diagram (Figure 2) shows the *a-priori* hypothesized structure of the relationships among the explanatory and dependent variables. LISREL uses the correlation matrix (Table 2) as the main input to solve for the parameter estimates of the direct and indirect effects. Validity and reliability statistics of the model, suggest a reasonable fit judging by the χ^2 = 16.73 (df = 16 and ρ = .40); GFI = 0.96; AGFI = 0.82. The root mean square residual is 0.13. Additionally, none of the modification indices exceed 7 and all of the standardized residuals fall within the range of ± 2.5. The sample size upon which the model was estimated is 62, which is somewhat relatively small. However, this concern is mitigated by the Tucker-Lewis Index (TLI = 0.99). The TLI is recommended for judging the overall fit of smaller sample-sized models, and values above 0.90 are deemed acceptable and are often considered to be indicative of good overall fit (Marsh, Balla & McDonald, 1988; Mueller, 1996).

FIGURE 2. LISREL Model

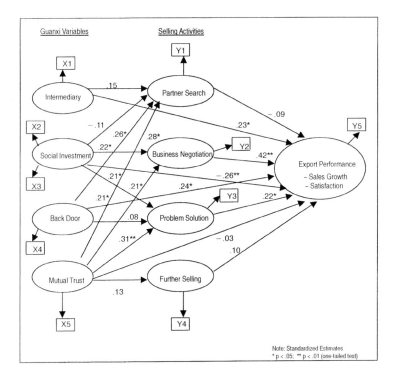

For each structural path, the standardized parameter estimate, t-value, significance level, and results concerning hypothesis testing are summarized in Table 3. As expected, intermediary positively influence export performance ($\gamma 5,1$), supporting H1a. Contrary to our expectation, social investment is inversely related to export performance ($\gamma 5,2 = -0.26$, $\rho = 0.01$), contradicting H1b. Back door positively influence export performance ($\gamma 5,3 = 0.24$, $\rho = 0.01$), supporting H1c. However, H1d is not supported suggesting that mutual trust does not directly influence export performance.

According to H2 and H3a, intermediary and social investment are expected to positively influence partner search; ($\gamma 1,1$) and ($\gamma 1,2$) respectively. However, these hypotheses are not supported by the data thereby rejecting·both H2 and H3a. But social investment does influence negotiation ($\gamma 2,2$) and problem solution ($\gamma 3,2$), implying that

TABLE 2. Correlation Matrix and Summary Statistics

Variable	X1	X2	X3	X4	X5	Y1	Y2	Y3	Y4	Mean	SD
X1: Business Agent										3.25	1.51
X2: Gift Exchange	.30*									2.65	1.20
X3: Business Visit	.33*	.42**								2.78	1.31
X4: Personal Contact	.49**	.50**	.43**							2.40	1.40
X5: Trustworthiness	.31*	.09	.13	.33*						4.03	1.31
Y1: Partner Search	.33**	.09	.19	.37**	.40**					3.20	1.18
Y2: Negotiation	.32*	.29*	.32*	.37**	.45**	.63**				3.12	1.22
Y3: Solution	.32*	.35**	.32*	.42**	.50**	.44**	.50**			2.73	1.25
Y4: Further Selling	.26*	.37**	.42**	.42**	.44**	.37**	.60**	.56**		3.33	1.08
Y5: Performance	.47**	.16	.32	.46**	.43**	.43**	.58**	.52**	.52**	2.78	1.32

* p < .05; ** p < .01 (two-tailed test)

H3b and H3c are supported. Of the two hypotheses concerning the influence of back door on selling activity, only H4a is supported while H4b is rejected. Concerning the influence of mutual trust on selling activity, it seems that mutual trust has a significant influence on partner search ($\gamma 1,4$), negotiation ($\gamma 2,4$) and problem solving ($\gamma 3,4$) but only a small and statistically insignificant influence on further selling ($\gamma 4,4$). Thus, H5a, H5b, and H5c are supported but H5d is rejected. The results also support H6b and H6c, suggesting that export performance is influenced significantly by business negotiation ($\beta 5,2$) and problem solution ($\beta 5,3$). However, contrary to a-priori expectation, partner search ($\beta 5,1$) and further selling ($\beta 5,4$), do not influence performance thereby rejecting H6a and H6d.

DISCUSSION AND CONCLUSION

Guanxi has traditionally been an integral part of doing business in China (Luo, 1997; Shi, 1997; Chen, 1996; Yeung & Tung, 1996; Ambler, 1995; Davies et al., 1995; Pye, 1992; Alston, 1989; Brunner et al.; 1989; Hwang, 1987). This paper investigates how New Zealand exporters perceive guanxi to affect the performance of their export activities to China. Following a literature review, four guanxi variables are identified and modeled through path analysis using LISREL. The data for the study comes from a survey which sought the perception of

TABLE 3. LISREL Model Results

	Standardized Estimate	t-value	Conclusion	
A. <u>Structural Model</u>				
Intermediary –> Export Performance (γ5,1)	.23	2.48*	H1a:	supported
Social Investment –> Export Performance (γ5,2)	–.26	–2.69**	H1b:	contradicted
Back Door –> Export Performance (γ5,3)	.24	2.29*	H1c:	supported
Mutual Trust –> Export Performance (γ5,4)	–.03	–.36	H1d:	not supported
Intermediary –> Partner Search (γ1,1)	.15	1.17	H2:	not supported
Social Investment –> Partner Search (γ1,2)	–.11	–.82	H3a:	not supported
Social Investment –> Business Negotiation (γ2,2)	.22	2.05*	H3b:	supported
Social Investment –> Problem Solution (γ3,2)	.21	1.81*	H3c:	supported
Back Door –> Partner Search (γ1,3)	.26	1.79*	H4a:	supported
Back Door –> Problem Solution (γ3,3)	.08	.64	H4b:	not supported
Mutual Trust –> Partner Search (γ1,4)	.28	2.31*	H5a:	supported
Mutual Trust –> Business Negotiation (γ2,4)	.21	2.08*	H5b:	supported
Mutual Trust –> Problem Solution (γ3,4)	.31	2.76**	H5c:	supported
Mutual Trust –> Further Selling (γ4,4)	.13	1.14	H5d:	not supported
Partner Search –> Export Performance (β5,1)	–.09	–.87	H6a:	not supported
Business Negotiation –> Export Performance (β5,2)	.42	3.47**	H6b:	supported
Problem Solution –> Export Performance (β5,3)	.22	2.04*	H6c:	supported
Further Selling –> Export Performance (β5,4)	.10	.91	H6d:	not supported
B. <u>Measurement Model</u>				
Business Agent (λx1,1)	1.51	–		
Gift Exchange (λx2,2)	1.20	–		
Business Visit (λx3,2)	.55	3.56**		
Personal Contact (λx4,3)	1.40	–		
Trustworthiness (λx5,4)	1.31	–		
Partner Search (λy1,1)	1.18	–		
Business Negotiation (λy2,2)	1.22	–		
Problem Solution (λy3,3)	1.25	–		
Further Selling (λy4,4)	1.08	–		
Sales Growth (λy5,5)	1.32	–		
Satisfaction (λy6,5)	1.10	7.57**		

C. <u>PSI Matrix</u>

	Standardized Estimates				
	(1)	(2)	(3)	(4)	(5)
1. Partner Search	.75**				
2. Business Negotiation	–	.51**			
3. Problem Solution	–	–	.58**		
4. Further Selling	–	–	–	.52**	
5. Export Performance	–	–	–	–	.47**

* p < .05; ** p < .01 (one-tail tests)

New Zealand exporters on the importance of guanxi in their business dealings with China. Despite the exploratory nature of the study, several interesting results emerge.

Previous studies have shown that non-Chinese investors frequently use intermediaries to locate suitable venture partners and to establish connections in China (Keizer, 1992; Yeung & Tung, 1996). The findings of this study suggest that intermediary has no influence on locating and choosing suitable business partners for New Zealand exporters. One possible explanation for this finding is that New Zealand exporters are more likely to use the domestic trade promotion body (TRADENZ) which has offices worldwide for facilitating their export activities. This is especially the case when exporters are entering markets that they are not familiar with. Thus, NZ exporters do not make use of intermediaries as defined in this study.

Another interesting finding is that contrary to our expectation, social investment negatively influence export performance. This phenomenon could be explained by the fact that many exporters resent exchanging gifts with their business partners as this could be viewed as a form of bribery. In fact, several firms in our sample had written corporate policies which strictly forbid any form of gift reward. Thus, spending money on such things as gifts or social activities with business partners could be viewed as being wasteful and do not necessarily directly contribute to the firm's performance. However, indirectly, social investment does influence export performance through business negotiation and problem solution. The findings that gift exchange and business visit mitigate the negotiation process and problem solving confirm those of previous studies (i.e., Shi, 1997; Yeung & Tung, 1996; Yang, 1994; Leung et al., 1996; Davies et al., 1995).

Personal contacts with government officials in China usually facilitate business dealings because such contacts may help overcome numerous bureaucratic difficulties when doing business in China. For example, government contacts may help solve problems favorably and smoothly, while avoiding bribes and power abuse. The results confirms the positive and significant direct influence of back door on export performance. Additionally, the results show that back door mitigates partner search, which could suggest that firms which have close relation with local government are regarded as being advantageous and therefore has a positive influence on partnering.

The presence of relationship commitment and trust is central and

critical to successful relationship marketing and trust produces outcomes that promote efficiency, effectiveness and productivity (Wilson,
1995; Morgan & Hunt, 1994). The results illustrate a significant influence of mutual trust on export performance, mediated by three selling
activities. Trust positively influence export performance of exporters
by facilitating partner search, negotiation and problem solving. The
development and fostering of mutual trust is of paramount importance
in doing business successfully in China.

In sum, guanxi is an integral element of conducting business in
China. The overall conclusion is that exploring and maintaining an
effective guanxi relation with both Chinese business partner and local
governmental officials helps facilitate business activities and enhance
business performance. However, as with any research, the findings of
this study should be interpreted with caution and due consideration be
given to its limitations. First, care should be taken not to generalize the
present findings because this study investigates the experience of only
New Zealand (NZ) firms exporting to China. Given the fact that the
business environments faced by NZ firms may be different from those
faced by firms from elsewhere, the results are specific to NZ firms
only. The second limitation of this study is its exploratory nature
because of the small sample size upon which the analysis is based. The
sample size in the present case was limited by the small size of the
New Zealand economy and consequently, the small number of firms
exporting to China. The convention for path analysis is to use sample
sizes that are 5 to 20 times the number of parameters in a particular
model. Thus, we recommend that further testing be done using a larger
data base. Third, given the small size of our sample, we were constrained to keep our model relatively simple by including only four
guanxi variables and two export performance measures. We recommend that future investigations adopt a more comprehensive set of
guanxi variables and also use a broader measure of export performance.

REFERENCES

Aaby, N. & Slater, S.F. (1989). Management Influences on Export Performance: A
Review of the Empirical Literature 1978-1988. *International Marketing Review.*
Vol. 6(4): 7-26.

Alston, J.P. (1989). Wa, Guanxi, and Inhwa: Managerial Principles in Japan, China
and Korea. *Business Horizons.* 32 (March): 26-31.

Ambler, Tim (1995). Reflections in China: Re-orienting Images of Marketing. *Marketing Management*. 4(1) (Summer): 22-30.

Anderson, James & Narus, J. A. (1990). A Model of Distributor Firm and Manufacturer Firm Working Partnerships. *Journal of Marketing*. Vol. 54 (January): 42-58.

Anderson, J.C.; Hakansson, Hakan & Johanson, Jan. (1994). Dyadic Business Relationships within a Business Network Context. *Journal of Marketing*. 58 (October): 1-15.

Angelmar, R. & Pras, B. (1984). Product Acceptance by Middlemen in Export Channels. *Journal of Business Research*. Vol.12: 227-240.

Barnes, J.C. (1995). The Quality and Depth of Customer Relationships. In M. Bergadaa (ed.) *Proceedings of the 24th EMAC Conference*. ESSEC. Cergy-Pontoise.

Bauerschmidt, A.; Sullivan, D. and Gillespie, K. (1985). Common Factors Underlying Barriers to Export: Studies in the U.S. Paper Industry. *Journal of International Business Studies*. Vol. 16: 111-123.

Berry, L.L. & Gresham, L.G. (1986). Relationship Retailing: Transforming Customers Into Clients. *Business Horizon*. Vol.29: 43-47.

Bilkey, W.J. (1985). Development of Export Marketing Guidelines. *International Marketing Review*. Vol. 8 (Autumn): 31-40.

Bodur, M. (1994). Foreign Market Indicators, Structural Resources and Marketing Strategies as Determinants of Export Performance. *Advances in International Marketing*. Vol. 6: 183-205.

Bonoma, T. & Clark, B.H. (1988). Marketing Performance Assessment. Boston: Harvard Business School Press.

Brady, D.L. & Bearden, W.O. (1979). The Effects of Managerial Attitudes on Alternative Exporting Methods. *Journal of International Business Studies*. Vol. 10(3): 79-84.

Brown, L.R. & Yau, O.H. (1995). Development of án Attitudinal Model of Export Performance. In *World Marketing Congress*. Australia (Melbourne).

Brunner, J.A.; Chen, J.; Sun, C. and Zhou, N. (1989). The Role of Guanxi in Negotiations in Pacific Basin. *Journal of Global Marketing*. 3(2): 7-23.

Cavusgil, S.T. (1984). Differences among Exporting Firms Based on their Degree of Internationalization. *Journal of Business Research*. Vol. 18 (February): 114-119.

_____ & Zhou, S. (1994). Marketing Strategy-Performance Relationship: An Investigation of the Empirical Link in Export Market Ventures. *Journal of Marketing*. Vol. 58 (January): 1-21.

China Statistical Yearbook. Various issues. China Statistical Publishing House. Beijing, China.

China Yearbook. Various issues. Published by China Yearbook Ltd. Beijing, China.

Chen, M. (1995). Asian Management Systems: Chinese, Japanese and Korean Style Of Business. Routledge, London.

Davies, H.; Leung, K.P.; Luk, T.K. and Wong, Y.H. (1995). The Benefits of Guanxi: The Value of Relationships in Developing the Chinese Market. *Industrial Marketing Management*. 24: 207-214.

Diamantopoulos, A. & Inglis, K. (1988). Identifying Differences between High- and Low-Involvement Exporters. *International Marketing Rev*. Vol. (Sum): 52-59.

Dominguez, L.V. & Sequeria, C.G. (1991). Strategic Options for LDC Exporters to Developed Countries. *International Marketing Review.* 8(5): 27-43.

Donthu, N. & Kim, S.H. (1993). Implications of Firm Controllable Factors on Export Growth. *Journal of Global Marketing.* Vol. 7(1): 47-63.

Dwyer, Robert; Schurr, Paul & Oh, Sejo (1987). Developing Buyer-Seller Relationships. *Journal of Marketing.* Vol. 5 (April): 11-27.

Evangelista, M.K. (1994). Export Performance and Its Determinants: Some Empirical Evidence from Australian Manufacturing Firms. *Advances in International Marketing.* Vol. 6: 207-229.

Gronroos, C. (1995). The Re-Birth of Marketing Management: Six Propositions about Relationship Marketing. Working paper 307, *Swedish School of Economic and Business Administration,* Helsinki.

He, Xiaohong & Li, Jie (1996). A Taxation Dilemma of Foreign Direct Investment in An Evolving Market Economy. *Multinational Business Review.* 4(2): 36-49.

Hofstede, G. (1983). The Cultural Relativity of Organizational Practices and Theories. *Journal of International Business Studies.* Vol.(Fall): 75-89.

Holzmuller, H.H. & Kasper, H. (1991). On a Theory of Export Performance: Personal And Organizational Determinants of Export Trade Activities Observed in Small Medium-sized Firms. *Management International Review.* Vol. 31: 45-70.

Hwang, K.K. (1987). Face and Favor; The Chinese Power Game. *American Journal Of Sociology.* 92 (4): 944-974.

Jackson, B.B. (1985). Winning and Keeping Industrial Customers. Lexington Books. Lexington, Mass.

Keizer, D. (1992). China: Business Strategies for the 1990s. Pacific View Press.

Lee, Kam-Hon & Lo, Wing-Chun. (1988). American Business People's Perceptions Of Marketing and Negotiating in the People's Republic of China. *International Marketing Review.* (Summer): 41-51.

Lee, C. & Yang, Y.S. (1991). Impact of Export Market Expansion Strategy on Export Performance. *International Marketing Review.* 7(4): 41-51.

Leung, T. & Wong, Y. H. and Wong, Syson (1996). A Study of Hong Kong Businessmen's perceptions of the role of guanxi in the People's Republic of China. *Journal of Business Ethics.* 15(7): 749-758.

Lewis, I.M. (1976). Social Anthropology in Perspective. Harmondsworth: Penguin.

Lindsay, Cindy & Dempsey, Bobby (1983). Ten Painfully Learned Lessons about Working in China: The Insights of Two American Behavioural Scientists. *Journal of Applied Behavioural Science.* 19: 265-276.

Luo, Yadong. (1997). Guanxi and Performance of Foreign-invested Enterprises in China: An Empirical Inquiry. *Management International Review.* 37(1): 51-70.

Madsen, T.K. (1989). Successful Export Marketing Management: Some Empirical Evidence. *International Marketing Review.* Vol. 6(4): 41-57.

Marsh, H.W., Balla, J.R. & McDonald, R.P. (1988). Goodness-of-fit Indexes in Confirmatory Factor Analysis: The Effect of Sample Size. *Psychological Bulletin.* 103: 391-410.

McGuiness, N.; Cambell, N. and Leontiades, J. (1991). Selling Machinery to China:

Chinese Perceptions of Strategies and Relationships. *Journal of International Business Studies.* 22: 187-207.

Modern Chinese Dictionary (1977). Dictionary Editing Board of Chinese Language Research Institute in China Science Academy. China Commercial Publishing House, Hong Kong.

Morgan, M. & Hunt, D. (1994). The Commitment-Trust Theory of Relationship Marketing. *Journal of Marketing.* Vol. 58 (July): 20-38.

Mueller, R.O. (1996). Basic Principles of Structural Equation Modeling. Springer-Verlag New York, Inc.

O'Neal, C. (1989). JIT Procurement and Relationship Marketing. *Industrial Marketing Management.* Vol. 18: 55-63.

Piercy, N. (1981). Company Internationalization: Active and Reactive Exporting. *Journal of Marketing.* Vol. 15 (3): 26-40.

Pye, L. (1982). Chinese Commercial Negotiation Styles. Cambridge: Oelgeschlager, Gunn, and Hain, Inc.

Reid, S. (1986). Migration, Cultural Distance and International Market Expansion. In *Research in International Marketing.* P.W.A.P. Turnbull, S.T. (ed.). Croom Helm, London: 22-137.

Samiee, S. & Roth, K. (1992). The Influence of Global Marketing Standardization on Performance. *Journal of Marketing.* 56 (8): 1-17.

Seifert, B. & Ford, J. (1989). Are Export Firms Modifying their Product, Pricing and Promotion Policies? *International Marketing Review.* 6(6): 53-68.

Sheth, Jagdish N. (1992). Emerging Marketing Strategies in a Changing Macroeconomic Environment: A Commentary. *International Marketing Review.* Vol. 9(1): 57-63.

_____ & Parvatiyar, Atul (1995). The Evolution of Relationship Marketing. *International Business Review.* 4(4): 397-418.

Shi, X. (1997). Guanxi as Relationship Marketing in China: Cases and Implications From IT Consulting Services. *Paper prepared for the Academy of International Business Southeast Asia Pacific Area Conference.*

Stewart, S. & Keown, C. (1989). Talking with the Dragon: Negotiating in the People's Republic of China. *Columbia Journal of World of Business.* Fall: 68-72.

Summers, Lawrence (1992). The Rise of China. *International Economic Insights.* May/June (17).

Tornroos, J.A. & Moller, K.E. (1993). The Cultural Factor and the Formation of International Business Relationships in Industrial Markets. *Advances in International Marketing.* Vol. 5: 107-121.

Webster, F. (1992). The Changing Role of Marketing in the Corporation. *Journal of Marketing.* Vol. 56: 1-17.

Wilson, David (1995). An Integrated Model of Buyer-Seller Relationships. *Journal of the Academy of Marketing Science.* Vol. 23. No. 4: 335-345.

Wilson, David & Moller, K. (1991). Buyer-Seller Relationships: Alternative Conceptualization. In *New Perspectives on International Marketing.* Ed. S. J. Paliwoda. New York: Routledge, 87-107.

Wood, Andrew & Young, Ian (1994). Overcoming Hurdles to Enter China. *Chemical Week (China Supplement)*. August-September: 43-44.

Yang, M.H. (1994). Gifts, Favours and Banquets. Cornell University Press.

Yang, Y.S.; Leone, R.P. and Alden, D.L. (1992). A Market Expansion Ability Approach to Identify Potential Exporters. *Journal of Marketing*. Vol. 56: 84-96.

Yeung, I. Y. M. & Tung, R.L. (1996). Achieving business success in Confucian Societies: The Importance of Guanxi. *Organizational Dynamics*. 25(2): 54-65.

The Intertextual Construction
of Emerging Consumer Culture
in China as Observed in the Movie *Ermo:*
A Postmodern, Sinicization Reading

Stephen J. Gould
Nancy Y. C. Wong

SUMMARY. The rapid development of consumer culture in China is chronicled and caricatured in particularly revealing ways in the movie *Ermo.* It concerns the story of a rural Chinese woman, Ermo, who undergoes a metamorphosis in seeking to make enough money to buy a television set. Since popular culture texts, such as movies, often serve to mirror a culture back to itself, we conducted a discourse analysis of this film. We found that cultural intertextuality, that is the hybridizing construction of global and local meanings, was central. This intertextuality had two emergent themes: (1) longstanding versus postmodern narratives and (2) a Sinicization or Chinese indigenization of meanings. Managerial and research implications are drawn which direct marketing efforts toward the needs of Chinese consumers embodied in their indigenized and particular local expression of new postmodern lifestyles. *[Article copies available for a fee from The Haworth Document Delivery Service:*

Stephen J. Gould is Professor of Marketing, Baruch College, The City University of New York, 17 Lexington Avenue, New York City, NY 10010. Nancy Y. C. Wong is Assistant Professor of Marketing, University of Hawai'i at Manoa, College of Business Administration, 2404 Maile Way, C303, Honolulu, HI 96822-2262.

Address correspondence to: Stephen J. Gould, 99 Harris Road, Princeton Junction, NJ 08550 (E-mail: STARAMAN@AOL.COM).

[Haworth co-indexing entry note]: "The Intertextual Construction of Emerging Consumer Culture in China as Observed in the Movie *Ermo*: A Postmodern, Sinicization Reading." Gould, Stephen J., and Nancy Y. C. Wong. Co-published simultaneously in *Journal of Global Marketing* (International Business Press, an imprint of The Haworth Press, Inc.) Vol. 14, No. 1/2, 2000, pp. 151-167; and: *Greater China in the Global Market* (ed: Yigang Pan) International Business Press, an imprint of The Haworth Press, Inc., 2000, pp. 151-167. Single or multiple copies of this article are available for a fee from The Haworth Document Delivery Service [1-800-342-9678, 9:00 a.m. - 5:00 p.m. (EST). E-mail address: getinfo@haworthpressinc. com].

151

1-800-342-9678. E-mail address: <getinfo@haworthpressinc.com> Website: <http://www.HaworthPress.com>]

KEYWORDS. Consumer behavior, China, postmoderism

We live in confusing times. (Costa and Bamossy, 1995, p. 3)

INTRODUCTION

As events unfold, the economy and culture of the People's Republic of China continue an evolution that is marked by rapid growth and exposure to Western values and business systems (Ikels, 1996). Simultaneously, Chinese nationalism and values are being rigorously asserted so that there is a continual cultural negotiation among these sets of competing, yet interpenetrating philosophies and experiences (Belk and Zhou, 1987). Much of this contention is consistent with the central theme repeated throughout the developing world: instead of a global convergence of cultures, differences in meanings, norms, and values boldly assert themselves, even though superficially, outward appearances in terms of goods and activities seem to be the same (Costa and Bamossy, 1995). To consider this contested sphere and in particular reflect the development of the emerging consumer-oriented economy in China, we look at a comedic, satiric film, *Ermo*, which tells the story of a farming woman, Ermo, and her quest to acquire a Japanese television. The film was shot in 1994 and has since received a number of awards. It has been shown abroad, including on the American cable-movie channel, Cinemax.

As *Ermo* will exemplify in our later discussion, this central trend of global and local cultural interpenetration in China and elsewhere is supported by a number of theories. They tend to focus on economic and cultural development from the perspective of moving from mimesis of developed cultures to recognition of one's own cultural values (Azuma, 1984). Similar to these other theories, but perhaps more radical, is the theory of ethnoconsumerism which emphasizes the role of indigenous cultures in shaping their own marketplace norms, organizations and practices (Venkatesh, 1995). This view is also suggestive of current cross-cultural and poststructuralist thinking in which researchers emphasize socially constructed local meanings in seeking to comprehend consumer behavior (Applbaum and Jordt, 1996).

From another perspective, these developments may also be viewed in terms of intertextuality whereby overlapping cultural narratives interact and mediate consumer behavior in new and dynamically evolving ways (Gould, 1998). Thus, not only are consumers experiencing the liminality of individual transformational development, involving life-span roles and rites of passage (e.g., making the transition from being single to being married (van Gennep, 1960), but they are also undergoing the metamorphosis of a continual macrosocial liminality in which both such roles and the culture, itself, are being transformed (e.g., from a socialist to capitalist economy). While such postmodern liminality has been generally conceptualized in terms of the developed Western world, we may use *Ermo* as an exemplar of how such a phenomenon manifests in a non-Western locale.

CULTURAL INTERTEXTUALITY: ASSIMILATION INTO CONSUMER CULTURE VERSUS ASSIMILATION OF IT

Intertextuality on a cross-cultural basis embodies the encounter and mixing of cultures and their narratives through such agents as the mass media, consumers involved in tourism and emigration-immigration, and product export-import in which goods and other components of life come to incorporate aspects of more than one culture (Gould, 1998). Such intertextuality in the case we are considering here may be characterized as a dialectic between the broad sociocultural idea of assimilation into mass cultural phenomena, on the one hand, and the related but also opposing idea of appropriating such phenomena to one's own ends, on the other. In this regard, the Chinese move toward consumer, materialistic culture has been characterized as reflecting ambivalent feelings (Belk and Zhou, 1987). Indeed, one study of Chinese consumers found that such ambivalence is manifested as a market segmentation phenomenon. They tended to fall into three segments as determined by the interest and knowledge they had in consumption: (1) pro-consumers, (2) moderate consumers, and (3) anti-consumers (Sklair, 1994). Pro-consumers tend to be knowledgeable and have favorable attitudes toward advertising and consumption while anti-consumers tend to have unfavorable opinions with moderate consumers being somewhere in the middle. Sklair takes these results as evidence of a "culture-ideology of consumerism" which seems very applicable to *Ermo*.

However, while China is undergoing rapid change reflective of globalization, its local culture has been found to be quite strong and persistent. Most notably, in his two studies of Hong Kong consumers of pens and mini-cassette players, Yau (1994) found that Chinese cultural values had a positive impact on product expectations and satisfaction. Chinese values such as adaptiveness, sincerity, interdependence, face, group-orientation, Pao (reciprocity), continuity, harmony with the universe, conformity, and abasement (self-control) tend to be important. Yau suggests that these findings were due to cognitive dissonance, namely that people holding these values tend to reduce their expectations upon purchasing a product and therefore are also more satisfied.

We should note that what constitutes Chinese culture today are layers of meaning laid one upon the other from various capitalist, socialist and traditional roots. These layers render the events and meanings emerging in China extremely complex. Yet, while all these levels constitute the background in *Ermo*, it tends to focus on the emerging capitalism. Apart from an occasional flash on traditional lion statues or other aspects of Chinese everyday life such as the preparation and consuming of noodles, *Ermo* also shows how they are being incorporated, commodified and especially marketized in the capitalist ethos (e.g., Ermo moves from selling her own homemade noodles in the street to eventually making them in a restaurant). Thus, both the traditional and new market economies interpenetrate one another as indicated in the following analysis.

METHOD

Rationale and Procedure

To consider the state of contemporary Chinese consumption, we focused on the movie, *Ermo* ,because it telescopes and reveals in both broad strokes and subtle details much of what we view as the discourse and narrative of Chinese consumer behavior. Indeed, movies have been shown to be an important medium for interpreting and understanding consumer behavior and symbolism (Holbrook and Grayson, 1986). In this regard, *Ermo* captures in both an entertaining and informing manner the remarkable changes taking place in China.

Method of Analysis

We watched *Ermo* on videotape, which included English subtitles. However, we did not rely strictly on these subtitles. Reflecting the cross-cultural collaboration of the two authors, one of whom is ethnically Chinese and fluent in Mandarin, we also looked directly at the original language. Our collaboration allowed for an incisive, hermeneutic process of cross-cultural triangulation in the interpretation process in general between the two researchers, the other of whom is an American of European descent. This discourse analysis also involved going back and forth between the data and interpretation. In addition, the approach used here draws from that of Holbrook and Grayson (1986) who looked at themes and symbols in the movie, *Out of Africa*, to uncover the semiotics and meaning systems of consumer behavior.

To the degree that we identify intertextuality *a priori*, we also follow Belk and Coon's (1993) approach in taking prior theories and comparing them to the qualitative data at hand, a method also consistent with a grounded theory approach. Based on the data, theoretical approaches may or may not stand up to empirical scrutiny, and new approaches or themes may emerge as well. The data may also lead the researchers to look at other literature on an emergent basis (Belk and Coon, 1993). Based on literature review and our initial review of the movie, we expected that intertextuality would dominate, but our focus is in the manner and context in which the intertextuality is manifested.

SYNOPSIS OF PLOT

A brief synopsis of the plot is necessary for the reader to understand the analysis and interpretation to follow. However, first it is useful to characterize the movie in terms of its genre. *Ermo* is very much a satire or even a parody in which the behavior of Ermo and the other characters is comically held up for ridicule. On the other hand, in keeping with the uneven development of consumer culture in China, it is likely that some viewers will take the movie more literally than others. In fact, much of the behavior portrayed in the movie would seem to reflect actual events. Thus, were the character of Ermo to magically see this movie herself, she probably would not get much of it and would fail to see most of its humor.

Ermo is a married woman living in rural China. Her life is hard and physically grueling. She is married to an older man, nicknamed the Chief, who is very traditional in his ways and has difficulty in keeping up with his younger wife. He is also physically ill and must be cared for by her. They have an only son, Tiger. This family of hers is portrayed in contrast to another one headed by a man named Blindman. Blindman is around Ermo's age and is also highly energetic. He is rich by his village's standards since he owns a truck, which gives him access to the local town and allows him to earn money by transporting goods to it. In contrast to Ermo, his wife is seen to be fat and lazy and seems to do nothing but complain. They have a daughter Xiu who is a younger playmate of Tiger's. This fact is important for a son is valued in Confucian terms and therefore the lack of a son causes jealousy on the part of Blindman's wife for Ermo. It would also appear that each family has only one child in compliance with China's one-child policy (though this is not explicitly stated), a fact we conjecture precludes a plot in which Blindman's wife tries to have a male child in reaction to Ermo. Instead, the movie focuses on consumer behavior rather than reproductive activity as the central thematic element.

However, the jealousy flows both ways in the story as Blindman's wife uses the television he has provided her (the first one in the village) to assert her advantage over Ermo. She entices Tiger over to watch TV with her daughter and antagonizes Ermo who does not like these shenanigans. For the wife, it gives her the opportunity to operate on an equal footing with Ermo and in fact she expresses the idea that hopefully one day Tiger and Xiu will marry although at this stage both are elementary school age. Ermo responds very resentfully and tries to keep Tiger at home. This rivalry over television viewing eventually drives Ermo to want to purchase her own and to acquire the money to do so. Her behavior in this respect comprises the central dramatic force of the movie. She becomes obsessed and ruthless in her pursuit of it. This compels her to expand her business of selling noodles in the streets and with Blindman's help she soon ends up making them for a restaurant in the local town. It is in a retail store there that she sees a television that is the biggest around and that even the regional chief does not possess.

Another plot element in the movie concerns Ermo's affair with Blindman. They bond in their various shared experiences in going to town and working. Blindman also symbolizes the new in China while Ermo's husband, the Chief, represents the old and resistance to the new. However, this seemingly clear symbolism is problematic on such occasions as when the Chief shows pride with respect to Ermo's accomplishments or when Blindman treats Ermo almost as a traditional concubine. In this regard, when Ermo finds out that Blindman had set her up in the restaurant to give her more money (Blindman pays the restaurant manager who in turn adds this money to her salary), she leaves the job. She also ends their affair and goes back to selling noodles in the street, thus demonstrating her independence. Eventually, she saves enough money to buy the television and brings it home to the Chief and Tiger where the whole village is invited to watch it. The movie ends with Ermo and her family, asleep and displaced from their bed because the TV is on it (the irony is that there is no table or stand big enough in their house to place the TV). Moreover, the TV is left on and since the programming is over for the night, only static is coming out from it.

EMERGENT THEMES OF CULTURAL INTERTEXTUALITY

As we recognized *a priori*, the main overall theme of our study of *Ermo* reflects the evolving and omnipresent intertextual dynamics of much of daily life, namely the tension between global and local sites of both activity and meaning. This plays itself out in many ways from the standardization-localization decisions in marketing to the import-export exchanges of cultural products and meanings. We call this theme *cultural intertextuality*. Through it, culture is seen as a text and the interaction of cultures is seen as a mixing of texts to create new, hybrid forms and meanings. In this regard, even the most local of sites such as the world of Ermo becomes one that is defined by such interaction. Thus, Ermo is redefining herself and her world not necessarily by rejecting Chinese meanings in favor of foreign ones but instead by engaging in an integration process in which the new and old are mixed in various novel and often unforeseen ways. Culture is therefore not merely constructing the world for consumers, but it, itself, is also being reconstructed by the process of intertextuality. Further analysis within this broad framework of cultural intertextuality reveals two main emergent themes that we will focus on: (1) longstanding versus postmodern narratives and (2) Sinicization. The first theme concerns the degree to which consumers see themselves as carrying on their lives in terms of age-old narratives (i.e., longstanding ones such as marriage and traditionally defined roles) versus postmodern narratives in which the self is less defined and boundaries and roles are less crisply understood or grasped. The second theme concerns the particular aspects of Chinese culture that emerge, interact and sometimes reassert themselves in the face of the globalization taking place throughout both the movie and Chinese life in general. To paraphrase the saying, "The more things change, the more they stay the same," we might say in the present context, "The more things become global, the more they become Chinese." Thus, these two themes should be viewed as displaying how the cultural intertextuality manifests and expresses itself. Moreover, as we examine them, we note that while they stand as separate definable issues, they also overlap. For example, Sinicization may be seen to represent an effort to maintain longstanding narratives in the face of massive change.

Longstanding versus Postmodern Perspectives

Development, such as that taking place in China, requires the construction of new sociocultural and self narratives that describe everyday life. Recent thought has considered such new, emerging narratives as *postmodern* which suggests that consumers transform themselves in a self-liberating manner (Firat and Venkatesh, 1995). This means that there has been a displacement of fixed identities in favor of more fluid, role-based ones. At the same time, the Chinese flavor of old, even ancient-based, traditional narratives persists and there is a continual contest between the old and new. In this regard, Thompson and Hirschman (1995) suggest that old or longstanding narratives reflect what came before change and often blend with the newer ones. Indeed, the displacement of the old may not be as straightforward as postmodern theorists have held. Thus, the idea of longstanding versus postmodern narratives will serve as a conceptual framework for characterizing the issues of traditional Chinese versus newer Western-type values. In this regard, we identify two major elements: (1) gender and (2) postmodern *tribal* lifestyles versus demographics.

The Gender Narrative Element. One major narrative element that emerges in *Ermo* is that of gender which has its longstanding aspects of traditionally defined roles and also its postmodern aspects involving reconstructed roles. Ermo's assertion of independence and going out and getting work is attended with various degrees of resistance, especially from her husband, the Chief. He is generally a benign figure but he cannot fathom why she wants to work and is constantly trying to persuade her to stay home. However, he is also portrayed as having relatively little power and is an older character. While Ermo does have an affair with Blindman, she is seeking much more: the freedom to be not so much an *equal-to-any-man* participant in the newly emergent consumer culture, as much as a full one, regardless of gender distinction. Nor will she allow gender or other traditional hierarchical constraints, such as class, to stop her. She does this as a pure instinctual desire to get what she wants rather than with any self-conscious ideological thought (e.g., feminist). Her vehement assertion of her own will is not a declaration of gender independence *per se*, but rather a form of *non-gender-specific* self-expression in which she is simply following what she wants to do.

In summary, the gender narrative element in *Ermo* shares many similar elements with those across the contemporary world, including traditional versus modern roles, sexual aspects, and mothering and nurturing aspects. But unlike gender narratives in the West, for example, the narrative in *Ermo* seems to reflect a natural assertion of Ermo's personal desires rather than any self-conscious attempt to assert her status as a woman. Her being a woman may compound her challenges but this appears to be just another obstacle in an environment of obstacles, such as harsh physical conditions and competition in her selling of noodles.

The Postmodern Tribal Lifestyles versus Demographics Narrative Element. From a broad cultural perspective, Maffesoli (1996) suggests that people, at least in the West, are moving toward tribal social forms which are organized around communal phenomena, including consumption activities, that are not fully accounted for by socioeconomic or demographic variables. But do these ideas apply to an emerging culture such as China? To some degree the evidence provided by *Ermo* indicates "yes." What seems to be a major aspect of development is that old socioeconomic constraints are being broken down in the face of both production and consumption changes. Since *Ermo* involves both areas in very close knit ways, it is necessary to see how they play out in the film. They do so mainly through the interplay of the old and new. Ermo's husband, the Chief, represents the old order of China and the socioeconomic influence of class with its roots in production as the sole basis of status. Ermo in seeking to make money and buy the TV is really challenging the old order. She establishes contact with others on the basis of something newer: the evolving dynamics of both work and consumption. Moreover, she goes to work to acquire a specific good and is motivated not to have a career so much as to acquire something for her family and especially her son. It is quite possible in the context of her character that she would not work at all had the need for television not arisen, and indeed, we are left wondering at the end if she ever will go back to work. Her life is as much defined by her consumption orientation as her production one. Perhaps a new desire for another consumer good will drive her to seek work, once again.

This is not to say that the old order has no impact. Rather, there is a dialectic synthesis between the old and new which is rapidly leading to a tribalized, postmodern society. In some respects, this is very much in keeping with Chinese history. Indeed, some have suggested that China might break up due to regionalism or what might be called regional tribalism. On the other hand, the impetus for this current tribalism has more to do with the intrusion of the newly emerging consumer society. In this regard, the social vision painted in *Ermo* suggests something of what Chua and Tan (1995) speak of when they consider new social configurations, such as communitarianism, and other reinvented Asian traditions in Singapore. While the Singapore experience is quite different from China's, the attenuation of class influence in favor of other social signifiers seems evident in both. In *Ermo*, we see evidence of new consumption and wealth traditions being invented, as symbolized here by the ownership of a television and the dynamics surrounding its acquisition and use. Old ways of creating social inequality are giving way to new ones which reflect working to getting ahead for the benefit of one's family and consuming to demonstrate one's new status to others (Wong and Ahuvia, 1998).

Sinicization (Chinese Indigenization) and Materialism

Sinicization concerns how various consumer culture trends emerging in the world are assimilated or indigenized by the Chinese people. By this, we mean that whatever transpires in the everyday life of the Chinese consumer-worker is culturally reproduced or constructed in Chinese terms so that any phenomenon whether it originally emanates from abroad or not must be established in its *Chineseness*. In many ways, this issue parallels the issues discussed in the previous sections. Thus, while even the very making of this movie reflects the globalization and (post)modernization of consumer culture, its portrayal of emerging materialism in many respects embodies the dialogue of Chinese culture with this new world.

It should be noted, however, that what it means to be Chinese is itself undergoing change, is often reflected in newly created symbolism, and also shares in the aforementioned dynamics of tribalism in which ethnicity is reconstituted and informed by consumption. For example, the television takes on special meanings in *Ermo* which are invested in the concept of Chineseness. Moreover, similar to what we found with respect to the gender issue, much of what is happening with respect to Sinicization does not stem from some self-conscious notion of a separate Chineseness, *per se*, but rather is something that is emerging in the course of everyday events. Most of the time, Ermo seemed to simply act in an instinctive way. That it is seen as Chinese is based on our *etic* (researcher-based) interpretation rather than a direct *emic* (local) expression. There are no occasions in the movie when someone says, "This is Chinese." However, to a viewer, especially a foreign one, it is quite apparent that this experience reflects local Chinese ethnicity in many respects.

The Television as a Symbol. Consumer ethnography is often performed on the basis of products, which are viewed as manifestations of material culture (e.g., Gould, 1998). The central fact of Ermo's desire for a color television alone is very suggestive in light of research by Doran (1997, p. 130) which indicates that, "The television has emerged as perhaps the most symbolic purchase an individual or couple makes in modern China." She points out that this is not only due to the limited number of product categories available or to financial considerations but also to television being a symbol of economic and political freedom. However, while the television in *Ermo* is no doubt a metaphor for the contemporary world, it becomes in the context of the countryside in which Ermo resides, a part of the social fabric, an object of Chinese concern.

House Is a Hen, TV Is an Egg. Throughout the movie, Ermo's husband, the Chief, stood against her desire to spend her hard-earned money on a television, much less the biggest one in the village and even beyond. To express his personal philosophy on this, he often repeated the proverbial phrase, "A house is a hen and a television is an egg." In many respects, the television while being new is captured by the longstanding narrative of how things are valued in China. The house is a better investment since it will yield financial returns whereas the TV will not. The TV is a money user. However, the hen (house) will lay eggs in the future. This view expressed by the husband is indicative of the frugal nature of Chinese materialism in that seemingly extravagant expenditures must be justified as an investment. The Chief insisted that,

> When you have money, you should build a bigger house. That's the way it should be. The house is a chicken, the TV is an egg. Why do you want an egg?

Still at the film's end, even he enjoys his new found popularity in the village when everyone comes to see the TV and he allows, it "is not so bad after all."

SUMMARY INTERPRETATION

Ermo provides an excellent mirror of the liminal or transitional state of contemporary consumer culture in Mainland China. It also reflects the intertextuality of events and emerging cultural narratives. A most important element of this intertextuality is the diffusion of capitalism and its liminal disruption of longstanding narratives. In this regard, we emphasize that liminality has to be seen in two senses: (1) individual role liminality in which people undergo personal rite of passage transitions and (2) cultural role liminality in which people make transitions in roles due to changes in culture. Yet, such intertextuality and the resulting cultural role liminality also involve the assimilation of longstanding narratives or even the reverse, co-optation by them. Here, we can contemplate the sweeping power of economic change in its challenge to the enduring culture of China. It is not that capitalism goes against the grain of Chinese thought. Quite the contrary, commerce is fully integrated into Chinese culture. What is disruptive is the force of modern capitalism, which embodies telescopic change that is new to Chinese culture. Arguably perhaps, a consumer in traditional China (as symbolized by Ermo's husband, the Chief) would desire a bigger house and more land or goods that store value such as jade. However, now the desire for a class of goods, such as televisions, which are not so much a store of monetary value, is driving socioeconomic change. Instead, such goods must be seen as stores of cultural value (e.g., status symbols). Thus, the meaning of materialism is undergoing a transformation in which the focus shifts to acquiring goods that may be used up rather than held as enduring stores of financial capital. These new goods do, however, represent sociocultural capital which allow the consumer to express herself in new ways. This is one important meaning of the hen-egg metaphor in *Ermo*.

The expression of capitalism has itself undergone change throughout the world. It is not just developmental modernization that is important now in terms of the process, but also cultural postmodernization. China as seen in *Ermo* is making the leap to the postmodern age as symbolized by the television on a material-object level and the social order change on a more abstract human relations level. For the most part during the Communist era, China has been dominated by a political-economic organization in which individuals serve as functional members of its state-dominated society (Yang, 1994). In this regard, Ermo is a person who defines herself by her roles and develops relationships, which are based on those roles rather than as a mere functionary. In terms of the affectual (social and activity-centered) tribes of postmodernity that Maffesoli (1996) describes, she shares links with her fellow workers, Blindman, and anyone whom she encounters in everyday situations. The dynamic situations define these relations as much or more than any state or traditional links.

Thus, we would argue, for instance, that *guanxi* (reliance on people in high places) is hardly dead but may take new forms (cf. Yan, 1996). Ermo needed the support of people such as Blindman but in fact was trying on her own to outdo everybody with a bigger TV, including the county head. It will be interesting in this regard to observe the evolution of *guanxi* in postmodernizing China. Still, there also remains the Sinicization of this postmodernization. How Chinese people view and culturally produce what is going on around them is very much a product of assimilation in their own terms. For example, while *Ermo*, itself, is very much a Chinese movie, a Westerner can understand and enjoy much of it, in large part because of its globally contemporary themes. Yet, that same Westerner would miss other parts of it because it is locally Chinese in such aspects as its character, style, meanings and metaphors.

We should note a few limitations of this study. First, we only looked at one movie though we also reviewed the literature and related it to the movie text. Second, movies may have limitations in terms of how they reflect a culture in that they reconstruct social conditions in their own often-caricatured way. We believe our study is revelatory but that it should be considered as a benchmark in what we hope will be continuing research on materialism and symbolic consumer behavior in China. Third, while *Ermo* appears to be widely distributed, we cannot account for the generalizability of its meanings across China. Thus, we expect that regions across China will differ in developmental stages and/or other factors (e.g., North versus South China, Han Chinese versus ethnic minorities). Finally, we provided our own reading of the film. Thus, while we did stick to it as closely as we could, it is possible that other researchers might provide different readings.

IMPLICATIONS FOR MARKETING IN CHINA

Based on this study, we conclude that there are three distinct, although interrelated strategic and research implications for marketers in China: (1) incorporate tribalized lifestyles, (2) become more emic as opposed to etic, and (3) revisit standardization-adaptation strategy.

Incorporate Tribalization and Lifestyle Considerations. Managerially, marketers should utilize the tribalism concept to target consumers. It is not enough to consider Chinese consumers as members of some broad social class, but rather, they should be seen as a part of product and/or work-related lifestyle tribes which drive their behavior. Managers might construct product-lifestyle segment grids in which these tribalized aspects of consumption are reflected. The value of such analysis will become even more apparent as niche marketing evolves and consumers become more refined and differentiated from each other. While the socioeconomic variables still have their place, we expect that they may well be subordinate to the tribal-lifestyle variables. Thus, for instance, there is no question that gender remains important for Ermo's role in society. But the understandings of how that role is understood and how it plays out with respect to consumption is itself being transformed and tribalized. In some cases, it will pay for marketers to target men or women separately but often this will still be within the tribal or product domain influences that help determine how consumers function. For example, based on the case of *Ermo*, marketers of televisions would do well to study the *television* culture of China. We learn in the movie that a television is a social center (more so than in the West), that its size is a symbol of status, that a piece of furniture could be marketed to hold the television, and that consumers project the dramas of their lives on it, among other things. Such findings thus can inform the development of product and promotion strategies.

Take a More Emic Perspective. Emic analysis involves starting with an indigenous culture and analyzing the meanings, values and norms of that culture in its own terms. Etic analysis involves, on the other hand, the formation of researcher driven theories and then attempting to apply them across cultures. While this distinction has its limitations, we would suggest that our analysis of *Ermo* indicates that managers should be attentive on an emic basis to indigenous meanings even for products with standardized components and branding (cf. Wong and Ahuvia, 1998). Thus, for instance, the television is a relatively standardized product but may differ quite widely in perceived meanings. A television has a much greater and quite different symbolic significance to Ermo than it would to most Westerners. Thus, taking more such emic perspectives, researchers can then derive better etic interpretations and marketing strategies. For example, De Beers found that its global strategy of selling diamond wedding rings as a symbol of romance (etic meaning) does not work in China. In order to succeed, De Beers need to know the emic meanings of diamonds, love, and marriage in China (March 18, 1999, Far East Economic Review, p. 48).

Revisit Standardization-Adaptation Strategy. Another implication concerns the issue of standardization-adaptation (Jain, 1989). In this regard, the textual-discourse approach taken here has not been widely considered. Strategists need to look at countries and products as comprising an intertextual interaction in which the culturally constructed meanings of products are analyzed for both their global and local meanings. Thus, for instance, while television is becoming a very widely diffused consumer good, its particular meaning to Ermo appears to reflect emic Chinese perceptions that would not have much resonance elsewhere. In this regard, the nuances expressed in *Ermo* suggest that adaptation in terms of meaning, especially in terms of promotion and retailing, is required for marketing success. In fact, many aspects of consumer culture will create an adaptive situation regardless of the marketer's effort. For example, the rendering of the television as a status symbol appears to be as much a consumer creation as it is one created by marketers. Thus, the latter will often need to consider Chinese generated meanings and embrace them rather than attempt to impose their own meanings.

CONCLUSION

Based on our analysis of the movie *Ermo*, we find that economic modernization and the emergence of a consumer culture in China does not reflect a single headlong rush in one direction. Instead, there is a confluence of macro and micro level forces that is producing an intertextuality of cultural narratives in which China is at once unique, and yet, a participant in the broader cultural trends emerging on a global basis. This perspective also suggests that the study of cultural texts, such as those provided by movies, is helpful in formulating marketing strategies involving China and is especially helpful in framing standardization-adaptation decisions.

REFERENCES

Applbaum, K. and I. Jordt (1996). Notes toward an application of McCracken's cultural categories for cross-cultural consumer research. *Journal of Consumer Research*, 23(3), 204-218.

Azuma, H. (1984). Psychology in a non-Western country, *International Journal of Psychology, 19*, 45-55.

Belk, R.W. and G.S. Coon (1993). Gift giving as agapic love: An alternative to the exchange paradigm based on dating experiences, *Journal of Consumer Research*, 20(3), 393-417.

Belk, R.W. and N. Zhou, (1987). Learning to want things. In M. Wallendorf and P. Anderson (Eds.), *Advances in Consumer Research, Vol. 14* (pp. 478-481). Provo, UT: Association for Consumer Research.

Chua, C.B. and J.E. Tan (1995). Singapore: New configuration of a socially stratified culture, paper presented to the workshop on Cultural Construction of Asia's New Rich, Murdoch University, Western Australia.

Costa, J.A. and G.J. Bamossy (1995). Perspectives on ethnicity, nationalism and cultural identity. In J.A. Costa and G.J. Bamossy (Eds.), *Marketing in a multicultural world*, (pp. 3-25). Thousand Oaks, CA: Sage.

Doran, K.B. (1997). Symbolic consumption in China: The color television as a life statement. In M. Brucks and D.J. MacInnis (Eds). *Advances in Consumer Research*, Vol. 24 (pp. 128-131). Provo, UT: Association for Consumer Research.

Firat, A.F. and A. Venkatesh (1995). Liberatory postmodernism and the reenchantment of consumption. *Journal of Consumer Research*, 22(3), 239-267.

Gould, S.J. (1998). Deconstructing and inscribing cross-cultural consumption through drinking *Tahitian Tikis* tea: Is it too late or never too late to experience the *authentic* culture of Polynesia? In J.W. Alba and J.W. Hutchinson (Eds.), *Advances in Consumer Research* (pp. 31-36). Provo, UT: Association for Consumer Research.

Holbrook, M.B. and M.W. Grayson (1986). The semiology of cinematic consumption: Symbolic consumer behavior in *Out of Africa*. *Journal of Consumer Research*, 13(3), 374-381.

Ikels, C. (1996). *The return of the god of wealth: The transition to a market economy in urban China*. Stanford, CA: Stanford University Press.

Jain, S.C. (1989). Standardization of international marketing strategy: Some research hypotheses. *Journal of Marketing*, 53(1), 70-79.

Maffesoli, M. (1996). *The time of tribes*. London: Sage.

Sklair, L. (1994). The consumer-ideology of consumerism in urban China, in C.J. Shultz II, R.W. Belk, and G. Ger (Eds.), *Research in Consumer Behavior, Vol. 7* (pp. 259-292). Greenwich, CT: JAI.

Thompson, C.J. and E.C. Hirschman (1995). Understanding the socialized body: A poststructuralist analysis of consumers' self-conceptions, body images, and self-care practice. *Journal of Consumer Research*, 22(2), 139-154.

van Gennep, Arnould (1960). *The rites of passage*. Chicago: University of Chicago Press.

Venkatesh, A. (1995). Ethnoconsumerism: A new paradigm to study cultural and cross-cultural consumer behavior. In J.A. Costa and G.J. Bamossy (Eds.), *Marketing in a Multicultural World*, (pp. 26-67). Thousand Oaks, CA: Sage.

Wong, N. and A. Ahuvia (1998). From personal taste to family face: Luxury consumption in Confucianist and Western societies. *Psychology and Marketing*, 15(5), 423-441.

Yan, Y. (1996). *The flow of gifts: Reciprocity and social networks in a Chinese village*. Stanford, CA: Stanford University Press.

Yang, M.M. (1994). *Gifts, favors, and banquets: The art of social relationships in China*. Ithaca, NY: Cornell University Press.

Yau, O.H.M. (1994). *Consumer behavior in China: Customer satisfaction and cultural values*. London: Routledge.

The Influence of Hedonic Values
on Consumer Behaviors:
An Empirical Investigation in China

Cheng-Lu Wang
Zhen-Xiong Chen
Allan K. K. Chan
Zong-Cheng Zheng

SUMMARY. This study investigated the influence of hedonic values on the consumer behavior of young Chinese. The results show that hedonic values are negatively associated with utilitarian orientation and positively associated with novelty seeking, responsiveness to promotion stimuli, and preference for foreign brands. Personal income moderates the relationship between hedonic values and brand consciousness. Conceptual importance and managerial implications are discussed. *[Article copies available for a fee from The Haworth Document Delivery Service: 1-800-342-9678. E-mail address: <getinfo@haworthpressinc.com> Website: <http://www.HaworthPress.com>]*

KEYWORDS. Hedonic values, branding, Chinese consumer

Cheng-Lu Wang, Zhen-Xiong Chen, and Allan K. K. Chan are affiliated with the Department of Marketing, Hong Kong Baptist University, Hong Kong. Zong-Cheng Zheng is affiliated with the School of Management, Zhongshan University, Guangzhou, China.

Address correspondence to: Dr. Zhen-Xiong Chen, Department of Marketing, Hong Kong Baptist University, Kwoloon Tong, Hong Kong (E-mail: georgezx@hkbu.edu.hk).

[Haworth co-indexing entry note]: "The Influence of Hedonic Values on Consumer Behaviors: An Empirical Investigation in China." Wang, Cheng-Lu et al. Co-published simultaneously in *Journal of Global Marketing* (International Business Press, an imprint of The Haworth Press, Inc.) Vol. 14, No. 1/2, 2000, pp. 169-186; and: *Greater China in the Global Market* (ed: Yigang Pan) International Business Press, an imprint of The Haworth Press, Inc., 2000, pp. 169-186. Single or multiple copies of this article are available for a fee from The Haworth Document Delivery Service [1-800-342-9678, 9:00 a.m. - 5:00 p.m. (EST). E-mail address: getinfo@haworthpressinc.com].

INTRODUCTION

Consumption values have been regarded as important predictors of consumer behavior (Kamakura & Mazzon, 1991; Pitts & Woodside, 1983; Sheth et al., 1991; Vinson et al., 1977). For instance, Sheth et al. (1991) noted that consumer choice is a function of multiple consumption values such as functional value, emotional value, and symbolic or conspicuous value. Other researchers distinguished utilitarian values from hedonic values in consumption behavior (Batra & Ahtola, 1991). While utilitarian values are described as rational and concerned with "expectations of consequences," hedonic values are said to be related to consummatory gratification through the experiences of fun, fantasy and playfulness (Babin et al., 1994; Batra & Ahtola, 1991; Hirschman, 1982; Hirschman & Holbrook, 1982; Holbrook & Hirschman, 1982). Previous studies have defined hedonic consumption by the facets of consumer behavior that relate to the senses, the ability to fantasize and the emotional aspects of one's experience with products or shopping (Babin et al., 1994; Hirschman, 1982; Hirschman & Holbrook, 1982). The present study focuses on the impact of hedonic values on consumer need-satisfaction behaviors through consumption. We argue that consumers with stronger hedonic values tend to consider consumption as more than satisfying basic or survival needs. Their consumption behaviors are characterized by pursuing instant gratification, spending expressively or symbolically, and seeking enjoyment and fun.

The consumption values of Chinese consumers have attracted researchers' attention since the 1980s. It has been found that consumers in China are less inclined to value the hedonic functions of a product or the benefits of a product beyond its utilitarian functions (Tse, 1996; Tse et al., 1989). However, no systematic study of the relationship between hedonic values and Chinese consumer behaviors has been conducted. With increases in personal income and greater influences from outside China and especially Western cultures, the values of Chinese consumers have recently been changing in reaction to years of deprivation and institutionalized discouragement towards consumption in the past. More Chinese consumers have accepted buying for hedonic reasons rather than for only utilitarian need, especially the younger generation (Chu & Ju, 1993). There is a tendency for young Chinese consumers to pursue a "modern" lifestyle by spending on big brand name products and keeping up with the fashion trends (Ariga et al., 1997; Bow & Ford, 1993; Cui, 1997; Swanson, 1995). As such, it is important to examine the impact of hedonic values on product choice and consumption behavior of contemporary Chinese, especially young Chinese consumers.

The objective of this study is to investigate the relationship between hedonic values and various behavioral patterns, such as utilitarian orientation, consumer novelty seeking, responsiveness to promotion stimuli, brand consciousness and preference for foreign brands. This article reports the results of an empirical study conducted in China and discusses the managerial implications of segmenting China's consumer market and of promoting and positioning consumer products.

THE RELATIONSHIP BETWEEN HEDONIC VALUES AND CONSUMER BEHAVIOR: RESEARCH HYPOTHESES DEVELOPMENT

Hedonic Values vs. Utilitarian Orientation

The utilitarian orientation has been described as a tendency to emphasize the perceived functional value or physical performance features (e.g., quality and value) of products in choice behavior (Sheth et al., 1991). Traditionally, the functional value is considered the primary driving force of consumer choice (Sheth et al., 1991) and is more likely to be adopted by consumers with traditional lifestyles. People with greater utilitarian values tend to live simpler lifestyles and may consider consumption necessary for survival or as a tool to reach higher-order life goals rather than as the terminal goal of enjoyment (Tse, 1996). Consequently, they tend to be more value conscious and have more positive value perceptions regarding prices paid (Feinberg et al., 1992; Wakefield & Barnes, 1996).

In contrast, those who focus on hedonic values are "modern consumers" who tend to use surplus income to satisfy their ever-growing new desires for consumption (Campbell, 1987). As such, consumers with stronger hedonic values may not be satisfied by the functional value of a product. Instead, they may be more concerned with the expressive or emotional value of a product, such as brand, design, appearance and packaging, than with quality and price. They appear to derive their gratification from the immediate hedonic pleasure experience of consumption (Fischer & Arnold, 1990).

H1: The utilitarian orientation will be negatively associated with hedonic values.

Hedonic Values vs. Novelty Seeking

Consumer novelty seeking refers to a propensity to seek new experiences and novel stimuli and to try new products or change brands for increasing stimulation and variety (Hirschman, 1980; Katz & Lazarsfeld, 1955; Leavitt & Walton, 1975, 1988; McAlister & Pessemier, 1982; Raju, 1980). Consumers with stronger hedonic values tend to enjoy more colorful lifestyles. Consequently, their behaviors are likely to be motivated by exploration, novelty and variety. It is expected that these consumers are likely to be the pioneers in new product diffusion processes. This is because a new product or a different brand may provide them with more ways to satisfy their needs for optimal stimulation (Raju, 1980), innovation (Leavitt & Walton, 1975, 1988) and sensation seeking (Zuckerman, 1979).

On the other hand, consumers with weaker hedonic values tend to be value consciousness (Lichtenstein, Netemeyer, & Burton, 1990) and display propensities for repetitive behavior (Raju, 1980). They are less likely to change brands or try new products and are more likely to be among the late-coming majority or behave as laggards in the market (Robertson, 1967). While Chinese people were not likely in the past to switch to other brands or products unless there was extreme dissatisfaction (Kindel, 1983; Yau, 1988), this value has recently changed in that young consumers have become more willing to try new brands for the sake of variety (Swanson, 1995). As a result, it is expected that the tendency to try new products or brands is related to the consumption value that one endorses.

H2: Novelty seeking will be positively associated with hedonic values.

Hedonic Values vs. Responsiveness to Promotion Stimuli

Researchers have further suggested that novelty seeking behavior in consumers is related to responsiveness to promotion stimuli or to being prone to promotion, which refers to a tendency to use promotion information as a basis for making purchase decisions (Feinberg et al.,

1992; Wakefield & Barnes, 1996). Individuals with a greater novelty-seeking tendency may be interested in promotion stimuli that offer stimulation and added value beyond the typical utilitarian functions of products. Since consumers with stronger hedonic values seek novelty and variety in trying new products, they are expected to be more sensitive and responsive to promotion influences in their product choice and brand-switching behavior.

H3: Responsiveness to promotion stimuli will be positively associated with hedonic values.

Hedonic Values vs. Brand Consciousness

While the systematic study of hedonic consumption began in the late 1970s (Hirschman, 1982; Hirschman & Holbrook, 1982; Holbrook & Hirschman, 1982), it has roots in research on consumer motivation (Dichter, 1960) and product symbolism (Levy, 1959). Since products have long been known to possess symbolic or conspicuous consumption value in excess of their functional utility (Veblen, 1899), "hedonic consumption acts are based not on what consumers know to be real but rather on what they desire reality to be" (Hirschman & Holbrook, 1982). A consumer's choice of a product or a brand is frequently based on the congruency between the consumer's lifestyle and his/her consumption values and the perceived symbolic meaning of the product or brand (Levy, 1959, 1963; Hirschman & Holbrook, 1982). Consumers with stronger hedonic values are expected to be more brand-conscious and to choose a product or a brand based on its symbolic or expressive value more than its functional value.

H4: Brand consciousness will be positively associated with hedonic values.

Hedonic Values vs. Preference for Foreign Brands

Research also indicates that foreign brands often trigger cultural stereotypes and influence product perceptions and attitudes. For instance, the French pronunciation of a brand name was found to have positive effect on the perceived hedonic value (e.g., aesthetic sensitivity, refined taste and sensory pleasure) of products and on the attitude-toward-the brand (Leclerc et al., 1994). In China, imported products are typically associated with high fashion or with those who have high social status (Bow & Ford, 1993; Li & Gallup, 1995; HKTDC, 1994). As such, many products that are made in China are purposely given brand names that look or sound like foreign brands. For some products, such as clothing and cosmetics, the symbolic or hedonic values associated with a foreign brand can be a key determinant of brand selection, especially for consumers who have strong hedonic values. Since consumers often use brand names to express their lifestyles, it is expected that consumers with strong hedonic values also show a preference for foreign brands.

> *H5: Preference for foreign brands will be positively associated with hedonic values.*

The Moderating Effect of Personal Income

Consumer behavior is a function of both willingness and ability to purchase a product. Therefore, personal income has been traditionally considered important in predicting consumer behavior and has been incorporated into market segmentation decisions. Consumers whose value systems derive from basic needs (needs for food, shelter and security) tend to have lower income than those who value psychological growth (Mitchell, 1983). In China, for instance, while high-income consumers are eager to buy brand name products, the average consumers have limited purchasing power (Chin & Towler, 1995). Those with low personal income may not be able to afford to buy famous brand-name products, even though they have a willingness to buy them. In other words, it is expected that personal income will moderate the relationship between hedonic values and brand consciousness.

> *H6: The relationship between hedonic values and brand consciousness will be stronger for consumers with higher personal income than for those with lower personal income.*

RESEARCH METHOD

Sample

The target population for the current study was young consumers in the 18 to 30 year-old age group in four major cities in China: Beijing,

Shanghai, Guangzhou, and Chengdu. Beijing is the capital city located in the north part of China; Shanghai is a commercial center located in the Eastern region of the country; Guangzhou is the largest city in South China (which has been greatly influenced by the West due to its closeness to Hong Kong); Chengdu is the largest city in Southwestern China, which represents the more traditional part of the country. These four metropolitan cities represent regions with different geographic, political and commercial backgrounds.

The total sample size consisted of 960 consumers, 240 in each city. In order to ensure the representativeness of the sample, a stratified sampling plan was followed based on the population distribution in the districts of each city. Table 1 indicates the sampling allocation in one of the cities, Beijing, as an example of our sampling method. First of all, we determined the numbers of subjects to be interviewed and the numbers of sampling communities for each district based on the distribution of the population in the city of Beijing. For example, we sought 23 subjects from one community in the Eastern District (9.14% of the population) and 70 subjects from the four communities in the Chaoyang District (29.24% of the population). Households within each district were randomly selected and visited by our interviewers. Only the target subjects (i.e., people whose ages were within the range of 18-30) within the sampling communities were interviewed. In the case when no target subjects were at home during the visit, a nearby household was visited.

TABLE 1. The Sample Allocation for the City of Beijing

District	Population	%	Allocation of sample	Number of sampling communities selected
Eastern district	1,129,170	9.14	23	1
Western district	1,430,008	12.35	30	2
Chongwen district	733,820	6.33	15	1
Xuanwu district	1,052,570	9.08	22	2
Chaoyang district	3,387,990	29.24	70	4
Haidian district	3,053,620	33.26	80	4
Total	11,587,240	100.00	240	14

Note: There are 6 districts in Beijing; our sample size for Beijing is 240.

Interview

Interviewers were university students recruited from the four cities where the survey was conducted. All interviewers were trained in interviewing skills in a short-term training program before they started the formal interviews. After the training program, each interviewer was asked to do an initial interview and the results were checked by researchers through telephone calls to the respondents. The results showed that the quality of the initial interviews was satisfactory.

Measures

A questionnaire composed of several multi-item scales was developed by the researchers based on the relevant literature and in-depth interviews with a sample of 30 young Chinese consumers. These scales measured the variables of hedonic value, utilitarian orientation, novelty seeking, responsiveness to promotion stimuli, preference for foreign brands, and brand consciousness. All variables were measured on a 6-point scale (1 = "Strongly Disagree" and 6 = "Strongly Agree"). The Cronbach alpha of these scales ranged from .65 to.78. Sample items of the measures are as follows:

Hedonic Value: "I would like to earn more and spend more to enjoy myself." "Consumption itself is an enjoyable experience."

Utilitarian Orientation: "When I choose a product, I emphasize quality rather than packaging or appearance." "How a product works is more important than how it looks."

Novelty Seeking: "I prefer to buy a new product that has not been tried by other people before." "I would like to try different brands rather than always use the same brand."

Responsiveness to Promotion Stimuli: "I am more likely to buy a product when it is promoted on TV or other media." "I would like to try a product when it is promoted in a store."

Brand Consciousness: "I am willing to pay more for buying products with famous brand names." "Brand is not as important as a product's price."

Preference for Foreign Brands: "It is worth buying a foreign brand product although it is more expensive than a domestic brand product." "Foreign brands are usually better than domestic brand."

Five demographic attributes were also included in the measure and used as control variables in the regression analysis. Age and education were measured by number of years. Gender was coded with 1 designating men and 0 designating women. Marital status was coded with 1 designating single and 2 designating married. Personal income was measured by the range from RMB 299 to 5,000 *yuan* per month. The demographic information is presented in Table 2.

Analysis

Multiple regression procedures were used to test the hypotheses. H1 to H5 were tested by hierarchical blocked regression analysis. In this regression model, demographic variables (controlled variables) were entered, as a first block, into the model. The hedonic value variable (independent variable) was entered as the second block. The

TABLE 2. Summary of Demographic Characteristics of Respondents

Demographic Variables	Beijing	Shanghai	Guangzhou	Chengdu	Mean (%)
Age					
18-23	51.1	51.0	50.9	50.9	51
24-30	48.9	49.0	49.1	49.1	49
Gender					
Male	50	50	50	50	
Female	50	50	50	50	
Marital Status					
Married	18.4	12.1	20.9	23.8	18.8
Single	81.6	87.8	79.1	76.2	81.2
Education					
Junior higher school	4.2	5.8	20.5	9.4	10.0
Senior higher school	45.6	60.3	53.8	44.6	51.2
University	50.2	33.9	25.6	45.9	38.8
Occupation					
White collar	45.2	34.9	37.3	49.3	41.6
Blue collar	6.7	16.5	20.9	23.2	16.7
Private business	9.0	9.0	14.9	6.4	9.8
Student	39.0	39.6	26.9	21.2	31.8
Personal income					
(Yuan/Month)					
Below 500	19.3	9.4	6.4	43.6	20.9
501-900	45.0	37.0	35.9	31.8	37.0
901-1,500	26.4	39.9	37.8	16.8	29.5
Above 1,501	9.3	13.8	19.9	7.8	12.6

five dependent variables tested in this model are as follows: utilitarian orientation, novelty seeking, responsiveness to promotion stimuli, preference for foreign brands, and brand consciousness. The purpose of using blocks in the regression analysis was to test the unique contribution (indicated by (ΔR^2) by the variables in each block.

H6 was tested by moderating the regression analysis. A three-step procedure was used in the analysis. We first regressed five dependent variables on four control variables (i.e., age, gender, education, and marriage). The independent variables of personal income and hedonic value were then added to the regression equation in step 2. In the final step, the interaction term of personal income*hedonic value was loaded into the equation. The moderating effect was tested by examining the change in the R-square attributable to the interaction term. If the interaction term added to the final stage of the regression analysis produced a significant R-square (i.e., significantly increased the amount of variance explained in the criterion variable–brand consciousness), personal income is indicated to be a moderator of the relationship between hedonic value and brand consciousness. Since a specific pattern of interaction was hypothesized in testing the moderation effect, one-tailed tests were used in significance testing.

RESULTS AND DISCUSSIONS

The descriptive statistics, such as means, standard deviations, and intercorrelations of all variables used in this study are reported in Table 3.

The results of the regression analysis as reported in Table 4 indicate that utilitarian orientation was negatively associated with hedonic value ($\beta = -.08$, $p < .05$) after controlling for demographic variables. Thus, H1 was supported. Table 4 also shows that, after controlling for demographic variables, hedonic value was positively associated with novelty seeking ($\beta = .12$, $p < .01$), responsiveness to commercial stimuli ($\beta = .09$, $p < .01$), and preference for foreign brands ($\beta = .16$, $p < .01$). Thus, H2, H3 and H5 were all supported. However, the result shows that hedonic value was not significantly associated with brand consciousness. Thus H4 was not supported. This result may not be surprising when we further consider the possible moderating effect due to personal income level, as we hypothesized in H6.

Table 5 presents the results of moderated regression analysis. The

TABLE 3. Means, Standard Deviations, and Intercorrelations of Demographic Information, Hedonic Values and Consumer Attitudes/Behaviors

	Mean	S.D.	1	2	3	4	5	6	7	8	9	10
1. Hedonic Values	4.2	0.63										
2. Utilitarian Orientation	3.15	1.27	−0.08*									
3. Novelty Seeking	3.45	1.19	0.15**	−0.01								
4. Responsiveness to Promotion Stimuli	3.68	1.22	0.08*	−0.02	0.11**							
5. Preference for Foreign Brand	4.11	0.83	0.15**	−0.09**	0.16**	0.09**						
6. Brand Consciousness	3.95	1.06	0.09**	−0.11**	0.19**	0.21**	0.32**					
7. Age	3.22	1.53	0.00	0.11**	0.03	−0.01	0.08*	0.09**				
8. Gender	1.50	0.52	−0.05	−0.10**	−0.01	0.03	−0.04	−0.02	−0.06			
9. Education	4.28	0.68	−0.02	−0.09**	−0.05	0.00	−0.04	0.06	0.06	−0.03		
10. Marital Status	1.19	0.39	−0.04	0.07	−0.01	−0.05	0.07	−0.02	0.46**	0.19**	−0.12**	
11. Income	4.59	2.65	−0.01	0.16**	0.02	0.00	0.11	0.07	0.19**	−0.13**	0.06	0.01

*p < .05; **p < .01.

TABLE 4. Regression Analysis of the Effect of Hedonic Values on Consumer Attitudes/Behaviors

Variables	Utilitarian Orientation β	Novelty Seeking β	Responsiveness to Promotion Stimuli β	Preference for Foreign Brand β	Brand Consciousness β
Control Variables					
Age	.06	.02	.08*	−.03	.10**
Gender	−.09*	−.03	.06	−.06	.01
Education	−.11**	−.05	.04	.00	.05
Marital Status	.08*	−.02	−.11**	.09**	−.08*
Personal Income	.10**	.05	.02	.09**	.07*
ΔR^2	.02**	.01*	.01**	.02*	.02**
Hedonic Value	−.08*	.12**	.09**	.16**	.03
ΔR^2	.01*	.01**	.01**	.03**	.00
Overall F	5.04**	2.85**	2.23**	4.3**	2.38**
d.f.	6,587	6,587	6,587	6,587	6,587

*p < .05; **p < .01.

coefficient for the interaction term (personal income*hedonic value) was significant ($\beta = .97$, $p < .01$). This interaction term, when added to the equation, accounted for 2 percent of the additional variance in brand consciousness, which is statistically significant ($\Delta R^2 = .02$, $p < .01$). The pattern of the interaction can be interpreted using the sign of the coefficient. The positive sign of the coefficient indicates that the relationship between hedonic value and brand consciousness was stronger for consumers who had higher personal income than for those who had lower personal income. Thus H6 was supported. This result also explains why we could not find a main effect of hedonic values on brand consciousness.

In sum, the results of the study reveal a negative relationship between hedonic values and utilitarian orientation. In addition, the results also show positive relationships between hedonic values and consumer novelty seeking, responsiveness to promotion stimuli and preference for foreign brands. However, the relationship between hedonic values and consumer brand consciousness is moderated by personal income.

TABLE 5. Moderating Regression Analysis of the Effect of Personal Income on the Relationship Between Hedonic Values and Brand Consciousness

Variables	β
Control variables	
Age	.12**
Gender	−.001
Education	.04
Marital Status	−.07
ΔR^2	.02*
Hedonic Value	.03
Personal Income	.07*
ΔR^2	.01
Hedonic Value * Personal Income	.97**
ΔR^2	.02**
Overall F	3.78**
d.f.	7,586

**p < .01; *p < .05.

IMPLICATIONS AND FUTURE RESEARCH DIRECTIONS

Consumer values and lifestyles have long been used in market segmentation research (Kamakura & Alfonso, 1991; Kamakura & Novak, 1992; Novak & MacEvoy, 1990; Plummer, 1974; Wells, 1975), and strong relationships have been found between values and consumer choice criteria (Pitts & Woodside, 1983). While the traditional market segmentation approach is more focused on the rational aspect of consumer behavior, the hedonic consumption perspective emphasizes emotional and symbolic consumption behaviors. As noted by Howard (1977), grouping consumers with similar values will provide groups with similar choice criteria and final behavior.

The present research has extended our knowledge of the relationship between hedonic values and various consumption behaviors in China. Previous studies have observed individual differences in hedonic consumption patterns among members of religious- and nationality-based ethnic groups (c.f., Hirschman, 1982). However, there is a dearth of empirical studies that have investigated the impacts of hedonic values on consumer choice and consumption behaviors. With a

Chinese sample, the present study provides evidence that hedonic values can be used to predict various consumer behaviors. The hedonic/utilitarian orientation can also be used to differentiate the consumer segment that enjoys consumption experiences from the more traditional consumer segment that considers consumption as a basic means to survive. In particular, people with stronger hedonic values tend to prefer the expressive functions of a product, such as product packaging and foreign branding. They also tend to respond quickly to promotion stimuli and are more likely to change their brand preference. They are more likely to set current fashions or to try new products in the early stage of the new product diffusion process. In contrast, people with weaker hedonic values tend to prefer the utilitarian functions of a product, such as the tangible product quality and physical performance. They are more value and price conscious and less likely to purchase expensive foreign brands. They are less likely to change their long-used brands and less likely to adopt new products. In addition, the relationship between hedonic values and brand consciousness is stronger for consumers with higher personal income than for those with lower personal income.

The results of the study also provide important managerial implications given that the effective penetration of China's emerging consumer market is an area of significant interest for multinational firms. In order to be successful in the Chinese market, understanding Chinese consumption values and their influences on consumer behaviors is a crucial issue. Considering the changing consumption values in today's Chinese market and the existence of different consumer segments in terms of different consumption values, marketers should be sensitive to different consumption needs and the product choice behavior of different segments. In particular, product designing, pricing, branding, packaging, and positioning strategies should be based on an understanding of the characteristics of the target market. For instance, when targeting today's young Chinese consumer who has stronger hedonic values, marketers should focus on symbolic or expressive meanings of a product or brand, emphasize the emotional or fantastical experience of consumption, appeal to the consumer's desire for exploration, novelty, variety and innovation in promotion messages. In fact, U.S. fast-food companies in China often position their products as a slice of American lifestyle rather than just as hamburgers or fried chicken (Cui, 1997). This experiential approach is surely different from a marketing strategy that targets more "rational" consumers with utilitarian orientations, to whom the product's tangible values such as quality, price, performance and even "traditional brand" are the big selling points.

It should be noted that this study is only the first step in investigating the relationships between the hedonic values of consumers and their consumption patterns. The measurement scales were developed based on characteristics of the Chinese culture and may not be directly applied to other cultures at this stage. Although our measurement of hedonic values is, in general, comparable to results from previous studies that measured the same construct with samples from the United States and Hong Kong (Tse, Hui and Pan, 1994), a continuous effort to validate the measures across cultures is desirable in future research. Moreover, with a focus on young Chinese consumers residing in urban areas, the sample used in this study may not be generalized to the whole population, and caution should be taken in interpreting the findings. For instance, previous research has suggested that age may positively relate to price consciousness and brand loyalty but negatively relate to hedonic choice behavior (Shim, 1996). Given that the young generation and people living in urban areas tend to be more responsive to Western cultural influences and more open to lifestyle and value changes than older Chinese in rural areas, managerial implications drawn from this study are limited to the sample population only. While young and urban consumers create the most promising and profitable target markets for many multinational companies, future research with more diversified populations, including other age groups and rural residential areas, is warranted.

REFERENCES

Ariga, M., Yasuo, M., & Wen, G. X. (1997). China's generation III: Viable target segment implications for marketing communications. *Marketing & Research Today*, 25 (1), 17-24.

Babin, B. J., Darden, W. R., & Griffin, M. (1994). Work and/or fun: Measuring hedonic and utilitarian shopping value. *Journal of Consumer Research*, 20 (4), 644-656.

Batra, R., & Ahtola, O. T. (1991). Measuring the hedonic and utilitarian sources of consumer attitudes. *Marketing Letters*, 2 (April), 159-170.

Bellenger, D. N., Steinberg, E., & Stanton, W. W. (1976). The congruence of store image and self image. *Journal of Retailing*, 52 (Spring), 17-32.

Bow, J., & Ford, M. (1993). Indonesia & China: The retail of two cities. *Asian Business*, 29 (10), 12-14.

Campbell, C. (1987). *The romantic ethic and the spirit of modern consumerism.* Oxford, England: Blackwell.

Chin, D., & Towler, W. (1995). Retail: Opportunities and obstacles, *Institutional Investor*, 29 (11), C13, C16.

Chu, G. C., & Ju, Y. (1993). *The Great Wall in Ruins: Communication and Cultural Change in China.* State University of New York Press.

Cui, G. (1997). The name game. *The China Business Review.* November/December, 40-43.

Dichter, E. (1960). *The strategy of desire.* New York: Doubleday.

Feinberg, Fred M., Kahn, B. E., & McAlister, L. (1992). Market share response when consumers seek variety. *Journal of Marketing Research*, 29 (2), 227-237.

Fischer, E., & Arnold, S. J. (1990). More than a labor of love: Gender roles and Christmas gift shopping. *Journal of Consumer Research*, 17 (3), 333-345.

Hirschman, E. C. (1980). Innovativeness, novelty seeking, and consumer creativity. *Journal of Consumer Research*, 7 (3), 288-295.

Hirschman, E. C. (1982). Ethnic variation in hedonic consumption. *Journal of Social Psychology*, 118 (2), 225-234.

Hirschman, E. C., & Holbrook, M. B. (1982). Hedonic consumption: Emerging concepts, methods and propositions. *Journal of Marketing*, 46 (3), 92-101.

Hong Kong Trade Development Council Research Department (1994). *China's Consumer Market*, August, 2-9.

Holbrook, M. B., & Hirschman, E. C. (1982). The experiential aspects of consumption: Consumer fantacies, feelings, and fun. *Journal of Consumer Research*, 9 (2), 132-140.

Howard, J. A. (1977). *Consumer Behavior: Application of Theory*, New York: McGraw-Hill.

Kamakura, W. A., & Mazzon, J. A. (1991). Value segmentation: A model for the measurement of values and value systems. *Journal of Consumer Research*, 18 (2), 208-218.

Kamakura, W. A., & Novak, T. P. (1992). Value-system segmentation: Exploring the meaning of LOV. *Journal of Consumer Research*, 19 (1), 119-132.

Katz, E., & Lazarsfeld, P. F. (1955). *Personal Influence: The Part Played by People in the Flow of Mass Communications.* New York: The Free Press.

Kingdel, T. I. (1983). A partial theory of Chinese consumer behavior: Marketing strategy implications. *Hong Kong Journal of Business Management*, 1, 97-109.

Leavitt, C., & Walton, J. (1975). Development of a scale for innovativeness. In Mary Jane Schlinger (Ed.), *Advances in Consumer research* (Vol. 2, pp. 545-554). Ann Arbor, MI: Association for Consumer Research.

Leclerc, F., Schmitt, B. H., & Dube, L. (1994). Foreign branding and its effects on product perceptions and attitudes. *Journal of Marketing Research*, 31 (2), 263-270.

Levy, S. J. (1959). Symbols for sale. *Harvard Business Review*, 37 (July-August), 117-119.

Levy, S. J. (1963). Symbolism and life style. In Stephen A. Greyser (Ed.), *Toward scientific marketing*. Chicago: American Marketing Association.

Li, D., & Gallup, A. M. (1995). In search of the Chinese consumer. *China Business Review*, 22 (5), 19-22.

Lichtenstein, D. R., Netemeyer, R. G., & Burton, S. (1990). Distinguishing coupon proneness from value consciousness: An acquisition-transaction utility theory perspective. *Journal of Marketing*, 54 (3), 54-67.

McAlister, L., & Pessemier, E. (1982). Variety seeking behavior: An interdisciplinary review. *Journal of Consumer Research*, 9 (3), 311-322.

Mitchell, A. (1983). *The nine American life styles*. New York: Warner.

Novak, T. P., & MacEvoy, B. (1990). On comparing alternative segmentation schemes: The list of values (LOV) and values and life styles (VALS). *Journal of Consumer Research*, 17 (1), 105-109.

Plummer, J. T. (1974). The concept and application of life style segmentation. *Journal of Marketing*, 38 (1), 33-37.

Pitts, R. E., & Woodside, A. G. (1983). Personal value influences on consumer product class and brand preferences. *The Journal of Social Psychology*, 119, 37-53.

Raju, P. S. (1980). Optimum stimulation level: Its relationship to personality, demographics, and exploratory behavior. *Journal of Consumer Research*, 7 (3), 272-282.

Rogers, E. M., & Shoemaker, F. F. (1971). *Communication of Innovations: A Cross-Cultural Approach* (2nd ed.). New York: The Free Press.

Robertson, T. S. (1967). The process of innovation and the diffusion of innovation. *Journal of Marketing*, 31 (1), 14-19.

Sheth, J. N., Newman, B. I., & Gross, B. L. (1991). Why we buy what we buy: A theory of consumption values. *Journal of Business Research*, 22 (2), 159-170.

Shim, S. (1996), Adolescent consumer decision making styles: The consumer socialization perspective. *Psychology & Marketing*, 13 (6), 547-569.

Swanson, M. (1995). China puts on a new face. *China Business Review*, 22 (5), 34-37.

Tse, D. K. (1996). Understanding Chinese people as consumers: Past findings and future propositions. In Michael H. Bond (Ed.) *Handbook of Chinese Psychology*. New York: Oxford University Press.

Tse, D., Belk, R. W., & Zhou, N. (1989). Becoming a consumer society: A longitudinal and cross-cultural content analysis of print Ads from Hong Kong, the People's Republic of China, and Taiwan. *Journal of Consumer Research*, 15 (4), 457-473.

Tse, D., Hui, M. and Pan, Y. (1994). "Consumption Values in Consumer Behaviour: A Comparison of Chinese and American Consumer," Unpublished Manuscript.

Veblen, T. (1899). *The Theory of the Leisure Class*. New York: MacMillan.

Vinson, D. E., Scott, J. E., & Lamont, L. M. (1977). The role of personal values in marketing and consumer behavior. *Journal of Marketing*, 7 (April), 44-50.

Wakefield, K. L., & Barnes, J. H. (1996). Retailing hedonic consumption: A model of sales promotion of a leisure service. *Journal of Retailing*, 72 (4), 409-427.

Wells, W. D. (1975). Psychographics: A critical review. *Journal of Marketing Research*, 12 (May), 196-213.

Yao, O. H. M. (1988). Chinese cultural values: Their dimensions and marketing implications. *European Journal of Marketing*, 22 (5), 44-57.

Zuckerman, M. (1979). *Sensation Seeking: Beyond the Optimum Level of Arousal.* Hillsdale, NJ: Lawrence Erlbaum.

Twenty Years of Research on Marketing in China: A Review and Assessment of Journal Publications

Ming Ouyang
Dongsheng Zhou
Nan Zhou

SUMMARY. This paper reviews research on marketing in China by examining publications in leading English language academic journals from 1978 to 1998. It summarizes the papers that have been published, identifies the contributing individuals and institutions, examines the importance these journals have given to China-related marketing research, and compares the research with research published in leading journals in other business disciplines. The paper concludes by discussing the future of research on marketing in China. Future reviews should include research on marketing in China published in leading Chinese language academic journals. *[Article copies available for a fee from The Haworth Document Delivery Service: 1-800-342-9678. E-mail address: <getinfo@haworthpressinc.com> Website: <http://www.HaworthPress.com>]*

Ming Ouyang, Dongsheng Zhou, and Nan Zhou are affiliated with the Department of Marketing, City University of Hong Kong.

Address correspondence to: Dr. Ming Ouyang, Department of Marketing, City University of Hong Kong, 83 Tat Chee Avenue, Kowloon, Hong Kong (E-mail: mkouyang@cityu.edu.hk).

All authors contributed equally to the paper; the order of the authorship is alphabetical.

[Haworth co-indexing entry note]: "Twenty Years of Research on Marketing in China: A Review and Assessment of Journal Publications." Ouyang, Ming, Dongsheng Zhou, and Nan Zhou. Co-published simultaneously in *Journal of Global Marketing* (International Business Press, an imprint of The Haworth Press, Inc.) Vol. 14, No. 1/2, 2000, pp. 187-201; and: *Greater China in the Global Market* (ed: Yigang Pan) International Business Press, an imprint of The Haworth Press, Inc., 2000, pp. 187-201. Single or multiple copies of this article are available for a fee from The Haworth Document Delivery Service [1-800-342-9678, 9:00 a.m. - 5:00 p.m. (EST). E-mail address: getinfo@haworthpressinc.com].

KEYWORDS. Research, China

INTRODUCTION

Since the introduction of the economic reforms and open door policy in the late 1970s, China's centrally-planned economy has been transformed into a market-oriented one. This transformation has led to a remarkable growth in GNP, averaging about 10% annually in the past two decades. It has made the country a large potential market for many products and services. It has also attracted a great deal of attention from marketing researchers. Many of them consider the country a natural experimental field in which to do research and to test and develop marketing theories and concepts (see, e.g., Belk and Zhou 1987; Tse et al. 1989). Though much research has so far been done, there has not yet appeared a comprehensive review of this work.

This paper tries to fill this gap by taking an inventory of the publications on China-related marketing topics in leading academic journals since the economic reforms. We attempt to achieve four objectives. First, we summarize the work that has been published, the topics covered in the work, and the places the papers have been published. Second, we identify the individuals and institutions that have contributed to the creation of this particular body of marketing literature. Third, we examine the importance the journals have given to China-related marketing topics. Fourth, we compare this work with research published on China-related business topics in other leading journals.

METHODOLOGY

In order to survey what research has been done on marketing in China during the past two decades, we searched through 27 English language, refereed marketing and international business journals published in the United States and Europe covering the period of January 1978 through September 1998. These 27 journals represent a broad spectrum of the marketing discipline and are listed in Appendix 1.

Among these journals, five (i.e., four marketing journals and one international business journal) were viewed as first-tier journals. The four first-tier marketing journals are *Journal of Consumer Research (JCR), Journal of Marketing (JM), Journal of Marketing Research*

(JMR), and *Marketing Science (MS)*. The first three, i.e., *JCR*, *JM* and *JMR*, had been viewed in previous studies as the most prestigious marketing journals (Clark 1985; Coe and Weinstock 1983; Luke and Doke 1987; Fields and Swayne 1988). The fourth one, *MS*, is a relatively newer journal published since 1982. It focuses on quantitative research methods in marketing. An indicator of the significance of *MS* is its Impact Factor shown in the Social Science Citation Index (see Appendix 2).

The first-tier international business journal used in the study is *Journal of International Business Studies (JIBS)*. In the past two decades, *JIBS* has published many papers on China. We read the *JIBS* abstracts carefully and only used those papers that were judged by at least two of the three co-authors to be related to marketing in China.

The other 22 were regarded as second-tier journals. Again, we used the Impact Factor in the Social Science Citation Index to cross-validate our choice of journals, as many of these journals are indexed there. The indices from 1995 to 1997 generally confirmed that these journals have been widely cited by researchers (see Appendix 2).

To address the question of comparing research on marketing in China with research on China in other business disciplines (accounting, finance, management, management science, etc.), we focused on publications in English language, first-tier business journals. We believe that, while this approach does not represent a perfect proxy, the number of papers published on China-related issues in these journals provides a good picture of the recognition and importance of the issues in business disciplines.

We developed our list of top journals in business disciplines based on the past literature. In accounting (Brown and Gardner 1985), the list includes *Accounting, Organizations and Society (AOS)*, *The Accounting Review (AR)*, *Journal of Accounting and Economics (JAE)*, and *Journal of Accounting Research (JAR)*. In finance (Mabry and Sharplin, 1985), we included *Journal of Finance (JF)*, *Journal of Financial Economics (JFE)*, *Journal of Financial and Quantitative Analysis (JFQ)* and *Journal of Money, Credit and Banking (JMB)*. In management, we included *Academy of Management Journal (AMJ)*, *Academy of Management Review (AMR)*, *Administrative Science Quarterly (ASQ)*, and *Strategic Management Journal (SMJ)*. In management science (Goh et al. 1997), we included *IIE Transactions*

(*IIE*), *Journal of Operations Management* (*JOM*), *Management Science* (*MS*), and *Operations Research* (*OR*).

RESULTS

General Findings

A total of 92 articles on China-related marketing issues were found collectively in 19 of the 27 journals. Among them, six articles appeared in our list of the first-tier marketing journals and 77 in second-tier ones. The first-tier marketing journals that have published China-related papers are: *JCR* (3 articles), *JM* (2 articles), and *MS* (1 article). There was no such paper in *JMR*. In *JIBS*, a total of 21 papers on China-related subjects were identified. After the screening process, nine of them were categorized as related to marketing in China.

As for the second-tier journals, 16 out of 22 were found to have published papers on marketing in China. The remaining six (i.e., about 30 percent of the total second-tier journals in our sample) did not publish China-related papers. The names of the journals that have publications on marketing in China are listed in Table 1.

What Has Been Done

The 92 China-related marketing papers cover the following areas:

Advertising. Advertising in China received the most attention. A total of 31 papers (i.e., 33 percent of the 92 China-related marketing papers) were found in this area. The most frequently examined issues were: the development of advertising (see Stewart and Campbell 1986); content analysis of advertisements (see Cheng 1994); attitudes toward advertising (see Pollay et al. 1990; Semenik et al. 1986); and advertising regulations (Chadwick 1997). The significant amount of papers published in this area may partly be due to the fact that there was a special issue on advertising in China produced by *International Journal of Advertising* in 1997 which included 6 papers.

Consumer Behavior. A total of 7 papers addressed this topic. Because of the great impact of the issue, four of these papers were published in first-tier journals: Tse, Belk and Zhou (*JCR* 1989); Schmitt, Pan and Tavassoli (*JCR* 1994); Schmitt and Zhang (*JCR*

TABLE 1. List of Journals Publishing Papers on Marketing in China

First-Tier Marketing Journals

Journal of Consumer Research (3)
Schmitt & Zhang, 1998
Schmitt, Pan, & Tavassoli, 1994
Tse, Belk, & Zhou, 1989
Journal of Marketing (2)
Klein, Ettenson, & Morris, 1998
Tse, Lee, Vertinsky, & Wehrung, 1988
Marketing Science (1)
Calantone, Schmidt, & Song, 1996

First-Tier International Business Journal

Journal of International Business Studies (9)
Chen & Chen, 1998
Luo, 1998
Tse, Pan, & Au, 1997
Pan & Tse, 1996
Pan, 1996
Tse, Francis, & Wells, 1994
Schroath, Frederick, Hu, & Chen, 1993
Shan, 1991
McGuirness, Campbell, & Leontiades, 1991

Second-Tier Marketing Journals

European Journal of Marketing (7)
International Journal of Advertising (20)
International Marketing Management (6)
Journal of Academy of Marketing Science (2)
Journal of Advertising (5)
Journal of Advertising Research (2)
Journal of Consumer Affairs (1)
Journal of Consumer Psychology (3)
Journal of Current Issues & Research in Advertising (3)
Journal of Business Research (4)
Journal of Global Marketing (6)
Journal of International Consumer Marketing (6)
Journal of International Marketing (4)
Journal of Marketing Education (2)
Journal of Product Innovation Management (3)
Psychology & Marketing (3)

* The numbers in the parentheses indicate the number of articles published in the journal.

1998) and Klein, Ettenson and Morris (*JM* 1998). Tse et al. (1989) conducted a longitudinal study of advertisements from Hong Kong, the People's Republic of China (or the mainland), and Taiwan. They found distinctive consumer cultures in these Chinese societies. Schmitt et al. (*JCR*, 1994) and Schmitt and Zhang (*JCR*, 1998) examined the relationship between language and consumer memory and consumer behavior. Klein et al. (1998) provided an initial test of the animosity model of foreign product purchase in China.

The Role of Chinese Culture in International Marketing Decisions. A total of 10 articles were related to this topic. One of them was published in a top-tier journal (Tse, Lee, Vertingsky, and Wehrung *JM* 1988). Tse et al. (1988) investigated whether or not a manager's home culture significantly influences his or her international marketing decisions.

New Product Development. There were 4 papers that addressed this issue. A paper by Calantone, Schmidt and Song (1996) was published in *MS*, a first-tier journal. In this paper, the authors conducted a cross-national comparison of factors affecting new product success. The remaining papers appeared in *Journal of Product Innovation Management (JPIM)*.

Foreign Firm's Entry Strategies into China. Eight papers in *JIBS* and 2 papers in *Journal of Business Research* (*JBR*) examined the issues related to FDI entry into the Chinese market, concerning where, when and/or how FDI entered the Chinese market.

Other Topics. The rest of the articles studied such topics as negotiations, firm performance, joint venture, change in firm structure, and technology transfer in connection with marketing in China.

Who Have Done the Work

A total of 139 researchers from 64 institutions collectively contributed to the 92 articles. Among them, 16 individuals were co-authors of the 6 papers in the top-tier marketing journals in our list while 19 individuals contributed to the 9 papers in *JIBS*. In the second-tier journals, a total of more than 100 individuals published 77 single-authored or joint-authored papers related to marketing in China.

Following practices adopted in previous studies (Peng et al. forthcoming), we examined both "total" and "adjusted" contributions of authors. In the "total" contribution category each author is assigned a full credit for every paper while in the "adjusted" category each author is assigned a discounted credit depending on the number of co-authors for a paper. For example, if a single author published an article, this author gets a full "adjusted" credit; and if an article was written by two authors jointly, each gets a half "adjusted" credit. Table 2 lists all the researchers who have contributed to one first-tier and two second-tier journal papers and their respective current institutions.

Two observations are made here. First, although authors from 17 different institutions are listed in Table 2, most were from universities in North America or Hong Kong. This is partly due to the fact that in the past few years, several of the authors publishing the most China-

TABLE 2. List of Top Contributors of Papers on Marketing in China

Researcher	Institution	1st tier total	1st tier adjusted	2nd tier total	2nd tier adjusted
Tse, D. K.	HKU	6	1.74	1	0.33
Pan, Y.	HKU/Oregon	5	2.17	3	2.17
Schmitt, B. H.	Columbia	2	.83		
Luo, Y. D.	Hawaii	1	1		
Shan, W. J.	JP Morgan	1	1		
Zhou, N.	City U of HK	1	0.33	4	2.17
Song, X. M.	Michigan State	1	0.33	2	1
Campbell, N.	Manchester	1	0.33	1	1
Belk, R. W.	Utah	1	0.33	1	0.5
Chen, H. M.	Chi-Nan U	1	0.5		
Chen, T. J.	Taiwan U	1	0.5		
Zhang, S.	UCLA	1	0.5		
Taoka, G. M.	Texas	1	0.5		
Lee, K.	CUHK	1	0.25		
Vertinsky, I.	UBC	1	0.25		
Wehrung, D.	UBC	1	0.25		
Swanson, L. A.	CUHK			3	3
Yau, O.	City U of HK			3	1.83
Jacobs, L. W.	Hawaii			3	1.58
Ho, S. C.	CUHK			3	1.5
Tam, J. L. M.	HKPU			3	1.5
Chan, K. K. W.	HKBU			2	2
Tai, S. H.	HKPU			2	2
Cheng, H.	Bradley			2	1.5
Kaynak, E.	Penn State			2	1.5

related marketing research changed their institutional affiliations from North America to Hong Kong. Second, there exist extensive co-operations between researchers from different institutions. Because research on China-related marketing issues requires a good understanding of Chinese culture, co-authorship from different institutions involving ethnic Chinese was common. For example, on average, 2.89 authors from 2.6 institutions co-authored one of the 6 papers appearing in first-tier journals, and ethnic Chinese were authors or co-authors in 5 out of 6 of these papers.

In addition to the number of papers an author has published, we used a citation index as another measure of the contribution of individual researchers. Paper citation indices have often been used to measure the importance of a scholar in a field (Robinson and Adler, 1981). In this paper, we used the Social Science Citation Index (SSCI) to find the number of citations made to these papers. We limited our search scope to the most recent period, i.e., from January 1996 to September 1998. Also, instead of giving one credit to the first author only as the SSCI has done, we gave one credit to each of the co-authors if a co-authored paper is cited by another paper. Table 3 lists the names of the most cited authors. When we estimated the current strength of institutions in term of their reputations based on these citation data, we found that more institutions in Hong Kong than in any other single location are contributing to the body of knowledge on China-related marketing (see Table 4).

How Important Is China to Marketing Researchers

As mentioned, three out of the four first-tier marketing journals studied here have published papers related to China. Longitudinally, the number of publications increased from four during 1978-1987 to 88 during 1988-1998. The increase is encouraging. Clearly, researchers in marketing are paying growing attention to China-related topics. However, aside from *JIBS*, publications on marketing in China seem to be more concentrated in certain top-tier and second-tier marketing journals, such as *JCR* (totaling 3 papers) and *International Journal of Advertising* (totaling 15 papers). Six out of the 22 (i.e., about 30 percent) of the second-tier journals in our sample have not published any China-related papers.

TABLE 3. Most Cited Authors of Journal Papers on Marketing in China: January 1996–September 1998*

Name	Total No. of Citations	Current Institution
1. David Tse	39	University of Hong Kong
2. X. Michael Song	20	Michigan State University
3. Mark E. Parry	19	University of Virginia
4. Yigang Pan	17	Univ. of HK/Univ. of Oregon
4. Nan Zhou	17	City University of Hong Kong
6. Russel Belk	15	University of Utah
7. Kam-hon Lee	14	Chinese University of HK
7. Ilan Vertinsky	14	UBC
7. Donald Wehrung	14	UBC
10. Weijian Shan	9	JP Morgan
11. Oliver Yau	7	City University of Hong Kong
12. Michael Y. Hu	5	Kent State University
12. Haiyang Chen	5	Youngstown State University
14. Hong Cheng	4	Bradley University
15. John C. Schweizer	4	Bradley University
16. Bernd H. Schmitt	3	Columbia University
16. Nader T. Tavassoli	3	University of Minnesota
16. J. Craig Andrews	3	Marquette University
16. Frederick W. Schroath	3	Kent State University
16. N. McGuinness	3	Acadia University

Source: *Social Science Citation Index 1996-1998.*

*We include only authors who have at least one "total" first-tier publication or one "adjusted" second-tier publication.

China-Related Research in Marketing vs. in Other Business Disciplines

Table 5 provides the number of papers on China-related issues published in first-tier journals in accounting, finance, management, and management science. It shows that first-tier management journals have published the most China-related papers while first-tier finance journals have published the least. This may not be surprising, because ever since China initiated its economic reforms, one of the country's focuses has been to implement modern or Western management theories and concepts, while its financial markets still remain fairly closed to outside interaction. By drawing comparisons with the total number

TABLE 4. List of Institutions with the Most Number of Citations: January 1996–September 1998

Institution	Total No. of Citations	Researcher
University of Hong Kong	56	Pan, Tse
UBC	28	Vertinsky, Wehrung
City University of Hong Kong	24	Yau, Zhou
Michigan State University	20	Song
University of Virginia	19	Parry
University of Utah	15	Belk
Chinese University of Hong Kong	14	Lee

of papers published in these journals, we conclude that marketing researchers have given China-related topics a modest attention.

CONCLUSION

Much more research can be done on China-related marketing topics. Past studies published in leading English-language academic journals have largely treated China as a homogenous market. However, there are 56 nationalities in China; significant cultural differences exist among various regions; and the level of economic development varies significantly from one area to another across the country. As the reforms deepen and the country continues its open door policy, domestic state, collective, and private enterprises, as well as foreign companies and Chinese-foreign joint ventures, compete with each other heavily. As a result, consumers with different cultural backgrounds, from different regions or working for different types of enterprises exhibit different behaviors when making consumption decisions; and companies also operate at different stages of corporate development and with different marketing capabilities.

How these companies will survive, grow and maintain sustainable marketing profitability in China's increasingly competitive and open marketing environment remains a challenging question for marketing researchers. We must also ask how future research on marketing in China will look like as a result. We expect to see a greater participation of researchers with Chinese ethnic background, using a variety of approaches, and studying in more areas of significance. And, we hope

Table 5. China-Related Publications in Other First-Tier Business Journals

	Accounting	Finance	Management	Management Science
	AOS (4) Firth, 1996 O'Connor, 1995 Skousen et al., 1988 Zhou, 1988	*JF* (0)	*AMJ* (7) Xie, 1996 Xin et al., 1996 Chen, 1995 Ralston et al., 1995 Yan et al., 1994 Earley, 1988 Shenkar et al., 1987	*IIE* (1) Courtney, 1994
	AR (2) Kachelmeier et al., 1997 Lyon, 1988	*JFE* (0)	*AMR* (2) Peng et al., 1996 Tung, 1981	*JOM* (0)
	JAE (1) Chan et al., 1997	*JFQ* (0)	*ASQ* (6) Farth et al., 1997 Boisot et al., 1996 _____, 1988 Earley, 1994 _____, 1989 Nee, 1992	*MS* (3) Hofstede, 1994 Shenkar et al., 1994 Ling et al., 1987
	JAR (0)	*JMB* (2) Feltenstein et al., 1990 _____, 1987	*SMJ* (3) Pan, 1997 Tan et al., 1994 Adler et al., 1992	*OR* (1) Zhao et al., 1991
Total	6	2	18	5
Average per journal	1.5	0.5	4.5	1.25

Abbreviations:
AOS: *Accounting, Organizations and Society*,
AR: *The Accounting Review*,
JAE: *Journal of Accounting and Economics*,
JAR: *Journal of Accounting Research*,
JF: *Journal of Finance*,
JFE: *Journal of Financial Economics*,
JFQ: *Journal of Financial and Quantitative Analysis*,
JMB: *Journal of Money, Credit and Banking*,
AMJ: *Academy of Management Journal*,
AMR: *Academy of Management Review*,
ASQ: *Administrative Science Quarterly*,
SMJ: *Strategic Management Journal*,
IIE: *IIE Transactions*,
JOM: *Journal of Operations Management*,
MS: *Management Science*,
OR: *Operations Research*.

to see more high quality publications on China-related marketing topics that include "Chinese characteristics" in leading academic journals in both Chinese and other languages. Therefore, future reviews on research on marketing in China should include publications in leading Chinese language academic journals for a more comprehensive picture.

REFERENCES

Belk, R. W. & N. Zhou (1987): "Learning to Want Things," in *Advances in Consumer Research*, Vol. 14, eds., M. Wallendorf & P. Anderson, Provo: UT: Association for Consumer Research, 478-481.

Brown, L. D. & J. C. Gardner (1985): "Using Citation Analysis to Assess the Impact of Journals and Articles on Contemporary Accounting Research," *Journal of Accounting Research*, Spring, 84-109.

Calantone, R. J., J. B. Schmidt, & X. M. Song (1996): "Controllable Factors of New Product Success: A Cross-National Comparison," *Marketing Science*, Vol. 15, 341-358.

Chadwick, J. (1997): "Navigating through China's New Advertising Law: The Role of Marketing Research," *International Journal of Advertising*, Vol. 16, 284-294.

Cheng, H. (1994): "Reflections of Cultural Values: A Content Analysis of Chinese Magazine Advertisements from 1982 and 1992," *International Journal of Advertising*, Vol. 13, 167-183.

Clark, G. L. (1985): "Productivity Ratings of Institutions Based on Publication in Eight Marketing Journals: 1983-1984," *Journal of Marketing Education*, Fall, 12-23.

Coe, R. K. & I. Weinstock (1983): "Evaluating Journal Publications of Marketing Professors: A Second Look," *Journal of Marketing Education*, Spring, 37-43.

Fields, D. M. & L. E. Swayne (1988): "Publication in Major Marketing Journals: 1960-1986," *Journal of Marketing Education*, Fall, 36-48.

Goh, C., C. W. Holsapple, L. E. Johnson, & J. R. Tanner (1997): "Evaluating and Classifying POM Journals," *Journal of Operations Management*, Vol. 15, 123-138.

Klein, J. G., R. Ettenson, & M. D. Morris (1998): "The Animosity Model of Foreign Product Purchase: An Empirical Test in the People's Republic of China," *Journal of Marketing*, Vol. 62, 89-100.

Luke, R. H. & E. R. Doke (1987): "Marketing Journal Hierarchies: Faculty Perceptions," *Journal of the Academy of Marketing Science*, Spring, 74-78.

Mabry, R. H. & A. D. Sharplin (1985): "The Relative Importance of Journals Used in Finance Research," *Journal of Financial Research*, Winter, 287-310.

Peng, M.W., Y. Lu, O. Shenkar, & D. Wang (1999): "Treasures in China House: A Review of Management and Organizational Research on Greater China," *Journal of Business Research* (forthcoming).

Pollay, R., D. K. Tse, & Z. Y. Wang (1990): "Advertising Propaganda and Value

Change in Economic Development: The New Cultural Revolution in China and Attitudes Toward Advertising," *Journal of Business Research*, 20(2), 99-110.

Robinson, L. M. & R. Adler (1981): "Measuring the Impact of Marketing Scholars and Institutions: An Analysis of Citation Frequency," *Journal of the Academy of Marketing Science*, Spring, 147-162.

Schmitt, B. H., Y. Pan, & N. T. Tavassoli (1994): "Language and Consumer Memory: The Impact of Linguistic Differences Between Chinese and English," *Journal of Consumer Research*, Vol. 21, 419-431.

_____ & S. Zhang (1998): "Language Structure and Categorization: A Study of Classifiers in Consumer Cognition, Judgement, and Choice," *Journal of Consumer Research*, Vol. 25, 108-122.

Semenik, R. J., N. Zhou & W. L. Moore (1986): "Chinese Managers' Attitude Toward Advertising in China," *Journal of Advertising*, Vol. 14, 4, 56-62.

Stewart, S. & N. Campbell (1986): "Advertising in China," *International Journal of Advertising*, Vol. 6, 317-323.

Tse, D. K., K. Lee, I. Vertinsky, & D. A. Wehrung (1988): "Does Culture Matter? A Cross-Cultural Study of Executives' Choice, Decisiveness, and Risk Adjustment in International Marketing," *Journal of Marketing*, Vol. 52, 81-95.

_____, R. W. Belk, & N. Zhou (1989): "Becoming A Consumer Society: A Longitudinal and Cross-cultural Content Analysis of Print Ads from Hong Kong, the People's Republic of China, and Taiwan," *Journal of Consumer Research*, Vol. 15, 457-472.

APPENDIX 1. List of Surveyed Journals

First-Tier Journals

Journal of Consumer Research (JCR)
Journal of International Business Studies (JIBS)
Journal of Marketing (JM)
Journal of Marketing Research (JMR)
Marketing Science (MS)

Second-Tier journals

European Journal of Marketing (EJM)
Industrial Marketing Management (IMM)
International Journal of Advertising (IJA)
International Journal of Research in Marketing (IJRM)
International Marketing Review (IMR)
Journal of Academy of Marketing Science (JAMS)
Journal of Advertising (JA)
Journal of Advertising Research (JAR)
Journal of Business Research (JBR)
Journal of Consumer Affairs (JCA)
Journal of Consumer Psychology (JCP)
Journal of Current Issues and Research in Advertising (JCI)
Journal of Global Marketing (JGM)
Journal of International Consumer Marketing (JICM)
Journal of International Marketing (JIM)
Journal of Marketing Education (JME)
Journal of Marketing Research Society (JMRS)
Journal of Product Innovation Management (JPIM)
Journal of Public Policy and Marketing (JPPM)
Journal of Retailing (JR)
Marketing Letters (ML)
Psychology and Marketing (PM)

APPENDIX 2. Selected Journal Impact Factors

	1995	1996	1997
Journal of Marketing	2.431	3.274	2.783
Journal of Consumer Research	1.274	1.621	1.381
Journal of Marketing Research	1.722	1.346	1.278
Journal of Product Innovation Management	1.035	1.214	1.038
Marketing Science	1.478	0.716	0.859
Journal of International Business Studies	0.768	0.889	0.793
Journal of Advertising Research	0.324	0.522	0.659
Journal of Advertising	0.518	0.582	0.477
Journal of Retailing	0.488	0.711	0.436
Journal of Business Research	0.315	0.407	0.401
Industrial Marketing Management	0.307	0.308	0.355
Journal of Marketing Research Society	0.232	0.164	0.185
Journal of Consumer Affairs	0.278	0.154	0.057

Source: *Social Science Citation Index Journal Citation Reports–Social Sciences Edition*, 1995, 1996, 1997

Index

Anderson, E., 85
"Asian Business Model," 23-24
Asian firms, corporate culture of,
    23-24,23t

Back door, defined, 134
Behavior(s), consumer, hedonic values
    effects on, 169-186. *See also*
    Hedonic values, influence on
    consumer behaviors
Belk, R.W., 155,190
BOT. *See* Build-operate-transfer (BOT)
Brand consciousness, vs. hedonic
    values, 173
Brunner, J.A., 135
Build-operate-transfer (BOT), 74-75
Business negotiation, defined, 135
Business performance, in China,
    factors affecting, 25-26

Calantone, R.J., 191
Chadee, D.D., 2,4,129
Chan, A.K.K., 4,169
Chen, Z-X, 4,169
Chi, P.S.K., 114-115
Child, J., 2-3,37
China
    entry strategy in, influences on,
        83-109. *See also* Market
        entry modes, in emerging
        markets, choice of
    foreign direct investment in,
        111-127. *See also* Foreign
        direct investment, in China
    influence of hedonic values on
        consumer behaviors in,
        169-186. *See also* Hedonic
        values, influence on
        consumer behaviors

international investors in, entry
    modes for, 57-82. *See also*
    International investors, in
    China, entry modes for
intertextual construction of
    emerging consumer culture
    in, as observed in *Ermo*,
    151-167. *See also Ermo*,
    intertextual construction of
    emerging consumer culture
    in China as observed in
market-focused organizational
    transformation in, 7-35. *See
    also* Market-focused
    organizational
    transformation, in China
marketing in, research on, review
    and assessment of journal
    publications, 187-201
    China-related research in
        marketing vs. in other
        business disciplines,
        194-195,197t
    China's importance to marketing
        researchers, 194
    completed research, 190,192
    general findings in, 190,191t
    introduction to, 188
    methodology in, 188-190
    participants in, 192-194,193t,195t
    results of, 190-196,191t,193t,
        195t-197t
New Zealand firms exporting to,
    study of, 129-149. *See also*
    Guanxi, impact on export
    performance
China's Law on Wholly Foreign-
    owned Enterprises, 58
Chinese firms, corporate culture of,
    23-24,23t

203

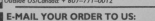

TO ORDER: CALL: 1-800-429-6784 / FAX: 1-800-895-0582 (Outside US/Canada: + 607-771-0012) / **E-MAIL: getinfo@haworthpressinc.com**

☐ YES, please send me **Multicultural Behavior and Global Business Environments**

___ in hard at $129.95 ISBN: 0-7890-1261-8. (Outside US/Canada/Mexico: $156.00)

___ in soft at $59.95 ISBN: 0-7890-1262-6. (Outside US/Canada/Mexico: $72.00)

- Individual orders outside US, Canada, and Mexico must be prepaid by check or credit card.
- Discounts are not available on 5+ text prices and not available in conjunction with any other discount. • Discount not applicable on books priced under $15.00.
- 5+ text prices are not available for jobbers and wholesalers.
- Postage & handling: in US: $4.00 for first book; $1.50 for each additional book. Outside US: $5.00 for first book; $2.00 for each additional book.
- Canadian residents: please add appropriate sales tax after postage & handling.
- Canadian residents of Newfoundland, Nova Scotia, and New Brunswick, also add 8% for province tax. • Payment in UNESCO coupons welcome.
- If paying in Canadian dollars, use current exchange rate to convert to US dollars.
- Please allow 3-4 weeks for delivery after publication.
- Prices and discounts subject to change without notice.

Signature _____

☐ **BILL ME LATER** ($5 service charge will be added).
(Not available for individuals outside US/Canada/Mexico. Service charge is waived for jobbers/wholesalers/booksellers.)
☐ Check here if billing address is different from shipping address and attach purchase order and billing address information.

☐ **PAYMENT ENCLOSED $** _____
(Payment must be in US or Canadian dollars by check or money order drawn on a US or Canadian bank.)

☐ **PLEASE BILL MY CREDIT CARD:**

☐ AmEx ☐ Diners Club ☐ Discover ☐ Eurocard ☐ JCB ☐ Master Card ☐ Visa

Account Number _____

Expiration Date _____

Signature _____

THE HAWORTH PRESS, INC., 10 Alice Street, Binghamton, NY 13904-1580 USA

FAX

Please complete the information below or tape your business card in this area.

NAME _____

INSTITUTION _____

ADDRESS _____

CITY _____

STATE _____ ZIP _____

COUNTRY _____

COUNTY (NY residents only) _____

E-MAIL _____
May we use your e-mail address for confirmations and other types of information?
( ) Yes ( ) No. We appreciate receiving your e-mail address and fax number. Haworth would like to e-mail or fax special discount offers to you, as a preferred customer. We will never **share, rent, or exchange** your e-mail address or fax number. We regard such actions as an invasion of your privacy.

☐ YES, please send me **Multicultural Behavior and Global Business Environments (ISBN: 0-7890-1262-6)** to consider on a 60-day **no risk** examination basis. I understand that I will receive an invoice payable within 60 days, or that if I decide to **adopt the book, my invoice will be cancelled.** I understand that I will be billed at the lowest price. (60-day offer available only to teaching faculty in US, Canada, and Mexico / Outside US/Canada, a proforma invoice will be sent upon receipt of your request and must be paid in advance of shipping. A full refund will be issued with proof of adoption)

Signature _____

Course Title(s) _____

Current Text(s) _____

Enrollment _____

Semester _____ Decision Date _____

Office Tel _____ Hours _____

(10)   09/00   BIC00